20x5

Theology In Africa

Centre for
Faith and Spirituality
Loughborough University

D1331308

By the same author published by Darton, Longman & Todd

The History and Religion of Israel (3 vols)
The Story of the Early Church

Theology In Africa

KWESI A. DICKSON

Darton, Longman and Todd
London

ORBIS BOOKS
Maryknoll, New York 10545

First published in 1984 by
Darton, Longman & Todd Ltd,
89 Lillie Road, London SW6 1UD
and Orbis Books
Maryknoll, New York 10545

ISBN 0 232 51551 4 (DLT)
ISBN 0–88344–508–5 (Orbis)

Phototypeset by Input Typesetting Ltd, London SW19 8DR
Printed in Great Britain by
Anchor Brendon Ltd, Tiptree, Essex

Contents

Part Three
Implications for Theological Education

Preface

In the *Directory of Theological Institutions* prepared in 1976 by the West African Association of Theological Institutions (WAATI), twenty-two such institutions were listed, with Nigeria having the largest number, thirteen, while Ghana had five, and Liberia and Sierra Leone two each. At the time the *Directory* was prepared there were other institutions which had not registered with WAATI. Thus these four West African countries have quite a number of seminaries, Bible colleges and university departments of Religion. The West African situation is just one element in the total story of the Christian theological presence in Africa, for the truth of the matter is that theological education is being given by a considerable number and variety of institutions. This considerable theological presence is the result of the great increase in the number and variety of Churches; the numbers of Christians have gone up impressively, and prognostications of future increase are being made.[1]

Given the fact of the great visibility which the Church and theological education enjoy in Africa, it is not to be wondered that in recent decades, especially since the fifties when the colonial powers began to give up their colonies in Africa, there should be such interest in assessing the Christian Church and its theological efforts. In the initial post-independence years sporadic indictments of the Christian Church were heard from some African politicians, but on the whole the Church's most dedicated questioners have come from within.

1. J. S. Mbiti, 'The Future of Christianity in Africa', in *Cross Currents*, vol. XXVIII, no. 4 (Winter 1978–9), pp. 387f.

PREFACE

This book is an attempt to articulate the questions which have been asked and to bring out their implications. Whether the questions have been articulated here with sufficient clarity and the assumptions regarding their implications correctly drawn may perhaps be considered by some to be debatable, but this book is an attempt to wrestle with the issue of Christian theology and the Church in Africa.

The opportunity to embark upon the assembling of material for this book came when I was appointed the Henry W. Luce Visiting Professor of World Christianity, Union Theological Seminary, New York, for the 1978/79 academic year. Not only did I teach the Old Testament, which is my principal area of theological interest, but also I had opportunity to organise my thoughts regarding the nature of the theological task facing the Church in Africa. I owe to Union, and to its President Donald Shriver, a great debt of gratitude. Union's library facilities were a great help, indeed.

Much of the material here has developed from papers I had published in journals and books or given at various conferences; it is also in part a rewriting of courses given at the University of Ghana and Union Theological Seminary. There is much here that is owed to others with whom I had at various times shared my thoughts on the subject of African theology. I do not presume to have exhausted the elements which should form part of the discussion, but it is hoped that what has been said here constitutes a true representation of the theological task facing the Church in Africa.

Unless otherwise stated the place of publication for books in both bibliography and footnotes is London.

KWESI A. DICKSON
University of Ghana
September 1983

Acknowledgement

The scripture quotations in this publication are from the Revised Standard Version of the Bible, copyrighted 1971 and 1952 by the Division of Christian Education of the National Council of the Churches of Christ in the U.S.A.

To my father
KODWO DOKU

Introduction

At the 1973 meeting of the Faith and Order Commission of the World Council of Churches which took place in Ghana I had the privilege to lead a study group which consisted of both Africans and Europeans, one of the latter being a Catholic priest from an Eastern European country. This priest got increasingly agitated as he listened to comments being made by African Christians, both Protestant and Catholic, on the uncertain nature of the Church in Africa and the need for taking a hard look at its received theology. During the discussion, and also in private conversation, he expressed his disquiet: Were not African Christians putting together a prescription for the dismantling of the world-wide Church in talking of African theology? Where would the Church be if every national group talked of a national theology? Even though I was not unfamiliar with this kind of reaction, this European priest's extreme agitation struck me very forcibly.

If he had not been so agitated he might have noticed and commented upon the fact that the Africans in the study group were not by any means unanimous regarding the shape which Christianity in Africa should take. An Ethiopian participant, for example, was somewhat irritated by the talk of Christianity taking account of African culture: had not the Coptic Church already done that? Indeed, in my judgement the explosive situation in the discussion arose, not so much from what the African participants thought of European Christianity as from what the African Christians, coming as they did from a variety of Christian traditions, considered to be the way forward for the Church in Africa.

For several decades discerning African Christians have raised questions regarding the validity of the expression of Christianity in Africa. In fact this questioning, in its unarticulated form, has been going on since the introduction of Christianity in Africa by European missionaries – and here I have Ghana in mind. The Akan lyrics which have been in use in the Methodist Church and which the missionaries did not work formally into the Church's worship (and, incidentally, the African leadership has not taken this step either since the Church became independent) is only one illustration of the theologising the Ghanaian Christians in the Methodist Church have been doing since the third decade of the last century when the first English Methodist missionaries came to Ghana. In more recent years, however, pointed questions have been asked by African Christians. Though there is a certain amount of unanimity regarding what needs to be done, there is not much agreement on how to proceed; all that one can say with certainty is that the majority of those who have expressed views on the subject see the need for the Church in Africa to become culturally authentic. This is not to ignore the significance of what African Christians in South Africa are calling Black theology, and which has been modelled, consciously or unconsciously, after the Black theology emanating from North America; Black theology has been adopted as a theological approach in South Africa, a part of the continent where there is much oppression of Africans by a white minority. Manas Buthelezi, a noted exponent of South African Black theology, has described this as 'a theology of social change for our situation (in South Africa)'.[1] Indeed, it has been suggested that Africa is more likely to produce theologies rather than a theology, given the great variety of religio-cultural, social and political realities in this vast continent.[2] While complete uniformity of expression may not be expected – or indeed be desirable, given the multi-faceted nature of

1. Alison Bareš (ed.), *Christian Theology and Theological Education in the African Context*, a Report of an All Lutheran Consultation at Gaborone, Botswana (5–14 October 1978).
2. E. W. Fasholé-Luke, 'The Quest for African Christian Theologies' in Gerald H. Anderson and Thomas F. Stransky (eds.), *Mission Trends*, no. 3 (New York, Paulist Press, 1976), pp. 135 ff.

the African scene – we would think that there is much in the African situation which could bring about a considerable unity in theological expression.

For the moment our concern is to note that theological discussions in Africa aimed at achieving a propositional articulation of faith – if such articulation be accepted as a necessary development – are at the preliminary stages, and different approaches have been espoused. Their validity will be examined in this study.

With respect to that European priest's misgivings in relation to the preservation of the oneness of the world Church, this is a concern that has surfaced again and again most recently, especially since Third World theologians began to articulate what they considered to be relevant theology in the circumstances of their socio-economic, political and cultural contexts. This concern is not unrelated to an observation recently made by Jürgen Moltmann in a critical review of certain expressions of Liberation theology: 'It would really be more meaningful to work in concert at a new construction of theology rather than in a rivalry to try to pass each other by on the "right" or in the "middle" and in the process step on each other's toes.'[3] Admittedly, Moltmann was not primarily raising the issue of theological catholicity; he was reacting to the criticism which certain protagonists of Liberation theology had levelled against him; thus he in turn points out the inconsistencies in the views of his critics. Strictly speaking, therefore, Moltmann's comments do not represent that position on catholicity which will presently be evaluated, though the reference to working 'in concert at a new construction of theology' does suggest a certain unease arising from the concern that a plethora of theologies could have the effect of sowing seeds of confusion.

Theological articulation has been done in the West for a long time, and theological education in the Third World has traditionally assumed the inviolability of the theological insights emanating from the West. It is not without a touch of exasperation that it has been observed: '[African theologians] continue to mouth the theological

3. In Gerald H. Anderson and Thomas F. Stransky (eds.), *Mission Trends*, no. 4 (New York, Paulist Press, 1979), p. 62.

platitudes they have picked up in universities, theological seminaries and colleges abroad or parade their erudition by quoting the latest theological ideas in Europe and North America.'[4] In consequence, theological education in Africa has generally had the effect of producing theologians who are more at home in Western theological thought, even if such thought pertains only to a certain level of their consciousness. True, one cannot ignore what has gone on before, even if it has come out of other contexts. Nevertheless, it cannot be seriously argued that in the interests of a uniformity of theological expression, and as a symbol of the oneness of the Church, the theological insights emanating from the West should be considered normative also outside the West.

There are at least three reasons why 'catholicity' must not be considered to be the *primary* goal of theological inquiry at this stage in the history of the development of theological thought. First, theology is done most meaningfully in particular settings: the cultural particularity is indispensable because theology is done by flesh and blood. As a result of a historical accident African theologians do theology in the medium of the languages of their erstwhile colonial rulers – English, French, Portuguese, etc. It is not always appreciated that to use someone else's language is to a large extent to have the train of one's thoughts set in a particular direction; language plays an important role in determining what parameters are to be taken into account in particular areas of study. This, in the African context, would explain why, for many African theologians, theologising has meant presupposing the traditional Western doctrinal statements but giving them what amounts to a thin veneer of traditional cultural coating, a basically unsatisfactory procedure. And language is only one of the characteristics which give a particular people its authenticity; history, traditional religion, social and political circumstances – all these and more constitute the setting within which peoples may be seen in their contextual reality. Thus it is essential that African Christians should be in a position to express in a vital way what Christ means to them, and to do so in and through a cultural medium that makes original thinking

4. Fasholé-Luke, in Anderson and Stransky, op. cit., no. 3, p. 137.

possible. Let Christ call them, rebuke them, accept them in his embrace; let him chasten them and carry them in his arms – but let all this be done in a medium that will give Christ's approach an eternal impact. The faith can be meaningful only when Christ is encountered as speaking and acting authentically, when he is heard in the African languages, when culture 'shapes the human voice that answers the voice of Christ'. To put this in another way, Christ must be heard to speak to African Christians direct.

Secondly, this quest for authenticity or selfhood is only at its initial stages as far as the articulation of Christian thought in Africa is concerned. Indeed, there are those who fear that the expression 'African theology', which has been in use for about a decade or two and which has come to be a source of some confusion for some African Christians, could very well become a slogan having little meaning unless some more serious thinking were done, and urgently, by African theologians. It needs to be observed that Western expectations in this regard may not necessarily accord with what African theologians might consider their work to consist in – and here we have in mind the mode of presentation of the implications of the Christian faith. African theologising may very well take the form of the kind of systematic presentation with which the world is familiar, with German theologians having the lion's share of achievement; or it may assume some other form; or a combination of several forms. It needs to be said that systematic theology, as traditionally conceived, is not an unavoidable form of presentation, contrary to what Western theologians tend to assume. As a matter of fact, not all theologising issues in a formal presentation. It would be an error if all theologising were to be constricted into propositional articulation, though some kind of articulation might become necessary in the interests of communication. In any case, the explication of the theological task in Africa is at its initial stages, and the outlines of what may be expected are not very clear. It is essential that every encouragement should be given to this experimentation for the enrichment of the world-wide Church.

For, and thirdly, there is no necessary correlation between a number of theologies emanating from different contexts and the breaking up of the Church's oneness. A distinction must be drawn between a unity of faith and diversity of doctrinal statements in such a way as not to see the two as cancelling each other out. The latter may perhaps get in the way of our visualising the unity, but they do not necessarily annihilate it. Thus the fourth-century controversies between *homoousians* and *homoiousians*, or more broadly the differences between the East and West on the subject of the Holy Spirit may be such as to make the reader wonder whether faith in Christ had not been lost in the welter of the theological disputations of that period; on the contrary, however, both sides in the controversy were attempting to state the same reality – as each saw it. To go back to that European priest, his kind of reaction may in fact be an impediment to the development of a world-wide Christian community, for the various authentic reactions to the same faith could be a means of arriving at a greater awareness of our oneness as we challenge one another with our views and begin to have a greater vision of the Christ who, in the final analysis, is too big for our theologies. The Church universal must be one whose *diverse* tongues complement one another as they express the Lordship of Christ.

The italicisation of 'diverse' calls for a further comment. Diversity often means greater richness, especially where each element in the mix represents a genuine and authentic creation, as already indicated. But I must not be understood to be saying that theological formulations emanating from the West have been devoid of the potential for universalism. To illustrate by reference to the Wesleyan tradition, to which I belong, there is the so-called Epworth Triangle which is a three-fold summing-up of the teaching of the eighteenth-century English reformer, John Wesley: (a) the priority of God's universal love; (b) the need for a personal faith; (c) no limitation can be put on God's grace as to its effect on man. As simply stated, these ideas could be the basis of a theology that recognises the particularity of our varied human and material circumstances. However, when one looks at them in the light of Wesley's understanding of them as it comes out in his writings they begin to strike one as having a narrower focus than one might suspect. For, as an example, Wesley's doctrine of holiness (related to (c) above) by which he taught, among other things, that holiness on earth was necessary in order to reach heaven, could drive a wedge between the sacred and the secular, the former representing God, the latter the world, as if the latter had no real value in relation to the former. African theologians agree – and indeed it is more or less generally recognised today – that the whole of life is to be seen in the light of God's love.

The subject of this study has come up again and again at quite a number of gatherings of African theologians. I have myself since 1955 attended a number of conferences, both in Ghana and elsewhere in Africa, at which the theological task facing the Church in Africa has been the main or subsidiary subject for discussion. Two of these conferences were hosted by the All Africa Conference of Churches, and at one other conference which took place in Ghana African theologians engaged Black American theologians in discussion on the subject. Much, then, has been said – though not half as much has been written – on the subject, but in very recent years I have formed the distinct impression that the discussions are beginning to stagnate. There are some reasons to explain this state of affairs. There is, to begin with, the fact that the questioners of the African Church's theological state have not been seriously engaged in discussion by the leadership of the Churches to which they belong. The questions being raised with regard to the Church's theology have largely gone unnoticed by the Church's leadership. Those questioners belonging to the denominational Churches are part of a system which, given its long history of development in the West, focusses attention on the inherited traditions. Indeed, many a questioner continues to live a Christian life which gives no indication whatsoever of a dissatisfaction with the Church's life and thought. Then, following from this, there is the tendency to use such an expression as 'indigenisation' which, unfortunately, is a potentially inhibiting term, since in using it some people assume, consciously or unconsciously, the normative character of Christian thought to be as it has developed in the West. To speak of the process of doing Christian theology in Africa as indigenising or translating Christian theology is to misunderstand the nature of the theological task facing the Church in Africa: this task consists not primarily in thinking through the theological deposit from the West;

it consists in thinking through faith in Christ. Yet again, the present stagnation may be accounted for by reference to the fact that recent discussants often seem to be unaware of past discussions on the subject. Again and again contributions made at conferences have not been such as to build upon the insights which have already been gained into the subject; that is why this study also attempts, among other things, to survey the thinking that has been done on the subject of Christian theology in Africa.

In view of the present state of the discussions it is perhaps not surprising that the phrase 'African theology' itself, which has been used a great deal in discussions over the last decades, is becoming in some quarters a source of confusion; for it has been pointed out by some that this expression is properly used when it designates the articulation of African traditional religious thought. The question of nomenclature may be important, but it must not be allowed to override the importance of the necessity to bring faith in Christ to bear upon the African life-experience, which is what the quest for an African Christian theology is all about.

The writing of this book was prompted in part by the conviction that there is a need to create more discussion and thereby, hopefully, to embroil the Church in Africa, particularly the historic Churches, in the task of re-examining the inherited expressions of faith in Christ.

In this connection some comments are necessary on certain expressions whose use in this book may be considered presumptuous, perhaps, and whose connotations may strike the reader as being somewhat imprecise. The book purports to be about Christian theology in *Africa*; needless to say, I do not presume to have detailed first-hand knowledge of the Church – in all its shapes and forms – in every African country. The only justification for being so bold as to use the expression is that the available literature provides such information about the shape of Christianity in diverse areas of the continent as to suggest that the expression of Christianity in Africa, wherever the traditional world-view persists, has been somewhat less than authentic and relevant; moreover, from meeting at conferences with Christians from many parts of the continent and exchanging views on the subject with them, it has been confirmed for me that there is a certain unity in the nature of the problems arising from the setting up of the Christian Church in Africa by Christian emissaries from outside the continent.

Another of the imprecise terms we have not been able to suppress is 'the Church (in Africa)'. The phrase is used here for the whole body of those who accept the Lordship of Christ and meet in groups of various sizes to celebrate this. This, however, is not meant to hide the fact that there is a bewildering array of Churches in Africa. This great variety of Churches has sometimes led to doubts being expressed as to the genuineness of some of them, especially the mushrooming new Church movements. It is getting increasingly difficult to characterise accurately the new Church movements in Africa. Various unsatisfactory expedients have been adopted, such as that they are at the opposite end of the spectrum from the 'main' (i.e. historic) Churches. In the wake of the veritable explosion of new Churches in Africa in the last several decades the accuracy of the expression 'main' as a characterisation of the historic Churches is called in question, for the great increase in Church membership in Africa in recent years may be accounted for primarily by reference to the membership of the new Churches. These new Churches have been variously characterised, and it is evident that there is need for delineating them more carefully, if for no other reason than that they range over a broad spectrum of shades and forms. The expression 'Spiritual Church' which was once preferred is going out of use, for good reason. Equally inappropriate is 'sect', not only because of the pejorative connotation often given it, but also by reference to the recognised characteristics of sects.[5] The expression 'Independent Church' is not entirely accurate as a blanket term since not all the new Churches are independent; there is, for example, the First Century Gospel Church which is run from the headquarters of its

5. Brian Wilson, *Religious Sects*, World University Library 1970. One may refer to just one of the stated characteristics: Sects, Wilson states, are 'movements of religious protest . . .' (p. 11); evidently not all these Church movements have been protest religious movements.

American founder, Pastor Clark.[6] Nevertheless, it has proved to be a convenient expression, being widely used to describe those new Church movements which have come about in a development which has been generally separate from that of the denominational Churches from the West. No serious study of Christian theology in Africa can with any justification ignore these Churches and their life and thought. They enjoy considerable visibility, and there are some members of the historic Churches who at the same time belong to these newer Churches, and evidently treasure the latter affiliation. While at one time it was thought that these Churches catered almost entirely for the unlettered members of society, now it is a well-known fact that their membership includes many well-educated and highly-placed members of society.

There is also such an imprecise expression as the 'early Church'; whenever it has been used here its connotation, it is hoped, has been self-evident. Possibly other expressions and ideas might be found to be imprecise, but then this would be a measure, on the one hand, of the enormity of the undertaking, and on the other, of the groping which is being done by a Church which has not quite found itself.

6. Incidentally, the adjective 'independent' does not strictly speaking fit the historic Churches either for the simple reason that they have not, by and large, succeeded in developing away from the life and thought of the parent Churches in Europe, even though they are, in general, no longer directed from abroad.

Part One

Theology in the Shaping

1

Some Factors Restated

Every Christian theologises.

Here is a statement that stands a fair chance of being considered melodramatic, for to the uninitiated, whether Christian or non-Christian, the word theology is intimidating: it conjures up visions of learned debates and abstruse dissertations on Christian belief, often seemingly calculated to mystify rather than to enlighten. And, of course, any one who has gone through formal theological training in our time will testify that the student of the Christian faith is being called upon to bring an increasingly diverse set of disciplines to bear upon the study of the faith. Indeed, theological study has become a considerably complex and awesome undertaking. Students of theology, particularly those in seminaries in the Western world, will witness to the great variety of specialists which seminaries employ for the edification of their students. It would seem, then, that theology is done by particular people: those who have received special training.

However, it needs to be recognised that it is not only those who have undergone special training who do theology or may theologise. Every Christian theologises, and the justification for this assertion is that, though ultimately the questions raised by theology (Greek: *theos* = god) are about God, essentially theology has to do with the meaning of human existence; and, theology does not always issue in a propositional articulation of the implications of faith.

Thus theology may be done at more than one level. There is the level at which reflection upon one's faith may not issue in the expression of one's thinking in coherent language. The reflection may be done in song, or in prayer, in action or in meditation: the song one has often sung in Church may suddenly come alive out of a conscious or unconscious relating of its thought to oneself and one's circumstances; one's prayer may reflect one's understanding of the meaning of faith in one's life; one's actions may be founded upon a particular view of life which flows from certain religious convictions; and one's meditation may become, as some of the saints have taught, a losing of oneself in the eternal. The understanding of faith revealed may not be considered to be illuminating by all; some might even consider it erroneous in the light of *their* own understanding of the Christian faith. This does not mean, however, that only certain individuals may theologise while the rest applaud the periodic theological popes; every Christian has a right to, and does indeed theologise, often through unhurried situational reflection. It is this reflection that may consequently give way to theological articulation. That this is exemplified by reference to the writing of the books of the New Testament will presently be noted.

For most people, however, theology much more readily implies articulation, in coherent language, of the Christian faith, and the uninitiated might be forgiven if they felt sometimes that theologians seemed to be more concerned to display erudition and opacity, especially where a philosophical vehicle of presentation has been made into an end rather than a means to an end, that is, the communication of Christian reflection.

Three things have so far been said about theology: it entails reflection; the reflection has situational reality; and, there is the communication of this reflection. The mode of communication may vary: there may be communication through coherent language, so that others might read and reflect upon someone else's reflection; as already indicated, there may be communication through living one's reflection. In a sense all theology must involve communication by living – it should be possible to gain an insight into one's theology through one's mode of life and interaction in society. Unfortunately, things are not always what they seem. Where theology tends to be considered merely as an intellectual exercise, unrelated to the living of faith, it might not be considered needful for one's mode of life to be an actualisation of one's theology; indeed, one's practical living might very well be in contradistinction to one's expressed theological position. Furthermore, there is always a temptation for the Christian to interpret situational reality so narrowly that it becomes the reality in which *others* are situated without his being aware, or indeed willing to admit, that by his own mode of life he might be contributing to that very situation, or that in other ways a particular situational reality at which theological analysis or action is aimed is closely paralleled by the mode of existence in which he might be indulging. In any case, communication is an important goal of theologising for this is the means by which others are enabled to grasp the essence of one's reflection, and to evaluate it in the light of their own circumstances.

We wish now to explore in some detail what we have called situational reality, for one of the most important assumptions underlying this study is that theology is done meaningfully only in context, or with reference to a situation or set of circumstances: not only does reflection necessarily need this situational reality for it to be vital, but also the communication of the reflection becomes most meaningful only when it is done in and through this reality. It is necessary, in the light of this, to raise the question of whether this emphasis on the situation in any sense receives support in what are usually considered to be the factors that shape theology – the 'situation', in the context of this study, being the life-circumstances of the African since one of our purposes here is to examine the relevance of Christian theology, as traditionally conceived, in the Church in Africa. It must be pointed out that our intention is not to undertake an elaborate analysis of these factors; the interested reader will find in such a work as Macquarrie's *Principles of Christian Theology*[1] much detailed material on the subject. Our interest is limited – to look at the main factors or working materials, having in mind what has been said above about situational reality.

The Scriptures

The first of the working materials to be considered is the Scriptures, not only because for many this is a primary formative factor, but

1. John Macquarrie, *Principles of Christian Theology*, S.C.M. 1966.

because to start at this point provides us with the opportunity to mention at these initial stages of our inquiry certain matters which we consider most essential for an appreciation of the concerns underlying the doing of Christian theology in Africa.

The importance of the Scriptures has been given striking expression at various times in the history of the Church. An extreme example is to be found in the Westminster Confession which has put the matter as follows:

> The whole counsel of God, concerning all things necessary for his own glory, man's salvation, faith, and life, is either expressly set down in Scripture, or by good and necessary consequence may be deduced from Scripture; unto which nothing at any time is to be added, whether by new revelations of the Spirit or traditions of men.[2]

It is perhaps needless to point out that this view of the Scriptures constitutes an over-emphasis and, consequently, a distortion. While it recognises that the Bible is the Word of God which was mediated first through his chosen people, and then through Christ to mankind as inheritor of God's grace, it nevertheless is such as to encourage extreme attitudes, such as that which in some quarters has resulted in the view that the Bible is literally inerrable. This, as it is well known, was the position adopted in a Swiss Confession of the seventeenth century which said, among other things, that the Hebrew manuscript of the Bible was inspired not only with regard to the consonants but also with regard to the vowel points.[3] Biblicism of this type is simply not helpful, for indeed the Bible does contain inaccuracies and various other kinds of infelicities, as biblical criticism has shown. This fact, however, does not negate the value that Christians attach to the Scriptures. Moreover, this kind of extreme attitude is one of the surest ways of drawing attention away from some very important biblical notions. It is an attitude that constricts the circle of theological vision, increasing its concentration, but at the expense of its breadth. As an attitude it may

2. 1.6; *The Proposed Book of Confessions* (The Presbyterian Church of the United States), p. 80.
3. *Formula Consensus Ecclesiarum Helvetiarum Reformatorum*, 1675.

have come about as a result of zeal for God's Word, but it turns out, paradoxically, to diminish the breadth of that Word; it in fact fails to take notice of certain insights into biblical study and teaching.

One of these insights is that God is concerned also with peoples outside the covenantal relationship with Israel.

The issue of the relationship between the people of Israel and the *goyim* is raised, in various ways, in both Testaments, and it is a commonplace that two attitudes can be discerned in the Scriptures.[4] There is an attitude which is strongly condemnatory of the life and thought of other peoples. According to this, Israel stands in a special relationship with God, a relationship which is epitomised by the images of choice and covenant. Indeed, the Deuteronomist takes the extraordinary step of referring to the Israelites as 'sons of Yahweh',[5] a phrase which implies a special bond between Yahweh and the Israelites, 'a people holy to the Lord'.[6] The Deuteronomic construction of the history of the Israelite settlement in Canaan is to a certain extent a theological statement which sees the people of God achieving an inevitable and speedy victory over the inhabitants of the land; surely, the possession of the land by the Israelites could not be thwarted by those who did not know Yahweh! It is in keeping with this that the Israelites are forbidden to adopt pagan practices;[7] they would have only themselves to blame if they went after other gods: 'Like the nations that the Lord makes to perish before you, so shall you perish, because you would not obey the voice of the Lord your God.'[8] Indeed, dedicated Yahwists considered the other peoples' gods to be powerless, even non-existent.[9] In view of this the exile of 586 B.C. was an uncomfortable experience, for it seemed as though the Babylonian victory was indicative of the supremacy of the Babylonian deities. Quite possibly some of the exiles lost faith in a God who could not protect his own. Others – and these would

4. Owen C. Thomas (ed.), *Attitudes Towards Other Religions* (S.C.M. 1969), pp. 12f.
5. Deut. 14:1.
6. Deut. 14:2.
7. Deut. 8:19–20; 18:9–14; etc.
8. Deut. 8:20.
9. Isa. 44:6.

seem to have exerted some influence – were led by the experience to the conviction that their survival would depend on their adhering strictly to their traditions; hence the strict observance of the circumcision rite and the sabbath, the rewriting of the existing records of Israel's history to reflect the Deuteronomic teaching which held that obedience to God deserved reward, while disobedience deserved punishment, and Nehemiah's insistence that those who would come to live in Jerusalem must have authentic Jewish ancestry.

If the attitude just surveyed bespeaks a theological discontinuity between Israel and other peoples, there is material in the Scriptures suggestive of an attitude which is the opposite of this. Not only did God create mankind, but also when man repeatedly disobeyed God he was not cast off.[10] It is affirmed more than once in Genesis that it is by God's action that mankind is diverse. In the story of the Tower of Babel man's cultural striving is critically viewed, and though human pride is deprecated, cultural development *per se* is not condemned. Then comes the promise to Abraham according to which by Abraham 'all the families of the earth shall bless themselves',[11] a promise that links up with the story of the creation of mankind. Many an Israelite prophet surprised his contemporaries by asserting that Yahweh's own people, as well as the non-Israelite peoples, deserved to be punished; the fact that Israel was Yahweh's own people would not save her from being severely punished. Indeed, Israel seemed to be less responsive to God's demands than 'peoples of foreign speech and a hard language'.[12] It is in line with this that Malachi declares:

> For from the rising of the sun to its setting my name is great among the nations, and in every place incense is offered to my name, and a pure offering; for my name is great among the nations, says the Lord.[13]

This passage has been interpreted in essentially two ways. According to one interpretation, Malachi is commending the

10. Gen. 1–11.
11. Gen. 12:3.
12. Ezek. 3:6.
13. Mal. 1:11.

worship practices of the Jews of the diaspora, 'nations' being on this understanding a reference to the peoples among whom Jewish settlements were to be found.[14] According to another interpretation, Malachi is commending the universal worship of the heathen: Jewish worship is not acceptable before God because it is corrupt, while heathen sacrifices are pure in God's sight because they are in accordance with what is prescribed in pagan cultic regulations. When the latter interpretation is viewed against the background of Malachi's severe criticism of his people's cultic practices, it gains in validity. In effect Malachi is saying that God is close to all peoples in the particularity of their differing life-situations. It may be pointed out in this connection that the people of Israel were not averse to appropriating other peoples' religio-cultural practices to express their understanding of God;[15] the very concept of Yahweh was enriched through contact with Canaanite life and thought, as such images as the vineyard,[16] and Israel as Yahweh's bride[17] indicate.

These then are the two attitudes, the presence of which in the early Church explains the genesis of the controversy which was 'resolved' by the Jerusalem Council as recorded in Acts 15.

It is being suggested here that at a deeper level the biblical attitude is more open and universalistic than exclusivist – all peoples stand in a close relationship with God. That many in the early Church understood Jesus' message in this way is attested in Luke's Gospel which again and again shows that Jesus was able to rise above the narrow-mindedness that saw God as reserving his love and mercy for the people of Israel.

This is a biblical fact of which theology must take account; for if indeed God is concerned with all peoples, then there is a theological continuity between the people of Israel and the *goyim*.

Secondly, even when it has been allowed that the Scriptures

14. S. W. Baron, *A Social and Religious History of the Jews* (New York, Columbia University Press, 4th ptg. 1962), p. 127.
15. J. Gray, *The Legacy of Canaan* (Leiden, E. J. Brill, 1957), pp. 140 ff.; H. Ringgren, *Israelite Religion* (Philadelphia, Fortress Press, 1966), pp. 176–7.
16. Isa. 5:1 ff.
17. Hos. 1:1 ff.

contain this important strand which sees a theological continuity between ancient Israel's traditions and those of other peoples, it still remains a fact that the Scriptures are a *particular* witness to the revelation of God made through *particular* events.[18] The question then arises of why store should be set by such notions as are found in the Scriptures considering that we live in times which are different, in some very fundamental respects, from those of ancient Israel. To say simply that being a Christian compels one to abide by the Scriptures is only to give a partial explanation, because the fact of the particularity of the Scriptures as an Israelite phenomenon would remain. Here is an issue which for reasons of space we cannot discuss in detail; it will suffice to bring out its bearing upon the subject of this study, Christian theology in Africa. Given the particularity of the Scriptures in terms of their historical and cultural background, it is not sufficient for the Church in Africa – or anywhere else, for that matter – merely to accept the tradition of a covenantal relationship between God and Israel. It is of fundamental importance that the Christian Church, wherever it is found, should *experience* the approach of God to humankind; it must *relive* here and now the outgoingness of God for the Scriptures to become for it the *living* Word of God. An important consequence of this is that, the message of God in the Scriptures must be heard and appropriated in the context of every people's circumstances; the Scriptures must be heard speaking to people in the particularity of their life situations. Thus in addition to the theological continuity there is a hermeneutical or interpretative continuity between Israelite traditions in the Scriptures, and the life and thought of other peoples.

In the light of this, theology must be an exercise in relevance; it is to be done in and through concrete life experiences. To put this in another way, to do Christian theology presupposes an awareness, among other things, of the Scriptures as a living Word – a Word that has power to challenge people everywhere today.

In the third place, it is essential that in emphasising the import-

18. James Barr usefully cautions against undue emphasis on 'events' with reference to the biblical material; see his *The Bible in the Modern World* (S.C.M. 1975), ch. 5.

ance of the Scriptures sight should not be lost of the full implications of Jesus' teaching on the 'spirit of truth' which 'will guide you into all the truth'[19] after his earthly ministry was over. In the light of this teaching we may conveniently speak of the Christ of history and the Christ of experience. There is the Christ of history who lived on this earth and taught, interacting with people and sharing their joys and sorrows. He went into 'alien' situations, much to the distress of the religious purists of his time. He reacted to kings and children, and was as likely to commend a Jew as a non-Jew. As it has been observed, it is perhaps unlikely that the first generations of Gentile believers would have committed their lives to a mythological figure. But, as Form Criticism has shown, the Gospels assumed their shape out of the religious experience of the Christian community – an experience which cherished the Christ of history and which was at the same time made up of a further unfolding of what Christ meant to them in their life and work. The Gospels are written from the point of view of faith and have the aim of eliciting commitment from their readers. Already, then, in the Gospels Christ's words about the 'spirit of truth' are exemplified. The revelation of God in Jesus was not to be limited to the days of Jesus in the flesh. In the light of the history of the Church one cannot but take seriously Jesus' promise that when his earthly existence was over the Spirit would be present with the disciples and would lead them into all the truth. Jesus was not referring to the revelation of an entirely new truth; he was speaking of light being thrown on the truth already revealed to his disciples. So then the Gospels constitute a stage – and a most important one, of course – in the process whereby the revelation of God is made increasingly clear to mankind. Jesus' own teaching, therefore, constrains the Church in every land to be guided into a constant renewal of its life and thought. To say this, however, is at the same time to be painfully aware of the ease with which claims have been made, in the history of the Church, for the Spirit's guiding when in fact it would be truer to say that the Spirit was 'being identified with man's own possibilities'.[20] Granted that

19. John 16:12f.
20. Hans Küng, *On Being a Christian* (New York, Pocket Books, 1978), p. 471.

in our sinfulness we sometimes find it convenient to label our desires as God's leading, nevertheless that teaching of Jesus on the Spirit of truth is clear warrant for hoping for constant guidance and enlightenment. No confessional statement on the Scriptures is complete without reference being made to the Spirit who renews.

Lastly, in the light of what has been said so far about the Scriptures, there is an aspect of New Testament study which is relevant here. One of the results of the critical study of the New Testament is that response to Christ preceded the articulation of faith. The writers of the various books had had an experience which each endeavoured to put into categories which would do justice to that experience. It is because of this that though the New Testament has for its background a common redemptive experience, yet it is by no means homogeneous in ideas. It suited the experience of the author of the Letter to the Hebrews, it must be presumed, to see Christ as the high priest who offers the supreme sacrifice for the sake of mankind. To John, who was evidently steeped in Greek philosophical thought, as well as in Hebrew thought, Jesus was the *logos*, the ground of the universe, the Way, the Truth and the Life for those who believed in him. Paul, versed as he was in Jewish law, experienced in Christ the fulfilment of our moral striving. Other New Testament writers could be referred to in order to underline the fact that response to Christ could not be in exactly the same terms for all, even though it meant for all a sense of salvation. Each of them had this experience of Christ which then issued in the narrating, in a distinctive way, of the story of the salvation that Christ brings.

Experience
It is to be expected that experience should now be highlighted as one of the factors in theological formation, for from comments already made it is evident that it is indispensable in the theologising process. Theologising is preceded by some experience of the life of faith, an awareness of the significance of one's faith. This experience, which is characterised by an openness to fresh dimensions of one's faith, may take the form of a revelation, the breaking in of the

holy upon human consciousness in such a way as to constitute an irreversible religious experience, with important consequences. The Scriptures give us several instances of revelatory experiences. Isaiah's may be cited in illustration, for it has dimensions which are of great significance. In the midst of the Temple activity Isaiah had an experience which was overwhelming – so overwhelming that he could only describe it in terms which the reader can only partly understand. Overcome and conscious of his own sinfulness and that of the community, he is cleansed by God for a task of service to others in God's name.

There is a subjective element in experience, of course. Only Isaiah could be fully aware of the impact of what happened to him in the Temple; in a sense it was an inward experience. This is not to say, however, that the ultimate basis of faith is a person's private convictions, as some have tended to suggest; such extreme subjectivism is unsatisfactory from two points of view. In the first place, it ignores the fact that there are adequate historical grounds for justifying faith. History is capable of leading the inquirer to the conviction that Jesus Christ not only lived, died, rose up from the dead and empowered his disciples to speak in his name to all, but also – and having in mind the subject of this inquiry – interacted with non-Jews, could ride rough-shod over the susceptibilities of those religious leaders who had made virtue out of their narrow-mindedness, and could startle with such pronouncements as that being a Jew was not an automatic qualification for a place in the kingdom. In other words, individual experience must not be presumed to be necessarily inconsistent with the facts of the past. Secondly, experience becomes meaningful, its full dimensions unfolding, in relation to on-going human circumstances. Thus Isaiah's experience blossomed in relation to concrete human situations. Again and again he cites historical occasions to show that the God who came to him in the Temple in such a way as to result in an experience which he could not communicate with any precision was also the God who was involved in the happenings of life, so that the birth of a child to a young woman becomes pregnant with meaning,[21] and the reign

21. Isa. 7:14ff.

of a foreign king provides an illustration of that human arrogance that presumes to ignore Yahweh's sovereignty.[22]

The facts of the past and individual experience, then, must be held in a balance. To emphasise the latter at the expense of the former is to land oneself in that extreme form of subjectivism which makes a person's private convictions the ultimate basis of faith; and to put undue emphasis on the facts of the past could lead to the position associated with those of the dialectical school of theology which postulated that kind of transcendentalism that practically rendered human experience of no account; it would mean setting God entirely apart from our human experiences and circumstances.

Tradition

This is an area of inquiry where questions are most likely to be raised, especially regarding the need for theology to keep within established Church traditions. In view of the nature of our concerns in this study (which has to do with Christian thought in Africa) the question of tradition becomes a particularly important one. On the basis of Christ's own teaching the Church has lived in the belief that the Spirit continually reveals fresh meaning in the teaching of Christ; in listening to the word of Christ afresh lies the Church's authority. But what precisely is the nature of this authority? Much discussion has centred on this question. On the one hand, there has been the tendency to regard the Church as the first source of Christian teaching and tradition. To be sure, those who give the Church this role recognise the importance of the Scriptures, but they consider the Church's interpretation of the Scriptures as primary authority, though there are those who concede co-ordinate authority to the Church's interpretation. On the other hand, in some quarters this tendency is strongly resisted, as is seen in the following statement to be found in the Scots Confession:

As we believe and confess the Scriptures of God sufficient to instruct and make perfect the man of God, so do we affirm and avow their authority to be from God, and not to depend on men

22. Isa. 10:5ff.

or angels. We affirm, therefore, that those who say the Scriptures have no other authority save that which they have received from the kirk are blasphemous against God and injurious to the true kirk, which always hears and obeys the voice of her own Spouse and Pastor, but takes not upon her to be mistress over the same.[23]

In these two positions we have the battle lines of the Catholic 'Scripture and tradition' and the Reformed 'Scripture only' drawn.

Of course, the situation has changed since the pre-Tridentine era. It is now generally believed that to draw a sharp distinction between Scripture and tradition and to see them as two unrelated sources rivalling each other is no longer possible; for historical research has shown that the New Testament writings are themselves already the outcome of, and witness to, tradition; indeed, the canonisation of the New Testament was itself part of the development of tradition. Furthermore, since the Second Vatican Council, Catholic teaching has stressed that there is a very close connection between Scripture and tradition: '. . . there exist a close connection and communication between sacred tradition and sacred Scripture. For both of them, flowing from the same divine wellspring, in a certain way merge into a unity and tend toward the same end.'[24] Thus Scripture and tradition 'form one sacred deposit of the Word of God, which is committed to the Church'.[25] Through the Scriptures the Holy Spirit guides the Church to reflect, so that doctrines obscurely stated in the Scriptures are elaborated by the Church and promulgated. Incidentally, to recognise that the distance between Catholic and Reformed positions on tradition has to a considerable extent been narrowed is not to say that no differences in outlook remain. Thus, while the Reformed teaching seeks to find a direct support in the apostolic witness of Scripture, the Catholic Church tends to perceive the apostolic witness in the life and faith of the whole Church as it has struggled throughout the centuries, and continues to struggle, to grasp the fullness of the divine truth. Furthermore, while Reformed thinking is along the lines of maintaining a balance between the

23. *The Proposed Book of Confessions*, ch. 19, p. 56.
24. *Dei Verbum*, 9.
25. *Dei Verbum*, 8.

theologically trained minister of the Gospel and the total Christian community with respect to discovering afresh the Word of God, the Catholic Church stresses the special services of those who have accepted pastoral responsibility and are therefore considered best suited to make provision for the right interpretation of the Word of God. These differences, however, do not negate the fact that there is considerable post-Tridentine consensus that through the Word of God the Holy Spirit guides the Church to reflect on its heritage. It is in consequence of this reflection that doctrines and confessions of faith are elaborated and worked out.

Some comments on the value of tradition may now be made. In the first place, tradition can be a good thing, for it guards against subjectivism. It provides a person (or a Christian community) with the opportunity of pitting his (their) thinking against that of the Church as it has developed over the centuries, so that the individual experience is tested and tried. This is not to say that the individual experience is *ipso facto* suspect; the point is that just as it would be inexcusable to dismiss individual experience out of hand, so also would it be wrong to assume that there is nothing to be learnt from the accumulated experience of the Church. But – and secondly – tradition could be the death of tradition, if it is not put into its proper perspective. To cling tenaciously to tradition in an unimaginative way, in the sense of the past being made into an unimpeachable norm for the present, is to prevent tradition from *growing* and speaking in authentic accents. For – and thirdly – the development of doctrine and the production of confessions is a dynamic process; the Church must always confess its faith or make doctrinal statements in the language of today. A confession of faith is after all an interpretation of the Word of God at a particular time within a particular set of circumstances; it is an expression of salvation as it is being lived in the Church at a given moment in its history. It is in the light of this that historical confessions raise questions of meaning in today's world. With respect to Christian doctrine it only has to be noted that it has a history of interpretative efforts aimed at giving Christian teaching meaning at particular points in time and in particular places.

However, to conclude from this that there have been discontinuous stages of the restructuring of the Church's teaching is probably misleading, suggesting as it does an inevitable lack of homogeneity. What we noted above about the differing salvation experiences of the authors of the New Testament books might be recalled here: there was a common faith in Christ's saving power, but the expressions of this had a particularity in terms of each author's cultural and intellectual background. Despite the periodic restructuring of doctrine, there is a transcendent meaning which unifies the various efforts. This, I dare say, would be hard to concede where there was an unimaginative attachment to tradition. No formulation of teaching may be considered definitive in the sense that there will never be any need of further re-interpretation in a new social and cultural situation. It must be explained that this is not to suggest that interpretative exercises should never start from the possibility of a particular formulation having relevance in another context, for often the problems of one society may be a fair reproduction of those of another society, even one of another era. Nevertheless, different societies will have specific concerns which will make the re-interpretation of Christian doctrinal formulations necessary. This is a consideration of which the Church must take account if its presence in any particular cultural context is to be vital and constructive.[26]

Fourthly, there is a matter which will be very briefly referred to here without discussion in view of comments already made: it is not often realised how tradition, in the form of creeds, unconsciously influences the interpretation of the Bible, and thus prevents what may be described as a 'relevant reading' of the Bible, for the interposition of the creed and doctrinal formulations creates a new starting point of interpretation which exercises its influence by reference to formal faith positions. On this Nineham has observed:

> In reading the Bible Christians have usually taken for granted the truth of the classical creeds and of the formularies of the denomination to which they belonged, and, with varying degrees

26. Cf. Dennis Nineham, *The Use and Abuse of the Bible* (Macmillan 1976), p. 227.

of self-awareness, allowed them to influence and dictate their interpretation of the text.[27]

The working materials of the Scriptures, experience and tradition intertwine. The inner experience is important; it actualises Christ for the believer in a very intimate way. Also, the Christian is nurtured by the Church which is an extension of the Incarnation. From the very beginning it was in the Church that the facts of Christ's life and work were treasured, meditated upon and witnessed to; it is no accident that Paul refers to the Church as the body of Christ. This is not to say, as some, notably Rudolf Bultmann, have done, that the gospel incidents are merely an idealised reconstruction invented by the Church in the apostolic era. Every Christian must surely take the Church's tradition seriously as long as no authoritarianism is claimed which subordinates Christ to the Church. One possible way of relating the Scriptures, experience and tradition is to see the Scriptures in the centre, with the other two revolving around it, these two being channels which must not be confused with the source of flow.

Culture

From the point of view of this study, and in line with comments already made, culture is a most important formative factor; it has such ramifications that more space is devoted to it here than is given to all the other previously discussed factors together. The point has been made above that it is essential for theology to be expressed in the language of today, and that Christian formularies have to be restructured every so often in the light of new circumstances, in every age and place, and this implies in every social and cultural situation. This procedure is inevitable, for people function most efficiently employing language and thought forms in which they have been nurtured; and theology, involving communication, as it does, obliges us to come to terms with our cultural particularities. It is related of Tillich that during a visit to Japan he noted with bewilderment the unfamiliar nature of the cultural scene; the

27. Ibid., p. 37.

bewilderment eventually turned into a sense of depression at the
thought of his having to rewrite his theology in order to make it
truly catholic. There is a sense in which the catholicity Tillich
yearned for is a necessary theological function: there is one transcendent meaning of which different formulations are parts. In other
words, God's salvific activity in Christ is one. However, this activity
embraces different peoples who speak different tongues and live
their own differing but authentic life-styles, whom God in his
wisdom has created, a fact which obliges the Church to expect that
there will be different understandings and expressions of the same
fact.

To turn specifically to Africa, African peoples have 'their own
cultural traditions some characteristics of which will be highlighted
below.[28] The concerns so far raised regarding the theologian's
working materials inevitably lead to the awareness of the need to
give culture a meaningful role in Christian theology in Africa.
Indeed, to uninformed observers the only formative factor recognised by African Christians is African culture. When Dawson
described culture as a 'theogamy, a coming together of the divine
and the human within the limits of a sacred tradition',[29] he was
providing an accurate characterisation of African life and thought
– African culture and religion are bound up together, so much so
that the term culture is in the context of this inquiry properly used
as an umbrella description which subsumes religion: '. . . a man's
way of life is the way by which he apprehends reality. . .'.[30] Religion
informs the African's life in its totality.

There being this relationship between African religion and
culture, the question arises as to the role which traditional religion
is to play in the theologising process if African culture, as I am
suggesting, is to be considered as an important formative factor of
theology. In my judgement much of the difficulty that arises for
those, especially in the West but also in Africa, who give time to
considering the inescapable nature of the need to theologise in and

28. Chapter 2.
29. Christopher Dawson, *Religion and Culture* (New York, Meridian Books Inc., 2nd
    ptg. 1952) p. 54.
30. Ibid., p. 58.

through cultural particularities concerns this: if African traditional religion is an essential part of African culture, then is it being seriously suggested that theologising in the African context must take account of this religion, a religion that is reputed to be characterised by unsavoury ritualism, polytheistic excesses and which, because of its very 'positive' attitude to nature, seems to be infantile? Those brought up on the theology of Ernst Troeltsch[31] or on the dialectical theology of such scholars as Karl Barth[32] would have serious problems trying to surmount their doubts on this score.

As a matter of fact there is a wider issue to be raised: Is the Christian theologian to be concerned solely with the Christian faith in his theologising, or is he to put Christianity into the wider context of religion as an acknowledgement of God's rule over mankind?

Issues of importance are raised by the fact that all known peoples have some kind or other of religious beliefs. In the last decades much has been written on the subject of the religions of the world, though not all religions have been given the attention they deserve. The issue most relevant to our inquiry is that of the relation between Christianity and other religions. Given the constraints of space no attempt will be made to survey the great number of views which have been expressed on the subject. Though the inquiry at this point is into Christianity and other religions of mankind, it is to be understood that the intention here is to argue that African traditional religion (or simply African religion), like every religion, challenges the Christian theologian to gain a broader understanding of religion in order that he may realise the full implications of the Gospel of Christ.

It was fashionable at one time to divide the world's religions into Christianity and the other religions, on the assumed understanding that the latter were the work of the devil, and that their adherents were bound to perish.[33] The non-Christian world of religions was itself divided into the 'major' or 'higher' religions and the so-called

31. See pp. 32–3 below.
32. See pp. 38–9 below.
33. Cf. Küng, *On Being a Christian*, p. 91.

nature religions, with scholarly attention being devoted to the former; religions without readily discernible bodies of beliefs and creeds did not seem to sustain the interest of serious investigators, generally speaking. The story of the study of man's religions then reached a stage where it was found possible to speak of Christianity in relation to other religions, though Christian scholars often showed their lack of ease in so proceeding. Thus Emil Brunner restricted religions which could be placed side by side with Christianity to Zoroastrianism, Judaism and Islam: these other religions he considered to be 'prophetic' or 'revelation' religions. Brunner did argue that in a sense all religions have an important defect: they are both a search for God, and an organised attempt to escape from him. Nevertheless he proceeded on the basis of there being radical distinctions among religions; not only does he speak of only three religions in connection with Christianity, as already observed, but even as he criticises all religions he singles out the so-called primitive religions as being much less satsifactory in this regard than the 'higher' religions.

Since African religion has traditionally been viewed as a species of 'primitive' or 'nature' religion, it played little or no part in serious discussions on religion. I have used the qualifying word 'serious' in order not to be understood to be saying that no attempts had been made from the start of contact between the Western world and Africa to present to the Western world what European writers believed African religion to consist in. The point is, however, that most of these early efforts, as it is well known, failed to fathom the essence of African traditional belief; not only did this religion belong to the non-Christian world, but also it was not classed with the non-Christian 'major' religions. Even when the attitude which looked down upon all religions gave way to a fairer appraisal of man's religions by a process which it would take too long to trace, 'primitive' religion – and here we have specifically in mind African religion – failed to receive due recognition in books on the subject of the religions of mankind. Thus Guy, whose books on the New Testament have been used by many thousands of West African students as text books for pre-university examinations, does not have a section on African religion in his book *Our Religions*, a collection of essays published under his editorship.[34] In his *Religion and the Christian Faith*, Hendrik Kraemer, once Director of the Ecumenical Institute at Bossey, Geneva, admits being silent about African religion, the reason being that 'it is only recently that [the tribal religions of Africa] have entered into contact with religions belonging to more elaborate cultural systems'.[35] The conclusion is inescapable that from the point of view of Kraemer African religion, compared with the 'major' religions, appears unsophisticated and consequently uninteresting as a cultural phenomenon.

There are thus three main reasons why African religion has received insufficient attention in discussions on religion as a phenomenon, and in relation to the development of Christian theology. First, the evolutionary view of religion placed the so-called primitive religion close to the bottom of the scale, especially as ethnographic material presented the peoples whose religions were so categorised as having an inferior form of civilisation. In this connection the views of the German scholar Ernst Troeltsch are of interest. In his *The Absoluteness of Christianity and the History of Religions*[36] he sets out to demonstrate the absoluteness of Christianity in the stream of history. To do this, he argues, it is sufficient to count with the 'powerful, Christian, Platonic, and Stoic world of ideas on the one hand, and the Buddhist or Eastern world of ideas on the other'.[37] On the basis of these religious orientations he concludes: 'Among the great religions Christianity is in actuality the strongest and most concentrated revelation of personalistic religious apprehension.'[38] On the other hand, 'Polytheism and the numerous religions of uncivilised peoples are irrelevant to the problem of highest religious values'.[39]

34. H. A. Guy, *Our Religions*, J. M. Dent 1973.

35. Hendrik Kraemer, *Religion and the Christian Faith* (Lutterworth 1956), p. 405.

36. Ernst Troeltsch, *The Absoluteness of Christianity and the History of Religions*, Atlanta, John Knox Press, 1971; the third edition of the original German was published in 1929.

37. Ibid., p. 93.

38. Ibid., pp. 111–12.

39. Ibid., p. 92; also p. 108: 'As far as the practical solution of religious problems is concerned, the polytheisms and polydemonisms of the lowest stages of religion do not come into consideration.'

Christianity, then, is not only the culmination point, but also the point of convergence of all religious development.

Troeltsch's analysis is of interest for some reasons, not the least of which is that it implies the very evolutionism for which he criticises such writers as Hegel. His evolutionism becomes even more glaring when he ties Christianity to Western culture: as he puts it, there is 'a vital connection between Christianity and Western culture as a whole'.[40] With Christianity and Western culture so inextricably intertwined a Christian, in Troeltsch's opinion, can say little about his faith to those belonging to other civilisations, and likewise the latter cannot encounter Christ save as members of the Western world.[41] This conclusion, incidentally, opens up a whole new area of speculation, for it raises the question of the extent to which views such as Troeltsch's might have helped to shape European mission policy. Our purpose in making this reference to Troeltsch is limited, however: it is to show how evolutionism has contributed to the narrowing of the field of inquiry, to the disadvantage of theological thought. Kraft is right when he observes: '. . . the western Church (reinforced by ethnocentric theological thinking that is often insensitive to the validity of other cultures), along with a large percentage of the rest of the population, has for the most part retained the evolutionary position.'[42]

Again, African religion seemed to the early European writers to be a rather unattractive religion. Nineteenth-century Methodist missionary records with respect to Ghana and other West African countries often feature the word 'sanguinary' as a description of the local religion, a reference no doubt to the bloody sacrifices (both human and animal) which the inhabitants were found making to the various spirit powers.[43] Disquieted as the explorers and the missionaries were by such encounters, they considered African reli-

40. Ibid., p. 108; also p. 115.
41. See Troeltsch's other book, *Christian Thought: Its History and Application* (London University Press 1923), pp. 21–35.
42. Charles H. Kraft, *Christianity in Culture* (Maryknoll, N.Y., Orbis Books, 1979), p. 51.
43. Guy Hunter, *The New Societies of Tropical Africa* (Oxford University Press, reprinted 1963), p. 9ff.

gion to deserve to be classed with the work of the devil. It is undoubted that the negative impression about African life and thought created by the early records has not quite dissipated. Indeed, some Western theologians refer to African religion in such a way as to suggest that the prayer of the early missionaries that African religion should give way before Christianity has been answered! After all, missionaries had come to Africa for the express purpose of ending the 'unholy' reign of 'magic' which, as they saw it, had enslaved Africa's many millions; the Church, in the form in which the missionaries knew it, was to displace African life and thought. In the process much was done, often out of ignorance, and with mixed success, to discredit various facets of the African religio-cultural tradition; and when the Church was set up it had, unavoidably, a distinctly Western ethos.

Western unhappiness with African religion may be further explained by reference to two characteristics of that religion: it does not present the researcher with a body of beliefs, and it has no founder. Ancient documents and inscriptions aid considerably the study of a religion, and this is why among the religions most explored are Judaism and generally the religions of the East. African religion does not present the researcher with written documents, and though archaeology is beginning to make a meaningful contribution to its exploration African religion still does not enjoy the attraction that other religions – especially those of the East – have for students of religion. With respect to the genesis of the various religious traditions, it is not always recognised that some students of religion draw a distinction between religions that have simply 'happened' and those which have founders; to the phenomenologist the former are equatable with 'primitive' religion. When the religions of the world are looked at from the point of view of their founders and reformers African religion is placed at a disadvantage, because it has no founder.[44]

Times have changed, thanks in part to the increasing readiness demonstrated by Africans educated in Western-oriented educational institutions both in Africa and elsewhere to identify with African

44. Cf. Küng, op. cit., pp. 92–3; also p. 101.

life and thought, and in part by the increasing volume of discerning studies on African religion. Now this religion is better understood than before; though it may not have Western-type formulations and credal statements, it is nevertheless recognised that it has a coherence of its own.[45] Furthermore, it is clear that African religion is not about to disappear, either before the Christian Church's advance (and the Church has been making very rapid progress in Africa), or in the face of advancing technology, industrialisation and urbanisation. Herskovits' study of the Blacks in America,[46] and the life-styles among Black populations in the West Indies and Brazil and elsewhere, have demonstrated the resilience of African life and thought. It is not surprising that many African Christians hold on to the traditional religious presuppositions.[47] More recently archaeological discoveries have established Africa as indispensable for the study of human origins,[48] and there is expectation of light being thrown on African religion, as more discoveries are made, as

45. S. G. Williamson, *Akan Religion and the Christian Faith* (Ghana Universities Press 1965), p. 110.

46. M. J. Herskovits, *The Myth of the Negro Past*, Boston, Beacon Press, 1958.

47. H. Nwosu and O. U. Kalu, 'The Study of African Culture', in O. U. Kalu, (ed.), *Readings in African Humanities: African Cultural Development* (Enugu, Nigeria, Fourth Dimension Publishers, 1978), pp. 10f.

48. The world knows about the finds made by the Leakey family in eastern Africa; one of these was made by the staff of Dr Mary Leakey in Tanzania, on the basis of which Dr Leakey advanced the interpretation that the Homo lineage began almost 3.75 million years ago. Most recently two American scholars, Donald C. Johanson and Tim White, have named the species indicated by the reconstructed skull *Australopithecus afarensis*, after Afar, a region of Ethiopia where Johanson found some of the fossils. Johanson and White argue that the human–ape split took place about 10 million years ago, and *Australopithecus afarensis* (about 3.5 million years old on their reckoning) represented a previously unknown form of human ancestor; according to this reconstruction the human species emerged from more primitive ancestors perhaps some 2 million years ago. This reconstruction has been challenged by Richard Leakey who argues that mankind appeared about 4 million years ago, so long ago that there is no clear evidence of a fossil form that could have been ancestral to human beings. Whatever reconstruction may be put on the so-called *Australopithecus afarensis* find, it remains a fact that skeletal remains have shown that Africa is the place where increasingly archaeologists are going to concentrate their attention in connection with the quest for human origins.

to its earliest stages and development and its place in mankind's religious quest. A promising beginning has already been made with discoveries at the border between Natal and Swaziland which show that religious practices were being carried on well before 15,000 B.C.[49]

In the wake of this rekindled interest in African life and thought which is being demonstrated by people from a wide range of special-isations (anthropologists, linguists, musicologists, etc.), and given the fact that African societies, notwithstanding many impinging foreign ideas and institutions, have retained enough of the past to give their life-styles an unmistakable distinctiveness even in the urban areas (to the extent that many African Christians hold on to traditional religio-cultural ideas and practices while calling on the name of Christ), several writers, mostly African, have called for the working out of a Christian theology that suits the African situation, a theology which would give recognition to the centrality of Christ and at the same time express a genuine African apprehension of the Christian faith. The protagonists of African theology (this is the expression most often used to describe the envisaged theological expression) have in recent years proceeded on the basis of the presupposition that there is one God of the whole earth, and that every religion is to a certain measure an embodiment of the drama of God meeting man. The Ghanaian writer J. B. Danquah has stated: '. . . the Spirit of God is abroad, even in the Akan of the Gold Coast'.[50] In other words, there is one God of the whole earth whom the Akan also are seeking to worship;[51] in effect, there is Religion of which Akan religion is an expression. Unfortunately Danquah does not develop this thought beyond making that bare assertion. Cantwell Smith spells the thought out much more: if, he argues, God is the Father that Christ has taught us to believe he is, then surely he must be involved in the life and thought of all peoples.[52]

49. See T. O. Ranger and I. Kimambo (eds.), *The Historical Study of African Religion*, Heinemann, 1972; see further, pp. 72–3 below.
50. J. B. Danquah, *The Akan Doctrine of God* (Frank Cass 1966), p. 186.
51. See p. 123 below.
52. W. Cantwell Smith, *The Faith of All Men* (Mentor Books 1965), pp. 89ff.

Several questions, then, clamour for attention: Is African religion indeed an avenue of the revelation of God to man? What is the relation between the revelation in Christ and African religion? To move from the specific to the more general, what is the relation between theology and the religions of mankind? Is there a connection between the function of theology and the discipline of the history of religions?

The science of the history of religions consists in gathering information about various religions (though hitherto this science has paid little or no attention to African religion), and it does so with every scientific means available – linguistic, ethnological and historical approaches are all utilised in the collection of data. Then the historian of religions proceeds to interpret these phenomena which constitute ultimate reality for living people. He compares and interprets myths, symbols and rituals, the very things by which people the world over set much store and which are believed to determine the nature and destiny of man.

It must be emphasised that the historian of religions studies religions as they actually are, and not as they are claimed to have been in some ideal form in the past. This is an important point that cannot be over-emphasised. Statements about a religion must be such that their adherents could give assent to them; they must be statements about the religion as it is and as it actively affects the lives of its adherents, not merely as it once was or is thought or expected to be. The study of African religion tends to suffer in this regard, because there is a tendency to rely very heavily on some of the excellent studies made of it by past researchers, their efforts being taken, consciously or unconsciously, to reflect present conditions and practices; in other words, African religion has tended to be treated as an immutable phenomenon, and that is why the historical approach to its study, to which we have already made reference, is so welcome. Of course it is important to know what a particular religion was at one time, but that should not be considered to be the sum-total of the inquiry. The African religious situation reflected in the nineteenth-century missionary records is not quite the same as it is today. Too much has happened since then to have made it possible for African religion to remain untouched.

The 'sanguinary' practices referred to in past records, particularly
the shedding of human blood, is not overtly encouraged in traditional practices now, and where it occurs public opinion is as
unfavourable as the American public opinion is outraged by the
work of New York's arsonists. After all it is people of flesh and
blood who practise religion, so that studying a religion amounts to
studying a living people. The symbols and ritual practices are
important, but these are not in themselves religion. Religion is what
these things mean to those who live with them. Religion is interior
to people; this is not without prejudice to the need for studying the
observable externals, as long as the externals are not considered to
define the totality and essence of religion.

   The last point has been belaboured with African religion in mind.
It is a religion practised by a great host of Africans. Where it is not
overtly practised, its presuppositions nevertheless influence the life
and thought of even those Africans who have accepted Christianity,
as already observed; traditional ways and thought may continue to
shape their thinking and actions. The point being made is that the
historian of religions cannot on any ground whatsoever ignore the
necessity for taking African religion, and indeed the so-called primal
religions, seriously.

   When it comes to the work of the theologian we are inclined to
say even less, not because the nature of the theological task is self-
evident, but because evidently there has been quite a variety of
approaches. The following description of the theological task is,
therefore, not meant to be exhaustive; indeed it is confessedly
partisan. For the Christian theologian the ultimate reality is Christ.
This statement has increasingly raised for many the question of the
nature of the revelation of God in Christ and its relation to the
religions of mankind. Perhaps the most widely known position on
this has been championed by those of the school of 'dialectical
theology', of which the best-known representative is Karl Barth.
Dialectical theologians consider that there is a gulf fixed between
God and man, a gulf which only God, the wholly other, can bridge
through his revelation. Barth did hold the view that in a sense
Christianity was not unique; it was a manifestation of the universal
phenomenon of religion, and all religion is unbelief since it repre-

sents attempts at self-justification and self-assertion before God.[53] Nevertheless Christianity, he believed, could justifiably be considered the true religion on the basis of the criterion of Christ – it is only in this religion that there is the miracle of grace whereby the sinner receives justification. Thus to formulate theology from human requirement is unacceptable since it implies trimming down God's word to suit human needs.

This position is now believed by many – and I share their reservation – to involve severe restrictions on the concept of revelation; for it implies an exclusivist attitude that ignores the reality of mankind's religions.

Among the more challenging theologians of our time are those who have wrestled with the issue of Christianity in a world of religions in such a way as to challenge the exclusivism involved in the views of the dialectical school. One such theologian is John Hick who, in his *God and the Universe of Faiths*,[54] attacks the *extra ecclesiam nulla salus* doctrine. 'Do we', he asks, 'regard the Christian way as the only way, so that salvation is not to be found outside it; or do we regard the other *great*[55] religions of mankind as other ways of life and salvation?'[56] After a careful exploration of the issues involved, Hick comes to advocate a 'Copernican Revolution' in the theology of world religions, in consequence of which we will no longer view the Christian position as the centre, but as one of a number of positions all of which have the same central point of orbit – namely, God himself.

Hick's views are not new, and they have not escaped criticism; but however much they are criticised it has to be admitted that Hick takes the other ('great') religions of the world much more seriously than they are often done. He has provided a powerful statement of the theology of world religions.

Perhaps the most sustained advocacy, in recent times, for an inclusive understanding of theology has been made by the Swiss Catholic theologian, Hans Küng. Küng, to be sure, stands squarely

53. Cf. Küng, op. cit., p. 99.
54. John Hick, *God and the Universe of Faiths*, Macmillan 1973.
55. Our italics; would Hick include African religion in the discussion?
56. Ibid., p. 120.

in the tradition of those European scholars who consider it prudent to limit discussion on the theology of the world religions to the 'higher' religions. That he is inclined to limit discussion in this way is clear, as when he writes, 'Do not all religions – or, if not the nature religions, at least the ethically higher religions – start out from the same perennial questions which open out behind what is visible and palpable and beyond one's own lifetime?'[57] It is difficult to believe that there are religions which do not have precisely these concerns. Nevertheless, Küng's views on the world's religious situation, though they have some limitations, are important. His views may be briefly summarised thus: like Hick he expresses dissatisfaction with the statement *extra ecclesiam nulla salus*, doing so by asking in effect some pertinent questions: What is the Church to say to the fact that only a small minority of the world's population is Christian? Is there no salvation for the vast majority of God's created humanity? What about all those who lived and died *before* Christ? Are they damned? Can it be truly said that God is unconcerned about the majority of his creatures? Küng comes to the conclusion that the exclusivist attitude to the religions of other peoples is insupportable.[58]

The Catholic Church out of which Küng speaks[59] has wrestled with the issue over and over again and, most recently, has made the following statement in the Church's new Constitution:

> But if some men do not know the Father of our Lord Jesus Christ, yet acknowledge the Creator, or seek the unknown God in shadows and images, then God himself is not far from such men, since he gives life and inspiration to all (Acts 17: 25–28), and the Saviour wills that all men should be saved (cf. 1 Tim. 2:4). Those who, while guiltlessly ignorant of Christ's Gospel and of his Church, sincerely seek God and are brought by the influence of grace to perform his will as known by the dictates of conscience, can achieve eternal salvation. Nor does divine Providence deny

57. Küng, op. cit., p. 92.
58. Ibid., pp. 89ff.
59. The Catholic Church has withdrawn Küng's licence to speak in the Church's name.

the assistance necessary to salvation to those who, without having attained, through no fault of their own, to an explicit knowledge of God, are striving, not without divine grace, to lead a good life.[60]

This statement comes in a long line of Catholic pronouncements which go back several centuries, and which indicate the willingness of the Catholic Church to adopt a more flexible attitude to other religions and cultures. However, the passage quoted above has a certain ambiguity about it, an assertion easily substantiated by reference to the word 'guiltlessly': by whose standard would guilt or lack of it be determined? Presumably by reference to the Church's teaching; and thus the cutting edge of this broadmindedness is blunted by an inveigling attachment to tradition.

To go back to the two specialists, the historian of religions and the theologian (the former studies the religious behaviour of man, the latter the revelation of God to man): in the light of the comments so far made how may the relationship between the two be conceived? It has already been implied in the discussion so far that the Christian theologian must not simply write off the other religions. But how, in more positive terms, may his work be viewed in relation to other religions?

One may describe the relationship between the historian of religions and the theologian in terms of the necessity for the latter to endeavour to gain a thorough understanding of the non-Christian religions as they have been analysed by the former.[61] Different peoples have different religious traditions and experiences, and the theologian should seek to broaden his horizons by studying these diverse phenomena as indications of a world-wide human awareness of an other-worldly dimension to existence. Such a statement would seem to be a very helpful one, recognising as it does the value of other peoples' traditions. However, it needs to be carefully evaluated as to its real import, for it is capable of being understood in a negative way. It could, for example, be taken to mean that the

---

60. *De Ecclesia*, 11.16.
61. Cf. Joachim Wach, *Types of Religious Experience* (University of Chicago 1951), pp. 25-6.

theologian should give some kind of recognition in his work to other religious traditions while maintaining an essentially exclusivist stand. Those who would adopt this approach would find that they had been anticipated by Justin Martyr in the second century, and in the third by Clement and Origen of Alexandria, who brilliantly expounded the *logos spermatikos* doctrine. Utilising the Platonic–Stoic philosophy of their time these early Churchmen came out with the teaching that the pagans who taught good and beautiful things did so through the presence of the divine *Logos*: it was the *logos spermatikos* which had made it possible for them to have such noble thoughts; hence the good elements in other religions and cultures. However, no matter how noble their teaching might be, pagans have in part what Christians have in full. This early Church doctrine continues to find favour with some theologians; it has been championed in one form or the other at various times, up to the present.

That this understanding of the relation between Christian theology and religion has proved useful is beyond question, for after all it is the basis of all non-exclusivist Christian theological positions. However, as a way of relating the two areas it is basically unsatisfactory. It seems to me that it is not helpful enough to express the relationship simply in terms of a peaceful co-existence, for it would leave the history of religions and theology sparring at a distance without seriously engaging each other, and this would have certain consequences: the history of religions would remain a cataloguing of religious phenomena, while theology would continue to be understood – as it is now in some circles – only as dogmatics. Each would be continually tempted to keep the other at arm's length and, indeed, to consider it unimportant; each would consider itself to be essentially self-sufficient. Surely it is essential that the relationship between them should go beyond the level of co-existence, if for no other reason than that both deal with religion which informs life vitally.

Is the theologian adequately defined as a spokesman for a particular religion, that is, Christianity? Or is he one whose understanding of the revelation of God has been tempered and enriched by an insight into God's self-disclosure in other religious traditions?

Is the term theology fully meaningful when used in relation to the life and thought of strictly one group of people, that is, Christians?

The object of the theologian's study, as already observed, is the revelation of God, and this revelation can hardly be defined simply in relation to a contingent group, particularly as theology is understood to be a function of the Church; for the Church speaks and acts not for the sake of one contingent group, but for the sake of all. It is in consonance with the nature of the Church that John should speak of Jesus as 'the expiation for our sins, and not for ours only but also for the sins of the whole world'.[62] Paul struggles with this thought, coming back again and again to the view that God must be seen in his full majesty, and not merely as the God of the Jews only.[63] And here Paul had theologically respectable parentage in some parts of the Old Testament where God is portrayed as being concerned with mankind, as was remarked earlier.[64]

In this connection the views of Johannes Blauw and Wolfhart Pannenberg are of interest. Writing under the title 'The Biblical View of Man and His Religion'[65] Blauw makes the point that 'man in his religion is the man who – for better or for worse – is related to God . . . It is important to have an understanding of the religions of mankind in order that we may be able to *hear* in them the answer of men to God's question, Man, where art thou?'[66] Considering that the Bible itself shows an interest in man's religions, 'it is important to have a real knowledge of the religions of man, not only because of general interest, but in order better to be able to articulate the word of God which is for all men, as the word of God for *this* man in his particular position'.[67] Blauw goes on to develop the thought in a way that would be considered in some theological circles as betraying the Word of God: 'By going as far as possible with man

62. 1 John 2:2.
63. It is admitted that Paul is unable to draw out the full implications of this realisation; see p. 89 below.
64. See pp. 18–19 above.
65. Johannes Blauw, 'The Biblical View of Man and His Religion' in G. H. Anderson (ed.), *The Theology of the Christian Mission*, New York, McGraw-Hill, 1961.
66. Ibid., p. 39.
67. Ibid., p. 40.

into his religious home, its atmosphere and vocabulary, perhaps the way may be opened for a new understanding both of "this religion" and "this gospel" '.[68] Finally, seeing that the Bible teaches that man is sinful, how should we understand Col. 1:15–20 which speaks of reconciling all things to Christ? 'Do we not fall short of the glory of Jesus Christ,' he asks, 'if we exclude from "all things" . . . the extremely rich heritage of the manifold religions by assuming that they cannot be reconciled to him?'[69] In a similar vein Pannenberg has observed:

> . . . the question concerning the truth of the Christian faith cannot be answered by the mere assertion that Jesus Christ is the truth, but only with regard to the whole of the reality that we experience. Only in this way is the unity of truth, which is essential to it, guaranteed. If the Christian proclamation should abandon the consideration of the totality of reality experienced by its hearers, then it would neglect 'Christian solidarity with the godless', and could no longer raise a well founded claim to be speaking about *the* absolute truth. As a result, the Christian proclamation would gradually become fit for display in a museum.

Again: 'The ultimacy of the Christian revelation can be illuminating, not as a supernaturalistic presupposition, but only if it can result from an unprejudiced understanding of the total process of the universal history of religion.'[70]

Opinions such as these suggest that within the context of the theologian's discipline religious distinctions are much less meaningful than one might be inclined to think. The theologian might argue that his approach to religion is so radically different from that of the historian of religions that he does not need the expertise of the latter in order to theologise: the theologian, starting from the revelation of God, has a 'downward' approach, to borrow G. Van der Leeuw's terminology,[71] while the approach of the historian of

68. Ibid., p. 40.
69. Ibid., pp. 40–1.
70. Wolfhart Pannenberg, *Basic Questions in Theology*, vol. 2 (S.C.M. 1971), pp. 2, 69.
71. *Inleiding tot de Theologie*, 2nd edn (Amsterdam 1948), pp. 163ff.

religions is 'upward', or worldly in the sense that the material he studies constitutes, as some would describe it, organised human rebellion against God. But before the theologian sets himself apart from the historian of religions in this way – and this way of distinguishing between the two kinds of specialists has been advocated – he must make a distinction between the given of the revelation of God and the theology he works out. The given, which is the basis of the theologian's study, is outside of himself, but the theology of the theologian can be described with considerable justification as human; after all the theologian is human. This point hardly needs to be laboured. The theological conflicts of the early days of the Church; the different theories of atonement based upon the material circumstances prevailing in particular periods; the theological movement from the rationalistic liberalism of Schleiermacher, Ritschl and Troeltsch, to the transcendentalism of Barth, to existential theology represented by Bultmann, to the revolt against existentialism, etc.: we have in the story of these developments a clear indication that theology has always been done by human beings! It was perhaps not without a touch of exasperation that Butterfield observed:

> It was often noted in the earlier decades of the present century how greatly it had become the habit of Protestants to hold some German scholar up their sleeves, a different one every few years but always preferably the latest one, and at appropriate moments strike the unwary Philistine on the head with this secret weapon, the German scholar having decided in a final manner whatever point might have been at issue in a controversy.[72]

This passage has been quoted not with a view to decrying theological innovation; we have often been helped by the brilliant minds which the world of theology has known, and it would be foolish to deny this. The fact remains, however, that theologians are human, and their theology cannot be other than human, even though it may be a source of enlightenment for many. Moreover, there is much evidence forthcoming from the history of the Church to show

72. Herbert Butterfield, *Christianity and History* (New York, Scribner, 1949), p. 9.

that the work of theologians has not, in many instances, involved a contempt for the world; on the contrary, many theologians have shown a deep sense of commitment to the world of their day and have attempted to see the reality of the revelation of God in the particularity of their circumstances, either of their own or of their society.

If the theologian is as we have described him, then the history of religions which involves itself with that which determines the nature and destination of man, that which reveals the hopes and fears of man, should matter a great deal to him. He needs first to recognise the structures of religion as revealed by the historian of religions or he may not notice the absence of religion from his theology. In the context of Africa, Christian theology must of necessity take account of that understanding of religion which bears the stamp of an authentic African contribution.

2

The African Religio-Cultural Reality

To begin with, the expression 'religio-cultural' calls for a comment. Culture involves many things: language, morality, art and generally material creations, including implements (whether used in agriculture, art, or generally for the purpose of ensuring that life goes on). This means that the culture of a people embraces its economics, politics, legal systems, and all the other societal systems and arrangements set up to ensure the welfare of the community. Moreover, in some societies all this is inseparable from religion; certainly in African society culture and religion are not easily separated. Religion is a regular accompaniment in a person's life; the chief's role, the relations between members of a society, morality, the stages in a person's life (birth, puberty and marriage, and death), the practice of medicine, architecture, warfare, traditional education, etc.: all these areas are not dissociated from religion in traditional African society. This means, of course, that to write a fully informative account of African religion and culture in the space at our disposal is a well-nigh impossible task. I shall therefore content myself with highlighting three areas of life and thought which reveal important religious ideas and vital societal arrangements which ensure the preservation and perpetuation of society.

Religion and the Physical World
It has been said that one of the differences between primal and technological world-views is that, while in the latter nature is to be 'exploited for human ends', in the former, 'people live in a relation-

ship of mutual obligation with nature'.[1] These statements of attitudes are valid if taken to be general statements, of course. The Western world has had a long history of attempts to control nature by first probing its secrets, and then making it serve man's purposes; since nature is often encountered as being hostile Western man has seen his survival as depending upon nature being brought under man's control. In our time man's indifference and downright thoughtlessness has resulted in near-crisis environmental situations, especially in the West: excessive hunting of certain animal species; the use of defoliating agents; the pollution of rivers, sometimes through the clandestine disposal of harmful chemical wastes – these and other examples of the Western attitude to nature have been very much in evidence, and have been the subject of much discussion in recent years. Even though there are groups in the West which are busily inculcating an ecological awareness with a view to reversing these destructive trends, it is nevertheless true that the predominant attitude in the West is one of exploiting nature.

In view of this it is hardly surprising that Western evaluations of the 'primal' attitude to nature have often been negative. Karl Marx's evaluation is an illustration of this. Following the anthropologist, M. Morgan, he found fault with the 'primitive' way of life which, as he saw it, prevented 'primitive' man from recognising the essential differences between himself and his environment. 'Primitive' man's 'Natur-religion', as he termed it, was a falsification of man's view of his world.[2] Students of 'primitive' religion have proved Marx wrong, though his kind of evaluation has continued to be made.

This introduces a very important dimension of African religion, one which has been the source of much misunderstanding, that is, the fellow-feeling that the African has with nature, which has led sometimes to the description of African religion as 'nature' religion. This fellow-feeling is of course much less in evidence in the urban

1. J. B. Taylor (ed.), *Primal World Views* (Ibadan, Daystar Press, 1976), p. 125.
2. Leszek Kolakowski, *Main Currents of Marxism: The Founders* (Oxford University Press 1978), pp. 134–7. J–J. Rousseau's evaluation was perhaps extreme in the other direction – he idealised the 'primitive' attitude; see his *Discours sur l'origine et les fondements de l'inégalité parmis les hommes*.

areas of Africa than in the rural. In the cities evidence of pollution is not difficult to find, thanks to the technological borrowing which is being done, often unimaginatively, by African countries; hence the setting up of Environmental Protection, or similarly-named bodies, in some African countries. Generally speaking, however, the environment has a special meaning for the African; he loves the environment, he fears it, and he senses something mysterious about it. The elements, plants and animals, the land and all that is within and on it – these play a vital role in the African's apprehension of reality.

That this has led to much misunderstanding is well known, and it would do no harm to go over some of this here. The evolutionary theory of religion, to which reference has already been made, has contributed in no small way to African religion being misjudged as to its value. It is in line with this type of thinking that references to African religion as animism still continue to be made in some circles. Of course there is the animistic in African religion, as there is in Christianity and other religions, but this does not make African religion deserve the description of animism, any more than does Christianity. Another unsatisfactory – yea, erroneous – description is fetishism which is a term used to characterise a religious system in which objects such as wood, stone, water, etc. are feared in themselves because supernatural powers are believed to be inherent in them. It has been pointed out often enough that the various material objects which feature in African religious practices are not venerated for their own sake; they are the means by which the spirit powers which they represent are approached.

While on the subject of that misinterpretation of the nature of African religion which arises from a failure to appreciate the African attitude to his environment, reference must be made to certain related matters. The African's approach to the universe is in one sense undifferentiated and unspecialised. In the West it is customary to systematise and label, distinguishing the animate from the inanimate, the physical from the metaphysical, the sacred from the secular, the natural from the supernatural. To the African such distinctions are not as meaningful as one might expect, for the unseen powers are held to be active also in the natural order. This is easily illustrated by reference to the African sense of causation. There is no happening which is uncaused. Disease may be the result of invading bacteria and other micro-organisms, as the Western-trained doctor would explain it; the death of an old person from respiratory disorders may be the result of weakened body systems being unable to cope with the deleterious effects of, say, smog in London or Los Angeles. To the African, disease and death are caused *ultimately* by spirit powers; the universe is full of spirits which for one reason or the other may act for or against man. In other words, the African predominantly interprets his world theologically, rather than in scientific terms, in terms of *final* rather than material causes. This is not to say, however, that the African has no knowledge of what might be labelled scientific causes. To this point I shall return.

The description given above of the African world being undifferentiated recalls Levy-Bruhl's description of 'primitive' mentality as 'pre-logical'.[3] The only justification for referring here to a theory which has not stood the test of time is that it is illustrative of the tendency to judge African religion by non-African standards; also, it ignores certain considerations which have an important bearing upon our concerns here in this study. The crux of Levy-Bruhl's critique is that 'primitive' thought differs from the thought of 'civilised' man in quality. If this were so, then one could hardly communicate with the African or indeed learn his language, as it has been pointed out.[4] To refer to another element in Levy-Bruhl's analysis, there is his contention that the 'primitive' mind sees things so connected (e.g. man and his shadow, man and his name, etc.) that what affects one affects the other, not objectively but by mystical action. As Evans-Pritchard has pointed out, on Levy-Bruhl's reckoning when the Nuer say a twin is a bird they are identifying the two; in fact, however, though the Nuer may say this and act as though the twin and the bird were one, they are in reality aware

3. L. Levy-Bruhl included 'Negroes' among the peoples whose reasoning he so labelled; see his *Primitive Mentality*, Allen and Unwin 1923; New York, Macmillan Co., 1923, and *How Natives Think*, Allen and Unwin 1926.

4. E. E. Evans-Pritchard, *Theories of Primitive Religion* (Oxford University Press 1965), pp. 78ff.

that the two are different;[5] in other words, the Nuer do not contravene the law of contraries. Furthermore, as Evans-Pritchard has shown, the development of modern Europeans from their 'primitive' era could not have happened unless their 'primitive' forebears had had empirical knowledge, in addition to the 'mystical' notions, to guide them.

This last observation raises the issue of whether it is any more valid to describe the African's attitude to his world as unscientific, as has been done sometimes. It has been stated above that the African interprets his world theologically rather than in scientific terms, and it has been pointed out often enough that for the African the spirit world and the physical world interact. It is important that this point be qualified, otherwise it might suggest to some that the African has no interest whatsoever in natural causes. The world of natural phenomena may be viewed by the African as part of spiritual reality, but there is no question of one world being real and the other not. This may be illustrated by reference to the diagnosis of disease by medicine men in Africa, on which subject Horton has some very useful comments:

Through the length and breadth of the African continent, sick or afflicted people go to consult diviners as to the causes of their troubles. Usually, the answer they receive involves a god or other spiritual agency, and the remedy prescribed involves the propitiation or calling-off of this being. But this is very seldom the whole story. For the diviner who diagnoses the intervention of a spiritual agency is also expected to give some acceptable account of what moved the agency in question to intervene. And this account very commonly involves reference to some event in the world of visible, tangible happenings.[6]

5. See E. E. Evans-Pritchard's *Nuer Religion* (Oxford University Press 1956) and *Witchcraft, Oracles, and Magic Among the Azande* (Oxford University Press 1937); also M. Polanyi and H. Prosch, 'Truth in Myths' in *Cross Currents*, vol. XXV, no. 2 (Summer 1975), pp. 149ff.
6. Robin Horton, 'African Traditional Thought and Western Science, I', *Africa*, vol. XXXVII (January 1967), p. 53.

The African farmer knows when to prepare the ground, when to sow and where to sow what; likewise the fisherman knows where to fish for what types of fish, etc.

Without going into any more detail about the misrepresentations of African religion, especially where the attitude to the environment is concerned, we would say that the African's world coheres for him. The universe is for him a living universe, and he is part of it. To appreciate African religion one has to first appreciate this attitude to the environment.

God, the gods and Man

What used to be regularly singled out for comment as signifying the inferiority of African religion is no longer deserving of extensive comment: no one seriously believes now that the concept of God in African religion is a borrowed one. It is more important to our purpose to look at some of the typical views of him and their implications, though matters of controversy will not be avoided.

The concept of God is to be encountered all over Africa, and going with this belief are stories of his having *withdrawn* away from men: there are widespread stories of how God used to live with human beings in a primal state of peace; he then withdrew, far, far away from the world of humans.[7] What the reality is behind such stories is debated. That God is in African thought associated with the sky (though not *identified* with it) is demonstrated in many African God-names: not only do these names often imply brightness, but also in some cases they are interchangeable with, or closely related to, the descriptions of rainfall, thunder, lightning, etc.[8] Thus the stories are quite explicit on God being 'far away' from the world of man. Are these stories meant to say simply that man could not read God's mind and discover his intentions, and hence could not

7. Among the Akan of Ghana it was the pestle of the woman pounding *fufu* which finally drove God upwards. See Edwin Smith (ed.), *African Ideas of God* (Edinburgh House 1950), pp. 216 and 233; also G. Parrinder, *African Traditional Religion* (S.P.C.K. 1962; New York, Harper and Row, 1976), pp. 40, 41.
8. See my 'Introduction' to J. B. Danquah's *The Akan Doctrine of God*, 2nd edn, Frank Cass 1968.

use his power? Or are they a way of explaining what is a reality in African religion: the presence of a considerable number of lesser divinities? Some African writers have argued, putting together the views represented by the two questions above, that a system of intermediaries became necessary because for some reason or other man had failed to understand God.

Now the question of the relation between God and the lesser divinities is from our point of view not one that is answered by simply referring to the latter as intermediaries, though this would appear to be the answer most favoured by African writers. But before we give consideration to this issue, it must be pointed out that the myth of the withdrawn God does not mean that for the African God is to all intents and purposes a redundant God. The Asante of Ghana may not have temples to *Nyame*, but they have *Nyamedua*, a three-forked branch supporting a pot into which food items are put as offerings to God.[9] Sacrifices to God are not often encountered; indeed, according to Arinze, among the Igbo of Nigeria sacrifices made direct to God are so infrequent that the ordinary Igboman may not be aware that they are done at all.[10] It is significant that sacrifices are offered to him, even though infrequently. These and other bits of evidence which could be cited do show that the withdrawn God is still considered to be close enough to be approached formally in worship, and more especially inform-ally in ejaculatory statements featuring the God-name in unexpected situations, particularly stress situations.

Some methodological questions arise in the presentation of the concept of God in African religion; one of these, to which reference has already been made, is that of the relation between God and the lesser divinities. This matter is of some importance in view of the increasing readiness with which the term monotheism is used in some quarters to describe African religion. Though Danquah, in his exposition of the religion of the Akan, does not specifically

9. Geoffrey Parrinder, *West African Religion* (Epworth Press 1961), p. 15.
10. F. A. Arinze, *Sacrifice in Ibo Religion* (Ibadan University Press 1970), p. 54; cf. S. E. Ezeanya, 'God, Spirit and the Spirits' in Kwesi Dickson and Paul Elling-worth (eds.), *Biblical Revelation and African Beliefs* (Guildford, Lutterworth, 1969), pp. 38–41.

identify Akan religion as monotheistic, he strongly implies this in his argument, which was undoubtedly inspired by Schmidt's theory of *urmonotheismus*,[11] that the Akan did not originally know the worship of lesser divinities, and that this came in as a corrupting influence.[12] It must be added that Danquah does not provide any evidence to back up his claim. Danquah is not the only African writer to be drawn to Schmidt's conclusions. Idowu has been favourably disposed towards his primitive monotheism theory, and comes down hard on those who are inclined to deny Africans the ability to have a conception of God;[13] he argues, moreover, that in African religion God is the sole goal of worship, and this is done through the lesser divinities which are not worshipped as ends in themselves. Accordingly, Idowu describes African religion as diffused monotheism, a description which rests upon the role he considers the lesser divinities to play in relation to God.

Idowu and others describe African religion as monotheism in reaction to such descriptions as polytheism because of the latter's implied ranking of God with the gods, as Ellis did.[14] However, whether monotheism or polytheism is to be preferred depends in the final analysis on what definitions one gives these terms. While it is not my intention to give definitions here of these two terms, I would observe that there has sometimes been considerable haste in the application of these terms to African religion. Polytheism, as it will be admitted, does not quite do full justice to the deep respect Africans have for God, a respect which the limited attention paid to him in ritual would seem to belie. God is held very high in the thinking of the African, and this is evident from a study of the praise-names and attributes given to him,[15] as well as from a consideration of how his relation to man is conceived, as we shall presently

11. Wilhelm Schmidt, *The Origins and Growth of Religion: Facts and Theories*, trans. H. J. Rose, Methuen 1931.

12. See K. A. Dickson, 'Introduction' to J. B. Danquah, op. cit.

13. See his contributions in Kwesi Dickson and Paul Ellingworth (eds.), *Biblical Revelation and African Beliefs*, Guildford, Lutterworth, 1969.

14. A. B. Ellis, *Tsi-speaking Peoples of the Slave Coast*, Chicago, Benin Press, 1964 (reprint).

15. J. Mugambi and N. Kirima, *The African Religious Heritage* (Nairobi, Oxford University Press, 1976), pp. 122ff.

see. He is the one on whom 'you lean and do not fall';[16] he it is who responds when called,[17] the one who has always been there, 'the old, old one',[18] etc. On the other hand monotheism (whether qualified or not) as a description of African religion raises problems. One element which is missing in the discussion hitherto of the relation between God and the lesser divinities is *a consideration of how the relation is conceived and described in African religion itself.* It is not enough to say, as is usually done, that the relations within the world of spirits is patterned after the relations within human social structures:[19] just as in African societies the chief is at the head of the structure of society, with his wishes being communicated through a series of functionaries, so in African thought God acts through different levels of intermediaries, the lesser divinities being the first in line. The assumption seems to be, whenever this statement is made, that it does not need to be substantiated; its validity is apparently self-evident.

Among the Akan at least three expressions are used to describe the relation between God and the gods.[20] One of these is *Nyankopɔn ne mba*, sons of God, used to describe the lesser divinities, at least some of them. How this expression is to be understood is debated, especially when it is understood that in African languages words denoting familial relationships are often used in non-specific senses; so that 'son' could be used simply to mean one much younger than the user, without any familial relationship being implied. Thus the Earth Goddess is referred to by the Asante of Ghana as the wife of God, but it is to be seriously doubted whether 'wife' is to be literally understood. In fact, the use of 'sons of God' has been understood by some to indicate that the cults of the gods came later. However that may be, this description of the gods in Akan religion is more obviously suggestive; it is used specifically in connection with

16. Akan, *Twerampɔn*.
17. Akan, *Abomubuwafrɛ*.
18. Zulu, *Unkulunkulu*.
19. M. J. McVeigh, *God in Africa*, Boston, Claude Stark, 1974.
20. For this aspect of the discussion, I am indebted to K. K. Amos Anti; see his unpublished M. A. thesis, *Relationship Between the Supreme Being and the Lesser Gods of the Akan*, University of Ghana, 1978.

certain water deities – Tano, Bea, Bosomtwe and Bosompo; according to Asante traditions, these are 'God's sons'. Water deities in a sense partake of the nature of God – they derive from him and share his spirit. It needs to be remembered that one of the Asante attributes of God is *Amosu*, he who gives rain, and thus makes the rivers and the sea full of water and life. Not surprisingly, the Asante consider these water deities as intermediaries: the relationship between God and these gods is considered to be one of sovereign and delegated ministers. It is significant that the description 'sons of God' is in Asante tradition limited to just these water deities; it is not an expression used in tradition of all the deities known in Asante or among the Akan.

A second Akan expression which is used to define the role of the gods is *abrafoɔ*, executioners. We shall see later that the gods are believed to be interested in the moral living of humans; they are, like the ancestors, offended when there is a breach of conduct. As the Supreme Being hates evil, the gods, it is believed, become his executioners, bringing death and destruction upon offenders. It is often the medicine cults which are so described; the description is not applied to all gods. There is a third description, which is *akyeame*, linguists or spokesmen. In the Akan court the linguist is a very important personality. He is close to the chief, relaying his requests and pronouncements, and even sometimes acting for him in his absence. The use of this expression may very well reflect the belief that the ultimate is God, so that nothing is done or happens unless he has allowed it. In theory this last expression would imply that the gods are intermediaries between God and man; in practice, however, this inference may be drawn with caution, for unlike the two other expressions this one is not experientially and ritually exemplified in Akan religion.

Prayers offered in ritual situations are often such as to cause one to wonder whether the gods are not addressed as self-sufficient entities. Prayer, whether it is made as part of private[21] or

---

21. This usually takes place every morning at the house shrine, a way of saying 'good morning' to the deity, and it is done before the worshipper has spoken to anyone.

communal[22] worship, has basically the same characteristics: invocation, petition and conclusion, mainly.[23] I here discuss these characteristics without going into any great detail. First, if worship is being directed to several deities, the leader of the cult sometimes takes the precaution of apologising for his inability to remember each and every one of the deities by name; this is for the purpose of pacifying any deities who might be present unknown. Then, in relation to the petitions which include requests for material blessings (long life, children and generally the good things of life), for blessings upon those who wish the worshippers well and curses upon their detractors, the question arises as to whose will is done in prayer, the deity's or the petitioner's. Idowu[24] and Gaba[25] argue that since in African belief there is nothing that happens unless it has been permitted by God, it can be said that in prayer it is the deity's, not the petitioner's will that is done. This is possibly a simplistic explanation in view of the third element, the conclusion, which sometimes assumes the form of an urgent appeal for the fulfilment of the petitioner's desires; this appeal may give way to threats, such as 'if you do not fulfil our desire, we shall abandon you and look for another deity'; the converse is promises of greater devotion if the deity performs the petitioner's desires. The attempts to explain away the obvious implication of this conclusion are not convincing.[26] The attitude to which the three elements cited testify is one of looking upon the gods as ends in themselves, given the nature of the ritual verbalisations used. One suspects that the view which rejects the obvious implication that in some situations at least the gods are treated as being self-sufficient is a reaction, conscious or unconscious, to the categorisation made of African religion by Western writers: to accept the fact of the gods being approached as

22. This is more elaborate, and usually takes place on sacred days of the deity and at yearly festivals.
23. According to C. R. Gaba prayer among the Anlo of Ghana begins with a prelude, a statement of the condition which qualifies the petitioner to pray to the deity; see his 'Prayer in Anlo Religion' in *Orita* 11/2, December 1968.
24. E. B. Idowu, *Olodumare: God in Yoruba Belief* (Longman 1962), p. 116.
25. C. R. Gaba, op. cit.
26. Ibid.

ends in themselves would seem to be supporting the view that the African spiritual world is teeming with a host of capricious deities who spell chaos rather than order, a situation which would imply that African religion is an inferior world-view. Horton has in this connection observed that the available evidence

> ... gives the lie to the old stereotype of the gods as capricious and irregular in their behaviour. For it shows that each category of beings has its appointed functions in relation to the world of observable happenings. The gods may sometimes appear capricious to the unreflective ordinary man. But for the religious expert charged with the diagnosis of spiritual agencies at work behind observed events, a basic modicum of regularity in their behaviour is the major premiss on which his work depends.[27]

Our conclusion is that there are no easy solutions to the problem of the relation between God and the gods, and that it is much less enlightening than is thought to use such terms as monotheism and polytheism; in a sense they confuse the discussion. One might in this connection refer again to the Earth Goddess. As pointed out above, the Akan refer to this goddess as the wife of God, and in ritual prayers she is mentioned next after God. It has been suggested that perhaps at some time in the past there was equality between God and the Earth Goddess, *Asase Yaa*, until God gained ascendancy over the latter.[28] Whatever the truth of the matter may be, *Asase Yaa* is a distinct personality. She has a sacred day (Thursday) on which no one should go to the farm. She is propitiated when a girl whose first menstruation has not been announced becomes pregnant. There should be no sex on the bare ground; she is believed to frown upon this and punishes offenders severely.[29] Farmers beseech her when preparing the land for sowing, and she receives the dead after prayers have been made to her. It is difficult to get away from the fact that *Asase Yaa*, whose recognition involves the

27. R. Horton, op. cit., p. 52.
28. This suggestion was made by a colleague at the University of Ghana, Dr Patrick Ryan, s.j.; it remains tentative and unsubstantiated.
29. It is likely that originally sex on the bare ground, or in the bush, was believed to imply the Earth Goddess as a partner.

observance of taboos, is treated in many respects as a self-sufficient deity.

The most one can say is that God's self-sufficiency is never in doubt, even if other deities may be recognised and worshipful attitudes adopted before them. So much for the tradition of the withdrawn God, and its implications.

Another typical view of God is that he is *creator*. Here also there is almost continent-wide agreement; myths of creation abound. The creation of everything is his work. Some of the names given to God may appear to belie this. The Akan, for example, give God (*Nyame*, *Nyankopɔn*) the day-name *Kwame*,[30] while among another Akan people *Nyankopɔn* is associated with Monday.[31] These day-names are evidently not meant to suggest that there was a time when God was not; our opinion is that they are a reference to particular historical occasions of considerable importance of which we no longer have any knowledge. Similarly the Zulus may call God *Unkulunkulu*, the old, old one, but this is not to say they consider him the Great Ancestor, for in fact they also consider God as creator.

Next we shall consider the typical view which arises from the one just referred to: *man is created by God*. African creation myths make clear how man was created. Sometimes man comes as the summit of creation, as in the Bukusu (Western Kenya) myth of creation which states that when all else had been created God wondered for whom all that had been done, and consequently created man; and for man he then created woman as a companion.[32] To underline the tie that binds God and man the Akan hold the belief that there are three elements which go to make up a human being: the mother's blood, the father's spirit, and the soul; this last-named element comes from God – without this divine element in man his creation is incomplete. He is a human being who has this element of God in him. In this connection the subject of morality comes up: any person who does not abide by the moral codes of the community

30. This is the name given to the boy born on Saturday. Sometimes *Nyankopɔn Kweku* (Wednesday born).
31. *Kodwo*. See my introduction to J. B. Danquah, op. cit.
32. J. Mugambi and N. Kirima, op. cit., p. 6.

is said not to be a human being;[33] in other words, the fully human is a worthy being. Similarly the Yoruba believe that God puts in man what they call the 'oracle of the heart' to aid him in ethical living; one is good or bad in accordance with one's response to the guidance of one's inner 'oracle'.[34] Furthermore, there is the belief found among several African peoples of a deterministic kind: at the creation of man God gives him his destiny which will dictate his mode of life. This, of course, is an expression of God's overriding sovereignty – he creates and governs life. However, some of these same peoples hold the belief that there are in fact two destinies – the one given by God, and another chosen by man himself.[35] The placing side by side of these two destinies is evidently a way of saying that man is, despite God's sovereignty, accountable for his actions.[36]

Man, then, is of considerable importance not only because he is created by God, but also because he is a moral being with a sense of right and wrong. Man is so important in the African conception that it might be wondered whether in African thought man is not at the centre of reality. However, it cannot be said of African thought that it is humanistic in the sense that it is antithetical to religion; reality is regarded as fundamentally religious.

One methodological problem in the presentation of the concept of God in African religion is the relation between *God and evil*. In African thought evil can be caused by various spirit powers: the gods, ancestors,[37] witches and sorcerers,[38] and other baneful spirits. The question is whether all evil is ultimately to be traced to God, the creator of all things. This, unfortunately, is not an easy question to answer. Some African peoples believe in evil spirits who cause havoc; the Igbo, for example, offer such creatures as lizards and

---

33. Ɔnnyɛ nyimpa – Akan.
34. E. B. Idowu, op. cit., p. 154.
35. M. Fortes, *Oedipus and Job in West African Religion*, Cambridge University Press 1959.
36. Kwesi Dickson, *Aspects of Religion and Life in Africa* (Ghana Academy of Arts and Sciences 1977), pp. 7ff.
37. See pp. 67–70 below.
38. See pp. 62–3 below.

toads (creatures that are not consumed for food nor offered to other spirit powers) to evil spirits, thus making a clear distinction between such spirits and, say, God. And yet some believe that God is the source of misfortune and death, even though he is often believed at the same time to be good. The Akan, for example, have the saying, 'When God gives you disease, he also gives you medicine.' Perhaps the view that would find general acceptance is that while God may not be looked upon as the direct cause of evil, except perhaps in the form of natural happenings, people will turn to God for an explanation of otherwise incomprehensible events without necessarily considering those events as primarily attributable to him. The sovereignty of God has found expression in this and other ways in the history of religion.[39]

It would be useful, as an introduction to the next section of this review of African religious ideas, to raise the issue of what might be said to be the traditional presentation of the various strands of belief in African religion. Edith Clarke has objected to that presentation which sets out the main strands in the descending order of God, the lesser divinities, ancestors and charms/amulets. The ground of her objection to this is that it does not reflect the sociological importance of these strands. Functionally, she argues, the ancestors are very important, with God being relatively unimportant; hence a presentation that does justice to the sociological importance of the belief strands should begin with the ancestors and end with God.[40] This is an observation which, on the one hand, threatens to sow seeds of misunderstanding; in line with comments made above, we would insist that God is believed to have a more important role in African life and thought than Miss Clarke would have us believe. On the other hand, it is a fact that the ancestors are ever in the consciousness of the living; community is defined to include the ancestors, the real owners of the land who, for many African peoples, are the custodians of morality. In a sense, then, Miss Clarke's observation with regard to the ancestors is an acute one,

39. In Exodus not only does God seek to take out his people from Egypt, but he also hardens Pharaoh's heart, so he would not let his people go!
40. See 'The Sociological Significance of Ancestor-Worship in Ashanti' in *Africa*, III, 1930, pp. 431–70.

and in the section which follows the ancestors and their role will be brought out.

Man and Community

It is a commonplace that the sense of community is strong in Africa. A society is in equilibrium when its customs are maintained, its goals attained and the spirit powers given regular and adequate recognition. Members of society are expected to live and act in such a way as to promote society's well-being; to do otherwise is to court disaster, not only for the actor but also for society as a whole. Any act that detracts from the soundness of a society is looked upon with disfavour, and society takes remedial measures to reverse the evil consequences set in motion. This may be illustrated by reference to witchcraft.

A witch is one, usually a woman, who is believed to have such magical powers as enable her to influence others drastically, usually by remote control.[41] More specifically, the activities of witches are believed to take place at night when they have their 'spiritual' meetings.[42]

41. As to how a person may become a witch there are several possibilities: (a) One may be born a witch. If the pregnant woman is a witch she may employ certain herbal preparations as part of her pre-natal care to ensure the child is born a witch; or, as among the Asante, a woman who experiences child mortality may be bathed during pregnancy with substances from a pot supported aloft by the three-forked branch called God's tree (*Nyame dua*) – the child is expected in those circumstances to be born a witch. However, it is believed that child witches are incapable of exercising their powers before the age of puberty. (b) Witchcraft power may be inherited; or where there is no ready successor the witchcraft power may be left behind in some article (e.g. of clothing) which will give the eventual user the power. (c) One may purchase it. (d) It may be inadvertently acquired through swallowing food mixed with witchcraft substance. (e) It may be deliberately acquired from a lesser god – ardent devotees may be given witchcraft as a reward for service and devotion; or from another witch who after guiding the aspirant through rituals will put her fingers on the candidate's eyes for her to 'see properly'.

42. They are believed to assume certain forms (e.g. a snake), in which they attend the meetings which reportedly take place usually on the tops of certain trees, such as silk-cotton, baobab, etc. The focus of activity at these meetings is a pot which contains blood, bones and flesh – this is the source from which their spiritual power is believed to be replenished.

The most widely reported activity of witches is spiritual cannibalism; hence diseases which prove difficult to cure, the wasting away of the body, death, involuntary abortion, etc.: these would be considered to be the work of witches, as would also sudden material losses, such as when someone loses his property or wealth. Given the traditional African concern for the preservation of the integrity of the community, the work of witches is generally considered to be against society, and that in fact explains why witches are feared and their activities often decried.[43] Of course, contrary to popular opinion, witches may also do good; in other words, it is not true that they are believed to do nothing but evil.[44] Witches may work for beneficial purposes such as controlling malevolent people, enabling people to succeed in life, etc.[45]

In pursuance of the need to strengthen the community, children are brought up to recognise the roles they must play in society. Puberty rites are occasions not only for giving the adolescent a physical sign that marks his or her development[46] but also for inculcating certain teachings that will fit him or her into society. Apart from the adolescent group there are age sets and groupings of other kinds, such as title holders;[47] there are rules and regulations which members of the various groups observe; these groups,

43. At one time the cult of Nana Tongo of Tongo-Zugu near Bolgatanga, Ghana, which was regarded as 'witch-killer', was so popular in West Africa that in 1951 the Nigerian government banned it, as well as passing a law prohibiting the profession of witchcraft; in 1928 Kenya passed a law which penalised anyone claiming such supernatural powers. Nigeria has known a member of secret cults such as the Ogboni cult of the Yoruba and the Ndako Gboya cult of the Nupe in northern Nigeria. The Akan of Ghana have the *sumanbrafoɔ*, a term used to describe all witch-hunting god's like Kune, Tigare, Aberewa, Kankamea, etc.

44. See P. Hughes, *Witchcraft*, Longman, 1952, and J. Middleton and E. H. Winter, *Witchcraft and Sorcery in East Africa*, Routledge and Kegan Paul 1963.

45. Among the Asante of Ghana a distinction is maintained by some between those witches who undergo an initiation rite and those who do not: the latter are considered to have the less potent kind of witchcraft which can be used only to trade, to protect oneself and one's children, etc., while the former acquire that kind of power which enables them to cause physical and spiritual havoc.

46. I.e., by circumcision/clitoridectomy.

47. E.g., *Ozo* title holders among the Igbo; see E. Ilogu's *Christianity and Igbo Culture*, Leiden, E. J. Brill, 1975.

however, are all fully integrated into the larger society, and the concern of the groups, as well as of individuals, is to live and act in such a way as to contribute to society's equilibrium.

Perhaps this is the point at which to make some remarks on the opinion often expressed that in African societies women have an inferior status, a view that would seem to be supported by such a taboo as that a man departing on a journey may not tell his wife precisely what business he is going to transact for fear of jeopardising the success of the business, or by those African stories of the beginning which give woman an uncomplimentary role;[48] it has also been suggested that the fact that in Africa it is mostly women who are believed to become witches is indicative of a deep-seated antagonism, especially as witch-hunters are usually men. Do not African women in fact acquiesce in their being associated with witchcraft as a way of enhancing their standing in a society where they have an inferior status?

It is not possible to go into this matter in detail here. In my opinion such words of comparison as inferior and superior are out of place in the African context; they represent the importation of Western attitudes into a context to which they do not belong.[49] It may be confidently asserted that it is more correct to speak of complementary roles which African societies expect of the sexes in order to serve the greater purpose of enhancing society's effectiveness. Account must be taken of the fact that women in African societies do play diverse roles. They may be queen-mothers, wielding considerable influence in the state;[50] they may be priestesses,

48. In an Ngombe story an initial paradisiac situation was disturbed when woman was introduced into it (Edwin Smith, op. cit., p. 175); reference has already been made to the myth, widely known in Africa, which attributes God's departure from the human environment to the activities of a woman. What do these stories mean? According to Aylward Shorter, they associate women with 'the original sin because in the symbolic classification of male-dominated societies women represent the qualities of weakness and fickleness'. See his *African Culture and the Christian Church* (G. Chapman 1973), p. 65.

49. Cf. Charles H. Kraft, *Christianity in Culture* (Maryknoll, N.Y., Orbis Books, 1979), p. 59.

50. E. Meyerowitz, *The Divine Kingship in Ghana and Ancient Egypt* (Faber and Faber 1960), p. 29; and R. S. Rattray, *Religion and Art in Ashanti* (Oxford University Press 1959), p. 108.

being as prominent as men in the conduct of religious affairs,[51] or practitioners of medicine,[52] or mediums;[53] then there are female deities whose role in society is recognised by both sexes – the most significant of these is the Earth Goddess to whom reference has already been made. The Fon of the Republic of Benin have a dual deity, *Mawu-Lisa*, *Mawu* being female and *Lisa* male.[54]

To go back to the point made above regarding the need for members of society to live and act in such a way as to maintain society's equilibrium, there is the question of *how* members of society should behave in order for them to make this contribution. Do Africans have a sense of having done wrong or sinned?

On the subject of morality what comes to mind most immediately is the system of taboos which one readily encounters in African societies. There is no society in Africa which does not observe taboos. Examples of taboos are sex with a woman during her period, having sex on the bare ground, and a woman during her period preparing her husband's food. These particular examples have been selected for a purpose: to make the point that a great number of taboos revolve round sex and the relations between the sexes. Properly understood, these taboos are intended to regulate social relationships, and the fact that they are mostly inspired by religion underlines the point already made that in African societies religion and life are not easily separated. Unfortunately, however, for some reasons taboos have, in some circles, been taken to indicate a negative understanding of morality and, more than that, a lack of a sense of sin: the argument seems to be that taboos may be moral or a-moral, that is, they prohibit indiscriminately; and, since the breaking of a taboo spells danger for the culprit, it would seem

51. G. Parrinder, op. cit., pp. 37 and 101; also M. L. Daneel, *Old and New in Southern Shona Independent Churches*, vol. 1 (New York, Mouton Publishers, 1971), p. 90.
52. What Rattray says about medicine-men and their skill may be applied to medicine-women in Akan as well as other African societies – op. cit., p. 39.
53. Sundkler has noted that among the Zulu mediums women predominate; and among the Shona the female medium 'retains this function for life and the family is provided with a direct "channel of communication"' – M. L. Daneel, op. cit., p. 101.
54. P. Mercier, 'The Fon of Dahomey' in Daryll Forde (ed.), *African Worlds* (Oxford University Press 1963), p. 219.

that taboos encourage a negative motivation. In reaction to this evaluation of taboos Adegbola has observed that 'negative morality' may not be divorced from the idea of sin, for not only is it true that 'the tabu idea has an underlying agreement with the idea of sin as that which causes evil to happen', but also, and more specifically, the idea of sin bringing evil consequences upon others than the perpetrator is recalled in the African understanding of the breaking of a taboo endangering the community as a whole, and hence being an anti-social act.[55] Adegbola's comments need to be taken seriously; they caution against rejecting taboos out of hand as being of little value in assessing a people's sense of sin, for they are believed to have been instituted by the spirit powers to ensure the attainment of societal integrity.[56]

In this connection one issue that has been the subject of much comment in recent years is whether Africans have a sense of wronging God. Views on this have varied between two extremes: there is the one according to which *Kalunga* (God in Namibia) 'requires conformity not to any laws of his own — for he has made none — but to tribal ethics, such as the observance of the tribal custom, reverence for one's elders and especially for the tribal and family ancestors and the avoidance of ὕβρις, "insolence".'[57] Perhaps this is as it should be if indeed *Kalunga* 'is not an object of love, for he is not concerned with the individual but with the universe. He is not a lawgiver by whose precepts a man may order his life.'[58] In contrast to this is the view that God is the 'ultimate originator and

---

55. A. Adegbola, 'The Theological Basis of Ethics', in Kwesi Dickson and Paul Ellingworth, op. cit., pp. 116f.; also Swailem Sidhom, 'The Concept of Sin in the African Context', in *Communio Viatorum*, vol. 9, no. 4 (Winter 1966), p. 244.
56. One may refer to the view that was widely championed at one time that the terms used in certain strata of the Old Testament yield a defective sense of sin; it is more readily recognised now that whether the emphasis was on custom as the means by which the goodness or badness of an act was determined, or whether there was a tendency to define sin in terms of ritual omissions, the main thought is not only that Yahweh was the giver of the rules and regulations by which the Israelites were to live, but also that the integrity of Israelite society depended on their being observed.
57. Edwin Smith, op. cit., p. 149.
58. Ibid., p. 144.

upholder of the moral law'.[59] More recently Awolalu has expressed this latter view as follows:

> Although sin can be and is punished by either the divinities or the ancestors, we must realise that Africans believe that such sins are still regarded as offenses against God who is Creator and Sustainer of the universe and its inhabitants, who expects His creatures to maintain good relationship with one another and with the super-sensible world and on whose behalf the divinities and ancestors punish immoral deeds.[60]

The truth probably lies somewhere between these two extreme positions. That there is a sense of sin against God in Africa has been documented. Thus it is believed in Rwanda that disobedience to authority offends God, as also does theft in southern Tanzania.[61] However, the view that all offences are finally against God is to be seen in the context of the attempt to respond to the Western typing of African religion, which response has led to the creation of such expressions as 'diffused monotheism'; for, not all offences are in fact consciously believed to be against God. The lesser divinities are believed to be concerned also with morality, so that among the Igbo of Nigeria the Earth divinity, *Ale*, is considered to be the administrator of moral laws, and her priests guardians of public morality; as already indicated, there are things that must not be done if her anger is not to be incurred.[62] The gods are believed to manifest their anger when murder, or theft, or adultery, etc. has been committed.

In addition to God and the lesser divinities there are the spirit ancestors who also are believed to reward and punish because they are concerned with the effective discharge of moral obligations. The ancestors indeed loom large in the traditional conception of religion; to a very great extent community consciousness revolves around the recognition of the ancestors, and where the latter are referred

59. Ibid., p. 251.
60. J. O. Awolalu, 'Sin and Its Removal in African Traditional Religion', in *Journal of the American Academy of Religion*, 44/2, 1976, p. 287.
61. A. Shorter, op. cit., p. 63.
62. *Contra* A. B. Ellis, op. cit., pp. 10–11.

to as an explanation of some situation or other the explanation is accepted as valid.[63] The prominence of the role they are held to play in the life of the community will be raised only briefly here.

To begin with, the cult of the dead is not to be equated with the cult of the ancestors; in other words, to die is not automatically to become an ancestor. Indeed, some African peoples, such as the people of the Republic of Benin, make a clear distinction between the dead and the ancestors and have ceremonies to transform the former into the latter.[64] The ancestor is believed to manifest himself in the life of the living who from time to time formally commune with him, though there comes a time when he practically ceases to be an ancestor: this is when there is no one alive who knew him, though the 'living' ancestors may be asked in ritual to serve as a bridge to the forgotten ancestors who will not be mentioned by name.

There are several ways by which contact may be established with the ancestors. It may be done through putting food on standards representing the ancestors. At the beginning of the yam season the Fon of the Republic of Benin take goats and fowls to the shrine, and when these have been slaughtered the flesh is cooked and portions put on the ancestral standards; similarly the Igbo of Nigeria represent the ancestors by pillars or staffs placed inside the hut; whenever the members of the family are having a meal, food or wine will be put on these pillars. Sometimes blood features as a means of contacting the ancestors, especially in connection with the stool which, for an African people such as the Asante of Ghana, symbolises the ancestors; on certain important occasions the stools in the royal house are smeared with blood, the understanding being that the people, symbolised by the blood (the seat of life) are brought into close contact with the ancestors who are symbolised by the stool. Thus communion is achieved.

Another way – and perhaps the best known – by which communion may be achieved with the ancestors is libation. Usually the

63. K. A. Busia, *The Position of the Chief in the Modern Political System of Ashanti*. (International African Institute 1951), pp. 25f.
64. Meyer Fortes, 'Ancestor Worship' in M. Fortes and G. Dieterlen, *African Systems of Thought*, Oxford University Press 1965.

material used for libation is either water or some alcoholic beverage, the latter being more favoured. The libation could constitute a complete ritual act by itself, poured to the family, clan and tribal ancestors, the occasion indicating which categories of ancestors are to be so contacted. The family ancestors are called upon at the important moments of life, principally at birth, puberty and marriage, and death; they are also called upon on occasions when new undertakings are envisaged by members of the family, e.g. trade, travel, etc. The clan and tribal ancestors are contacted in situations of grave importance to the clan or tribe, especially on the death of a particularly important person such as the chief. Libation is usually poured by the head of the family, or tribe, or by the linguist or priest; however, ordinary individuals may also pour libation.

The offering of food or drink is accompanied by prayer. As to the content of prayers, petitions for children, good crops, health, etc. feature prominently.[65] To increase life, enemies (all those who work against peace and the well-being of the individual and the community) must be suppressed; hence prayers of libation often express the desire that the enemy may be destroyed: nothing should stand in the way of the society's well-being and security.

The question must be raised as to whether in contacting the dead the motivating factor is one of communion or propitiation. It will have been noticed that we have already used the word communion to describe the purpose of the contact made with the ancestors, and some would insist that this is the only way in which this contact may be characterised; that is, in contacting the ancestors the living are not expiating an offence or bribing them; their only desire, it is insisted, is to maintain filial relations with them. This interpretation has many proponents, though it is somewhat doubtful whether it can be considered to apply in every instance of the enactment of this rite. Many African peoples believe that the ancestors are custodians of law and custom, as already noted; they punish with sickness or misfortune those who infringe them. It is hard to imagine that

65. C. R. Gaba, op. cit.

there would be no occasion for propitiation.[66] The most one can say is that the African sense of community requires the recognition of the presence of the ancestors as the rallying point of the group's solidarity, and they, being the custodians of law and morality, may punish or reward in order to ensure the maintenance of the group's equilibrium.[67]

To complete this statement of African life and thought I offer a brief word on the traditional political system.

Roughly, there are two traditional political systems: some African societies have kings or chiefs while others, like the Kikuyu of East Africa, have ruling councils of elders; each political system is geared towards enabling individuals, families and clans and tribes to attain goals that ensure the welfare of all. As is well known, the family in Africa is not of the nuclear type; it is an extended family whose head has the duty, aided by others such as fathers and mothers, of socialising the younger members and generally ordering the affairs of the family. Similarly the clan has a clan head who enjoys recognition by members of the clan who, no matter how widely they may be scattered in a country, enjoy a common kinship through the totem. Kings (or chiefs) or councils of elders are at the head of the community as a whole. In many African societies the chief still has a certain primacy on ritual occasions because he is a sacred person,

66. Propitiatory sacrifices are indicated in an incident related by Busia: A slave woman bought by a chief had two daughters; the chief's successor married one, the other being married by a commoner. The chief's wife had four children, the other woman two. When the chief died both women refused to live with the deceased's sister with whom they had been living previously. Consequently the woman with four children lost two, and the other lost both of her children. When the local god was consulted its priest revealed that the ancestral spirits were angry because the women had left the chief's house; it was necessary that they should offer sacrifices and return. See K. A. Busia, op. cit., pp. 25f.

67. It will have been noticed that the phrase 'ancestor worship' has been avoided. It is a description of African religion, specifically of the attitude adopted towards the ancestors, which has been championed and decried with equal passion. It is certainly a misleading term, as are basically all religious terms and descriptions taken from a Western context and applied without qualification to African religion. Among the Akan the verb usually used to describe the process of contacting the ancestors is *frɛ* = call; never is the verb *som* (to worship) used; it would evidently be considered inappropriate.

sitting as he does on the stool that symbolises the ancestors. Usually it is males who become chiefs, though women play an important political role in more than one way.[68]

Those who govern have the responsibility of establishing and maintaining stability in their societies. In carrying out his duties the chief is expected not to isolate himself from the rest of the society; he is to make himself available to all. Contrary to the impression which has been created following the tendency for certain African leaders of today to claim to model their rule and policies on traditional patterns when their authoritarian rule could be given a much less flattering explanation, traditional Africa does not brook dictatorial rule. 'Rulers who impose their power end up being overthrown by more popular ones';[69] there are checks and balances which ensure that no ruler enslaves his people. Furthermore, the African concept of society encourages certain attitudes to property and the means of sustenance, as well as to other members of society with respect to their needs. Nyerere has pointed out often enough that African societies in various ways act to ensure the security of their members; a society in which there were extremes in terms of what its members had of the good things of life would be considered abnormal.[70] This is not to say that a person has no freedom to acquire property beyond the family property deposit; such acquisition, however, would not necessarily mean the dismembering of the group.[71] The important thing is that members of society should not be so disadvantaged as to be destitute. One cannot speak of classes in traditional Africa based on economic superiority or inferiority.[72] Whatever stratification exists is, as already observed, in the form of age sets, titled men, etc., and these

68. See pp. 64–5 above.
69. J. Mugambi and N. Kirima, op. cit., p. 15.
70. Julius Nyerere, *Ujamaa – Essays on Socialism* (Dar es Salaam, Oxford University Press, 1974), pp. 1ff.
71. For example, see Mary Douglas, 'Is Matriliny Doomed in Africa' in Mary Douglas and Phyllis M. Kaberry (eds.), *Man in Africa* (New York, Doubleday, 1971), pp. 123–37.
72. A. Shorter, op. cit., p. 27.

sets represent a new level of awareness of responsibility to the wider community.

If the above material has been presented in the present tense, it is not being suggested that African culture is an unchanging system, an impression created by some of the studies done on it. The survey of African religion done here is based partly upon sources which date from the beginning of this century, which would seem to cast doubt upon the wisdom of parading this as representing the religion on which fell the impact of the Western world, especially in view of the fact that no religion can be said to be impervious to external influences, though the extent of assimilation of new ideas will no doubt differ from one culture to another. However, two comments may be made in this connection. First, references dating from the inception of colonial rule and missions suggest that whatever changes have come about in African religion cannot be said to be dramatic though – and secondly – the full story of the history of African religion has hardly begun to be told. Students of African religion will readily admit that very little is known about the history of African religion, despite the publication of *The Historical Study of African Religion*.[73] This book, which is a pioneer study, makes basically two assumptions: that African religions are dynamic and have changed over time; and, historical research can demonstrate in what ways these religions have changed. However, fully half of the case studies presented in this book do not portray an historical time-depth greater than a century. What about all that vast stretch of time for which no archival or oral traditional sources exist?[74] It is in the light of this that the contribution by M. Poznansky is

73. T. O. Ranger and I. N. Kimambo (eds.), *The Historical Study of African Religion*, Heinemann 1972.

74. For a review of the book in question see Jan Vansina in *International Journal of African Historical Studies*, vol. VI, no. 1, 1973, pp. 178–80. Among other things Vansina points out that the book does not grapple with the issue of what religion is; he argues that once the question of definition is swept aside then we are left in the dark analytically as to what religion, supposedly the subject of the book, is. One sympathises with Vansina, though it must be observed that one of the problems the study of African religion has often encountered is its being typed on the basis of some assumed definition of religion.

perhaps the most important in the book:[75] it offers irrefutable proof that African religious beliefs are thoroughly indigenous; and, it demonstrates the need to exercise caution in interpreting those archaeological findings deemed relevant to religion, especially where the findings would seem to link up with the traditions of other peoples in the ancient world.[76] Allowance must be made, as Poznansky points out, for the possibility of independent development.

It may be stated in conclusion that as far as it is possible to determine, given the available pointers, Africa's religio-cultural tradition has a vitality that makes it an important area of study in any endeavour to understand the reactions of Africans in such a situation as arises from the presence of a new faith which is backed by a different cultural viewpoint.

75. M. Poznansky, 'Archaeology, Ritual and Religion' in Ranger and Kimambo (eds.), op. cit.
76. For example, some would trace African religion and culture to ancient Egypt – see E. Meyerowitz, *The Divine Kingship in Ghana and Ancient Egypt*, Faber and Faber 1960; also C. G. Seligman, *Races of Africa*, 3rd edn, Oxford University Press 1957 and *Egypt and Negro Africa*, Routledge 1934. Comparisons can serve a useful purpose, but from conversations with some of my black students in America I formed the impression that, consciously or unconsciously, comparison was felt to be necessary in order to lend 'respectability' or 'legitimation' to African life and thought. The importance of African life and thought does not lie in their sharing common characteristics with other ancient systems; it does not lie in their being presented as a system that is paralleled in several of its aspects in other ancient or modern systems. They have importance of their own.

3

The Colonial Factor – And Now

If in the previous chapter African religion has been spoken of in the singular it is because it is possible to speak in terms of a unity of religious ideas. However, the use of religions (in the plural) can be justified, for one should not assume a uniformity of religious ideas; attitudes to the spirit powers differ in intensity and variety from one area to another, from one African people to another. Indeed, the African continent has always been characterised by a lack of uniformity in many ways, a situation which was exacerbated by colonial rule, a subject to which we now turn as an element in the discussion of the realities of Africa; not only did the colonial period involve several European powers in the life of Africans but also the colonisers tended to have distinctive policies which served effectively to distinguish African peoples one from the other, with the result that it was only in the post-colonial period that the African states could begin to speak of African unity.

But, first, a word of explanation. Our interest in the colonial period is not simply in order to recount the facts of the past; indeed our survey will be a very brief one. A selection of facts has been made here having in mind the limits of this theological inquiry. Again, the colonial period is important for this study, but not in order to provide a ready explanation for every aspect of Africa's problems today. This is not to say that we have no awareness of the colonial legacy which in some respects still exercises a baneful influence in Africa; indeed, any discerning observer of the African scene will be aware that the phrase 'colonial mentality' which is used – often in jest – to describe a determined hankering after un-African ways of life and thought does represent a reality of which

African governments have taken little account in working out policies. Colonial rule brought about a cultural mix which has not
turned out to be a useful basis for real development, and which is
in many ways the cause of many problems in the socio-economic
and political life of African peoples. Indeed, to us the most interesting thing about colonialism is, paradoxically, that African peoples
themselves, to a significant extent, have kept up its momentum by
their unimaginative attachment to the life and thought of the erstwhile colonial masters. Europe may have underdeveloped Africa,
but the momentum of underdevelopment is in our time being kept
up, to a large extent, by African themselves.

Our real purpose, then, in providing the survey that follows is
two-fold: to describe a factor that impinged upon African life and
thought, and to raise the question of whether or not, in the light of
the colonial past (a confluence of foreign political and Christian
missionary influences) and its consequences, it is realistic to expect
the Christian Church in Africa to look upon African life and thought
as a necessary component of the theologising process.

The continent of Africa was divided into spheres of influence by
the European powers; the Berlin Conference of 1884–5 spelt out the
principle of partition. By that time the slave trade had officially
come to an end, thanks to the British – and other unsung – abolition-
ists. Each European country imposed its own administrative and
legal systems, with the result that African countries soon duplicated
the European differences in systems of government. Hence the
continent was polarised, its peoples looking up to the European
capitals of London, Paris, Brussels, Lisbon, Berlin, Madrid and
Rome. Of course, in a sense colonialism brought many and diverse
linguistic groups together: country after country came to be made
up of peoples with different cultural characteristics. However, colonialism succeeded in making a complex situation even more complex,
for it raised unrealistic territorial barriers; thus, as an illustration,
the Ewe people are to be found in Ghana, Togo and the Republic
of Benin. Furthermore, the colonial powers imposed their culture
upon the African territories which were under their control. This
brought about cultural contradictions; African cultures did not give

way as expected, with the result that they and Europeanism existed side by side.

In the wake of colonial domination, then, two developments became discernible: political plurality characterised Africa; and, the personality of the African began to experience certain distortions in as much as he was being made to believe that he could not live a genuine existence without his adopting European modes of life and thought. European political conflicts were projected upon Africa whose indigenous peoples were enlisted to fight European wars. Perhaps it will be useful to look briefly at the policies of particular European powers in order to see in a little more detail what colonialism meant in terms of its effect on the African's identity.

In a decree passed in 1792 which had its springs in the French Revolution of 1789 all those domiciled in the French colonies were deemed to be French citizens and were to enjoy all rights assured by the French constitution: '. . . the principle of "Identity" held that, in so far as all men were basically equal in their capacity for reason, all Africans were to be completely assimilated and made equal citizens of France. The principle of "Association" called for the deliberate creation of an African elite, which would accept the standards of the West and become "associated" with French rulers in the work of colonial development.'[1] The French took this step simply because they believed that their culture was superior. In 1901 the French West African empire was established, consisting of West African countries governed by the French; the formation of this group was meant to enhance the French image in that part of the world. That very few citizens of the French African colonies actually attained to French citizenship is not surprising, for only a small number of Africans had access to the kind of education which the French considered necessary for full citizenship. Those who did obtain that 'privilege' had the right to sit in the French parliament as Deputies. The feeling of cultural superiority which characterised French rule resulted in damage being done to such African institutions as chieftaincy. The chief lost much of the privilege of being

1. Irving L. Markovits (ed.), *African Politics and Society* (New York, The Free Press, 1970), p. 16; see also Harry A. Gailey, *History of Africa From 1800 to Present* (New York, Holt, Rinehart and Winston, 1972), pp. 182ff.

primus inter pares, becoming in the eyes of the elite the representative of a culture which was regarded as inferior to French culture. Under Charles de Gaulle the French colonial structure underwent drastic modification when the need for political autonomy for the African countries was recognised. Even so, the independent African countries were coaxed into a political organisation headed by France, which meant that France still maintained a considerable presence, and hence influence, in the former colonies. It is a measure of the genuineness of France's liberalisation policies that when in 1958 the West African country of Guinea opted out of the union of former French colonies France was furious and immediately cut off aid. It was unpardonable to fail to recognise the benignity of French paternalism!

The British colonial system of rule provides several contrasts. The British employed the system of indirect rule; that is, the local institutions were largely left intact, and were employed as the vehicle of government. Thus the chief's position was recognised and used as a link between the colonial government and the ruled.[2] This is not to say that chieftaincy went unscathed in its new role; it was not long before it was being looked down upon by the educated as being nothing more than an agency that did the 'dirty work' of the British for them. Chieftaincy was beginning to lose its authority with the people. Traditionally the chief's wealth lay in his people who worked for him and provided him with the means of sustenance;[3] now the chief accepts a stipend from the British government, and the erosion of his religious and political power is well in progress. It has often been remarked that official British policy was not in favour of turning British subjects into Englishmen; this opinion needs to be qualified, however. British policy was not specifically of the French 'assimilation' variety, though the British colonial government sometimes came out with policies which were not essentially different. This is illustrated by the report of a Royal Commission which inquired into the affairs of the former British

2. Gailey, op. cit., pp. 177f.
3. S. G. Williamson, *Akan Religion and the Christian Faith* (Ghana Universities Press 1965), pp. 117f.

colonies of East Africa[4] between the years of 1953 and 1955; the
report's authors noted that the way forward for the African populations was 'the emergence of a responsible African middle class who
can meet members of other races on equal terms . . . The first duty
of government is to create the conditions which make development
of a community of this kind possible.'[5] Furthermore, British mission
policy in the field encouraged attachment to British ways of life
among the African populations. And where British settlements were
established, as in Northern and Southern Rhodesia, and in Kenya,[6]
the interests of the Africans were subordinated to those of the
British, thus creating the preconditions for violent confrontations,
as took place in Kenya where there was a sizeable British settlement.

It would serve no useful purpose to go into similar detail with
respect to the other European colonisers. We refer to them here
simply in order to complete the survey of influencing agents. Portuguese policy in Angola and Mozambique could be described as one
of assimilation and paternalism;[7] Spain,[8] Belgium,[9] Italy,[10] and
Germany[11] – all exercised rule in Africa and left their mark, for
good or evil, on the countries which they governed. Africans,
whether they were under the British (whose policies were often
quite reasonable), or under the Portuguese or the Italians (the two
last-named European peoples were often very brutal in their rule)
were a subject people, and their countries were exploited for gold,
diamonds, slaves, etc.

It may be remarked, incidentally, that in some ways missionary
activity contributed to the expansion of European interests in Africa.

4. Kenya, Uganda, Tanganyika and Zanzibar.
5. Basil Davidson, *Can Africa Survive?* (Boston, Little Brown, 1974), p. 48.
6. The French also set up settlements in Algeria and Morocco.
7. According to the *assimilado* system 'all persons, no matter what their race, will
   be accorded the same status if they meet certain qualifications. To qualify for
   this status, an African had to adopt the European mode of life, speak and read
   Portuguese fluently, be a Christian, complete military service, and have a trade
   or profession' – H. A. Gailey, op. cit., pp. 194–5.
8. Western Sahara.
9. Congo.
10. Eritrea, Somaliland and Libya.
11. South West Africa and Tanganyika.

The missionaries often inculcated a policy which paralleled that colonial policy which, as we have noted, assumed as a necessary precondition for the development of Africa the creation of an African middle class which would fit into the world of the European. Thus, for example, the training of Africans for the Church's ministry in the early days of missions in West Africa aimed at creating an African ministry that had a European approach to the Gospel and as much as possible adopted a European mode of life; and, as late as 1971, Portuguese bishops in Angola issued a pastoral letter in which, among other things, they noted: 'What is absolutely necessary is that we build an African middle class . . . for only in this way can we fulfil our mission and justify the laws which we obey.'[12] Also, active support was lent to the missionary effort by the home governments. This was true, for example, of British missionary effort in West Africa[13] in the last century. This situation was even more to be expected where there were rival missions of different European origins; thus during the last century the British and French missionary groups in the kingdom of Buganda tended to reflect the aims of their respective home states.[14]

If the story of Africa's colonial period is important, the story of what has happened since the fifties of this century is even more important. Since Ghana achieved its independence in 1957 much has happened in Africa; Ghana's independence marked a turning point in Africa's history. Now most African countries have shaken off colonial rule, though perhaps it would be more accurate to say that the shaking off of foreign rule is under way.

One of the problems facing Africa is that the decolonisation of the continent is incomplete; there still are some African peoples in

12. Commenting on this Basil Davidson observes: '. . . what the bishops did not say . . . was what they meant by an "African middle class". I think they would have told you, had you asked, that they meant all that kind of Africans who were clerks, and plumbers . . . people who were beginning to live in towns above the hunger line, and even to enjoy a little material comfort.' Basil Davidson, op. cit., p. 49. Davidson comments further: '. . . what the colonial powers evidently wished to promote was no genuine kind of middle class, but convenient tools or intermediaries' – p. 50.

13. Gailey, op. cit., p. 12.

14. Ibid., p. 138.

a colonial situation. It was Kwame Nkrumah, the first Head of State of independent Ghana, who said, with considerable justification, that the independence of Ghana was incomplete as long as there were countries in Africa under colonial rule; the decolonisation of the whole of the African continent was a necessity. The White governments of South-West Africa (Namibia) and South Africa are doing all they can to delay the day of majority rule in those countries. Thus South Africa has pressed for elections in Namibia on terms which are not wholly acceptable to the main African liberation movement in Namibia led by Sam Nujoma. When Johannes Vorster, the former Prime Minister of South Africa, announced his resignation on 20 September 1978, after twelve years of rule, he announced also his rejection of the proposals by Kurt Waldheim, the United Nations General Secretary, for granting independence to Namibia. It is a measure of the intractability of the South African situation that, on leaving office as Prime Minister, Vorster became South Africa's President.[15] The policy of creating the Bantu Homelands (Bantustans) and giving Africans a type of education which is inferior to that being received by Whites, reinforces the view which some observers of the situation hold that the Whites are determined to put the Africans in such a position that they will come to accept White supremacy. The recent African terrorist activity in South Africa comes in the wake of increasing dissatisfaction on the part of the African population.

When Rhodesia, under Ian Smith, declared its independence from Britain, it soon became obvious to the leaders of the African population of that country that a situation had developed in which the Africans who formed the majority of the country's population had little or no say in the running of the country. Eventually Smith bowed to pressure and agreed to share power with some of the African leaders. When elections were held in April 1979 Bishop Abel Muzorewa, one of Smith's African colleagues, emerged as the country's new leader, a development which, however, did not reduce the determination of two other Africans, Joshua Nkomo and Robert

15. Vorster was to resign as President on 14 June 1979 as a result of a scandal over the use of government funds to buy friends abroad.

Mugabe, leaders of the main guerilla groups in the country, to fight on to rid the country of what they saw as an African sell-out to Smith and his White colleagues whose interests were entrenched in the constitution by which Muzorewa and his cabinet were to govern the country. Smith and Muzorewa had no difficulty recruiting Africans into the country's armed and 'auxiliary' forces, because of unemployment caused largely by the strains which the Rhodesian economy was experiencing as a result of the sanctions imposed by the United Nations; and Nkomo and Mugabe had no difficulty recruiting into the ranks of their guerilla armies, because of political motivation.[16]

It is an over-simplication to say that the southern African situation is a complex one. One thing is certain: in the cross-currents of the political activity and struggle stands the disadvantaged African.[17]

When it comes to the independent African countries one finds that often there is independence only in the sense that government is manned by Africans. In some African countries the influence of the European powers is quite strong; the 1978 military developments in Shaba province (in Zaire) suggest an inordinate amount of influence lying with France and Belgium in a country which was once ruled by the latter. Recent events in Ethiopia and the Horn of Africa show the extent to which a world power like Russia would go to try and gain a firm foothold in Africa; and, of course, America would not sit idly by when Russian influence appeared to be on the ascendancy in Africa (and Asia, or anywhere else, for that matter). Again, the tendency for African liberation groups to be unable, or unwilling, to work together is illustrated by reference not only to

16. Following the Lancaster House Conference in London in 1979, elections were held in Zimbabwe early in 1980 and Robert Mugabe became the country's Prime Minister.
17. There are a few other areas in Africa which are in a colonial situation: Western Sahara, a former Spanish colony which is now caught between Algeria, on the one hand, and Morocco (and until recently Mauretania), on the other; the islands of Reunion and Mayotte within the Comoros in the Indian Ocean which are under France; and Melilla, within Morocco.

Rhodesia but also to independent Angola whose armed forces are still fighting African dissidents based reportedly in Zaire.[18]

What all this means is that many independent African states are politically unstable; the causes of this instability are varied. There is, of course, interference from outside the continent, often by former colonial masters who seek to maintain their influence either through subversion (aided by some nationals) or aggression towards the enemies of their 'wards'. Moreover, there is a decided tendency for African states to adopt systems of government and ideologies which have their origin outside Africa; the assumption has often been that the concept of government or the socio-economic and political style fashioned in London, Paris, Moscow, etc. is the one which would do for Africa. Of course, where the educational system does not relate Africans firmly to their own background (i.e. where the colonial educational systems remain more or less intact) there will be the likelihood of Africans showing little inclination to be critical of the ways of life inculcated by their former rulers. Aspiring to the values and life-styles of the erstwhile colonial masters has proved to have divisive and dehumanising consequences.

While on the subject of instability, some comments may be made on a significant political development which has taken place in Africa during the last decade or two – the rise of military governments. Military governments have often come about in consequence, avowedly, of disillusionment with civilian rulers. However, it is no secret that military rulers in Africa have not proved to be any more innovative or honest. Indeed, African armies, as presently conceived and constituted, are among the least imaginative colonial legacies to Africa, in many ways. They are an incredible drain upon the resources of African countries, and vested interests have consistently kept military expenditures at a very high level; the more sophisticated the military implements purchased from the advanced countries, the more African countries become dependent upon those arming countries in order to keep the military implements in a workable condition, and to update them.

18. These dissidents are FNLA and UNITA elements who had been involved in the struggle for independence from Portugal.

THE COLONIAL FACTOR — AND NOW

This reference to huge expenditures which do not benefit the generality of the population necessitates commenting on the subject of economic development. One of the main goals of the struggle for independence was economic development and prosperity. This goal of economic development has proved to be an elusive one, and there are some reasons for this, such as the exploitation by foreign countries and multinational corporations; and the plundering of Africa which started centuries ago still goes on in various forms. But Africa's economic problems are not caused by external forces alone. It has already been indicated that African governments have not managed too well. There has not been a clear-cut determination to work out economic policies which would bring about the economic liberation of African countries. The result has been that in some countries the economy is largely controlled, overtly or covertly, by outsiders, and a sizeable proportion of the indigenous population lives in comparative poverty. Of course, African countries have suffered from natural causes. The Sahel drought and its effects on the living conditions of the local people are too well known to be spelt out here. However, African governments are to a considerable extent to blame for the economic misfortunes that have soured the euphoria of independence.

One of the insidious self-deceptions since independence comes from African governments' desire for foreign aid. Economic aid is not necessarily a panacea. African governments should be aware by now that true aid is simply not that which temporarily alleviates economic difficulties; of course, aid of this type may be needed sometimes in particular circumstances. True aid, however, is that kind which would permit further local development without the need for regular infusions from outside; this kind of aid does not do injury to the dignity of the recipients, nor does it create the preconditions for the development of a neo-colonial economic situation.

Another of Africa's problems concerns the development of an authentic African identity. Those African countries which had become independent increasingly felt the need for a continental unity as a greater insurance for stability than the regional groupings which often had ties with the erstwhile colonial masters. As observed earlier, Africa's tribal-cum-linguistic differences were exacerbated by the partition of Africa by Europe. The tribal and linguistic differences still exist, and former colonies to a considerable extent aspire to the values and life-styles of the former colonial rulers. This is one reason why even though the Organisation of African Unity has existed for almost two decades Africa's problems have increased, and not decreased. In this connection the main issues discussed at the O.A.U. meeting at Khartoum in Sudan in 1978 are of interest: these were 'the intervention of extra-continental forces in Africa's conflicts and affairs; and the inter-state tensions that span the continent from the Horn to Western Sahara and from the desolate lands of northern Chad to the thick tropical forests of Angola and Zaire. Underlying both issues was the broader question of the continent's non-alignment.'[19] Some would say that African countries have too many intra-mural problems to be able to function as a continental group able to solve the kinds of problems which have continued to plague the continent.

There are some aspects of this survey that have a distinct bearing upon our discussion of Christian theology in Africa, and these we now highlight in concluding this part of our discussion. There is the fact of the colonial past which remains in some respects a present reality. Evidence of influences from outside is to be encountered everywhere – in the schools, colleges and universities; in the civil service, military, Church, etc. Further, there is evidence that African life and thought have been influenced by various aspects of Westernism, such as money economy, Western education, and urbanisation, to name just these. With respect to the last-named area of influence, for long now there has been a drift of young people into the urban areas, a situation which is encouraged by the continued concentration of development in such areas. As skills become marketable the exodus from the rural areas goes on, and with this goes a diminution of family cohesion. It is not true, however, that with the scattering of members of families, clan and tribe individualism has become the distinctive style of life, any more than that the sense

19. *Africa* (an International Business, Economic and Political Magazine), no. 85, September 1978, p. 27.

of community has disappeared in the West; African cities teem with societies and groups which are surrogates for traditional groupings. Granted this, however, the Africa of today is not the Africa of yesterday. Times have changed.

In the light of this the question arises: Would it not be turning the clock back to look upon African life and thought as necessary ingredients of the theologising process?

There are at least two reasons why the answer to this must be in the negative, and these reasons constitute the presuppositions upon which subsequent exploration of Christian theology in Africa will be based. First, we have argued that African life and thought have been affected (even though the full extent of the modifications which have occurred has yet to be documented), though not overrun, by the modern influences to which we have referred. This fact has already been given recognition in some African countries whose schools, colleges and universities offer instruction in African life and thought; in Ghana the teaching of African religion at the University of Ghana was begun before the country became independent. Secondly, it is our conviction that there is such wisdom in African life and thought as would make for stability and self-authentication in today's world; in other words, the achievement of *selfhood* which has been delayed by the kind of socio-economic and political problems referred to above would be immensely facilitated by an appreciation and appropriation of some of the African religio-cultural values. Selfhood is a concept which is essential to this study of Christian theology; it may be given even greater particularity by its being juxtaposed with Senghor's term 'Africanity'. Selfhood has not been realised by the Church in Africa, which is not surprising, for without the achievement of national selfhood in the sense of the practice of that kind of life-style which exhibits a keen awareness of the values in African religio-cultural traditions, selfhood in the Church could hardly become a reality.

Part Two

Theological Uncertainty and Experimentation

4

Theological Unreality in the Church in Africa

Missionary activity in Africa in the modern period repeatedly raised the issue of what was to be made of the religio-cultural background of those who were being evangelised: Should not this background be eliminated as part of the process of preaching the Gospel?

This is an issue that dates from before the modern missionary period. That the early Church had to wrestle with it is amply evidenced in the New Testament. The Jewish Christians were divided on the question of whether or not there was a continuity between the Church's Jewish traditions and the non-Jewish traditions. While many, like Paul, were prepared to concede that Gentiles could become members of the Church, it is evident that Gentile admission was hedged about with precautionary measures. Thus Paul, the intrepid evangelist, believed that pre-Christian traditions, especially those outside Judaism, were valueless and must be discarded.[1]

Much later, in the sixth century, this issue formed the background to instructions given by Gregory I to Augustine who was then labouring as a missionary in southern England, and who was to become the first Archbishop of Canterbury: Gregory advised that Christian ritual should be adapted to local circumstances, and that pagan temples, instead of being destroyed, should be transformed

---

1. See Galatians 4:8–11, where Paul describes the Galatians as having been 'in bondage to beings that by nature are no gods'; he further underlines the pointlessness of the traditional religion of the Galatians when he describes their gods as 'weak and beggarly elemental spirits'.

into Churches.[2] The same issue was raised in the seventeenth century in connection with Jesuit missionary activity in China where Matteo Ricci's methods of evangelism were such as not to require his converts to make a break with Confucianism, and in India where Robert de Nobili adopted a Brahmin's way of life.[3]

Christian evangelism as it was carried out by European missionaries in the early days of missions in Africa, and also by those African preachers whom the missionaries had trained as their co-workers, tended to assume the destructiveness of African religion and culture. Consequently, little or no attempt was made to relate the Gospel to the African's life and thought. What is of interest in this connection is that policy statements made by missionary societies and European church leaders would have led one to expect a more positive attitude to indigenous traditions. A look at some of the past papal pronouncements, for example, shows clearly that *officially* an enlightened attitude was expected to prevail with respect to non-European peoples and cultures in the missionary drive;[4] in the actualities of the field situation, however, severely censorious attitudes prevailed.

What is known of missionary preaching, especially in the nineteenth-century Africa, reveals not only a lack of appreciation of African life and thought, but also a presentation of the Christian message that sometimes detracted from the fullness of its meaning and significance. This latter failing is not so readily documented, though indications of what the missionary theological approach might have been in the field are not entirely lacking; not only do the missionary records contain the occasional reference to biblical texts chosen for sermons and the gists of those sermons, but also there is the evidence of the Africans' understanding of what the missionaries said in their preaching, and their reaction to it. The

2. B. J. Kidd (ed.), *Documents Illustrative of the History of the Church*, vol. III, c. 500–1500 (S.P.C.K. 1941), pp. 42–3.

3. K. S. Latourette, *History of the Expansion of Christianity*, vol. III (New York, Harper, 1939), pp. 259–62, 339–42.

4. See Stephen N. Ezeanya, 'God, Spirits and the Spirit World', in Kwesi Dickson and Paul Ellingworth (eds.), *Biblical Revelation and African Beliefs* (Guildford, Lutterworth, 1969), esp. pp. 31–4.

latter could be regarded as unreliable evidence, since it may in fact amount to a misrepresentation of what the missionaries had said unless, of course, it can be shown to be otherwise by reference to other data. A few comments will now be made on this second failing.

In the surroundings of Africa which struck the missionaries with that kind of strangeness and unreality from which they felt they had to remove their converts, it would seem that the missionaries presented God as a transcendent God, one whose concern was to lift up the African from the world of human concerns in which God apparently had no interest.[5] That this was in all probability the predominant theological approach adopted by the missionaries may be deduced from certain historical incidents; it will suffice to refer to only two of these.

When in 1876 the British Methodist missionary, Thomas R. Picot, arrived in Kumasi (Ghana) to try and persuade the Asantehene, Mensa Bonsu, to accept a mission, the king made some very instructive comments which were based upon earlier missionary activity in his kingdom by Picot's predecessors. He stated that he would lend his support if Picot would 'act as [one of Picot's predecessors, T. B. Freeman] did to help the peace of the nation and the prosperity of the trade . . . Our fetishes are God's interpreters to us . . . They tell us too where the gold is with which we trade . . .'[6] Mensa Bonsu knew that in the traditional religion of his people the spirit world was considered to be linked to the physical world; he must have gained the impression, rightly or wrongly, that the religion being proclaimed by the missionaries, with its strongly other-worldly slant, was not such as could be relied upon.

The second incident has to do with Nigeria. In the middle of the last century the King of Dahomey (now the Republic of Benin)

5. In his report of 30 July 1838 the British Methodist missionary, Thomas Birch Freeman, wrote from the Gold Coast (Ghana): 'Blessed be God that the "swarthy Negro" can exalt in the idea, that he will soon exchange the burning wilds of Africa, for that heavenly country where the sun shall not light on him nor any heat . . .'

6. Kwesi Dickson, *Aspects of Religion and Life in Africa* (Ghana Academy of Arts and Sciences 1977), p. 19.

started making warlike preparations against Abeokuta whose leaders, in desperation, turned to the missionary Henry Townsend, who responded favourably – no doubt because he saw the success of Abeokuta against her enemies as crucial to the interests of the British missionaries in that area. With Townsend's help the Fon of Dahomey were defeated in 1850, and Townsend's reputation was considerably enhanced.[7] Contrary to what might have been expected, this enhancement of the British missionary's reputation did not result in any appreciable rise in the number of conversions to Christianity. A more than likely explanation for this is that the Yoruba, mindful of that missionary preaching which emphasised the transcendence of God, had not correlated this God's governance with Townsend's military skills; in other words, they had not come to look upon Townsend's God as having the powers of *Olodumare* or *Ogun*.[8] Thus, what the missionary was preaching was not seen to be related to the 'mundane' pursuits of warfare, trade, etc. In contrast to this, there is in our time active advocacy of the need to recognise that the Gospel has to do with the totality of man's life. The early missionaries, by and large, did not relate the Gospel and life, except where the latter was considered to be coterminous with Europeanism. This narrow correlation meant, of course, that the theological task of the missionary had been given a restricted focus; hence the conviction that it was God's desire that Africans should be taken out of their 'unwholesome' system of life and thought. That this contradicted and annulled the correlation of the Gospel and Western culture largely went unnoticed and unremarked.

Incidentally, the two incidents just referred to give indication of a potentially rewarding aspect of Church history and Christian theology in the African context which has largely gone unexplored. It has been commented often enough that in traditional Africa religion informs life in general, but seldom has the bearing of this upon African response to Christian missions been given any detailed consideration. Much of what was surely the African interpretation of missionary preaching tended to be viewed in mission records as

7. S. O. Biobaku, 'An Historical Sketch of Egba Traditional Authorities', in *Africa*, vol. 22, January 1952, pp. 47ff.
8. E. B. Idowu, *Olodumare: God in Yoruba Belief*, Longmans 1962.

insensitivity to the Gospel, and has not therefore been properly evaluated. Hence a potentially interesting and valuable aspect of Church history and theology has yet to be written. That Africans often interpreted what they were being told by Christian evangelists in the light of their own life and thought may not be doubted.[9]

The unenlightened nature of the theological stand adopted by some missionaries to Africa has had some consequences for the Church on that continent; in particular, it has resulted in a lack of cohesion in the Church's thinking and vision, situated as it is in the midst of the African religio-cultural reality which, overtly or covertly, exercises a great deal of influence. We shall proceed to illustrate further the missionary theological approach and the uncertainties it has given rise to.

Worship

First, worship. On the evidence of Thomas Birch Freeman, one of the most tireless of the nineteenth-century British Methodist missionaries to the Gold Coast (now Ghana), the missionaries saw their task as consisting partly in inculcating the worship patterns with which they were familiar in the British Methodist Church. Thus at a 'Special District Meeting' of missionaries and 'native assistants'[10] held at Cape Coast[11] on 12 March 1849 it was noted that local preachers (Ghanaian preachers trained by the missionaries but not ordained) were expected to preach 'English Methodism'.[12] This was the context in which worship was done in the Methodist Church in Ghana. In his time Freeman enjoyed the reputation – somewhat exaggerated, admittedly – of having a great understanding of African ways; on more than one occasion he voiced out his dissatisfaction with the rate at which European customs

9. Dickson, *Aspects of Religion and Life in Africa*, pp. 15ff.
10. These were Ghanaians trained and ordained as ministers but who were considered by the missionaries as their assistants.
11. One of Ghana's principal towns and the starting point of British Methodist missionary activity in Ghana.
12. See Kwesi Dickson 'The Minister – Then and Now' in J. S. Pobee (ed.), *Religion in a Pluralistic Society* (Leiden, E. J. Brill, 1976), pp. 166ff.

were being introduced, these being considered by him to have 'no connexion with Christianity' and 'may be . . . a fruitful cause of evil'.[13] And yet it was this same Freeman who wrote that in his first ten years in Ghana he yearned for the kind of worship which he knew in England, and that the yearning ceased after the British pattern had been reproduced in the Ghana mission area. As he himself put it, '. . . if our Public worship in Cape Coast is not heaven come down to earth, it is pretty nearly that of England come to Africa'.[14] This meant not only the teaching of English hymns for worship, but also in some instances the teaching of the English language as a means of facilitating the introduction of English patterns of worship. A Methodist missionary to Ghana wrote in 1840: '. . . I was delighted to hear them [the people of Cape Coast] sing the praises of God in the English language and pray in their own . . .'[15] While it is true that some concern was voiced by some missionaries over the introduction of the English language as an accompaniment to the inculcation of Christianity,[16] nevertheless missionary policy in the field was such as to preclude the working out of a worship pattern that took account of the African's life experiences. Thus traditional music was, generally speaking, kept out of the church. To be sure, traditional lyrics have been used in worship in the Ghana Methodist Church since before the end of the last century,[17] but it is a measure of the prevalence to this day of Western influence that these lyrics have not found a *formal* place

---

13. Dickson, 'The Minister – Then and Now', pp. 173–4.
14. 1854 Report of the Wesleyan Methodist Missionary Society, vol. XII.
15. Rev. Brooking; see Dickson 'The Minister – Then and Now', p. 171.
16. Rev. Wrigley expressed doubts in 1836, about a year after the inception of Methodist missions in Ghana, about the wisdom of placing emphasis on the English language in the teaching of 'divine truth' in Ghana. Missionary policy could not possibly have anticipated all situations in the actual fields of operation; hence the missionaries were often free to take decisions and adopt measures as they saw fit. Consequently, it comes as no surprise that sometimes opposed attitudes were demonstrated in the field.
17. On the evidence of Rev. Jacob Anaman (1866–1939) whose ministry began in the Methodist Church, Ghana; see A. A. Mensah, 'Leadership Roles in Worship', All Africa Conference of Churches Consultation on African Church Music, University of Ghana, 17–23 April 1976.

in the liturgy of the Church.[18] An aspect of worship which has intriguing possibilities and which was not examined in the context of Africa is preaching: what this should consist in, given the change in context from Europe to Africa, was not raised in the missionary period, and to our knowledge it has yet to be seriously raised.

Stages in the Christian Life

There is, secondly, the matter of the classical Protestant theological sequence of faith leading to salvation, followed by works and sanctification, which was the basis of much missionary teaching. If the early missionaries had not been preoccupied with ensuring that their understanding of the Gospel, and the Church ethos that went with it, was adopted wholesale by their African converts, they might have observed how this classical sequence was experienced by them. Methodist missionary records relating to Ghana note occurrences which could have been seen as indicating how the Ghanaian converts were appropriating Christianity. There are references to natural disasters (especially earthquakes) which drove crowds into the churches; there was also the ready acceptance of the 'class' system, whereby the church membership was divided into groups which would meet once a week to study the Bible and Church teaching, and to encourage one another in Christian living; each group would be led by a leader ('class leader'). Quite clearly the class system recalls the African family system within the larger settings of the clan and tribe.[19] The point is that in African society questions of the maintenance of life predominate, and in the context of the Church these issue in concerns of security in Christ. Hence priority would be given to questions of healing, church discipline and generally those intra-church 'societal' arrangements and groupings which underline and enhance the sense of belonging and

18. On the subject of the lyric see S. G. Williamson, 'The Lyric in the Fante Methodist Church', in *Africa*, XXVIII, no. 2, April 1958.
19. The family is the smallest group within which individuals are socialised and the needs of the group as a whole, and of its individual members, satisfied. It is significant that the Class system is strongly maintained in the Ghana Methodist Church even though English Methodism seems to be outgrowing it.

security. Questions of confessing the faith are distinctly secondary. That the concerns referred to continue to predominate accounts for the popularity of healing Churches in Ghana, and in Africa generally. On the whole, the historic Churches have not shown much interest in healing, being more concerned to preserve their European-oriented traditions.

A general comment may be made regarding this theological sequence of faith, salvation, works and sanctification: it is usually implied that chronological distinctions exist between these so-called stages in the Christian life. Such a view is highly questionable. Faith, salvation, works and sanctification interact with one another; the drawing of distinctions between them is an illustration of how the Church has listened ineffectively to the Scriptures. The sudden blossoming of relevant theology or theological activism in our time contrasts with the theological fashion that drew distinctions such as have been referred to when there was no warrant for so proceeding. And as noted, in Africa life is seen as a whole, undifferentiated into religion and life, into life in the spirit and life in the 'flesh'; it would be alien to the African to cut up life into watertight compartments, and the Christian Scriptures would give backing to this visualising of life as one whole. The delineation of steps in discipleship as referred to could lead to serious contradictions in the African convert's life.

Bible translation

Then, thirdly, there is the matter of Bible translation. As already indicated, the European missionary's language was inculcated as part of the task of missions; for some time the missionary's language was considered the most suitable medium of worship. Thus in Ghana Methodist missionaries were very slow in acquiring the local languages, a fact which led one of the Methodist missionaries, Daniel West, to write in 1857: 'I cannot but express my surprise that in these eighteen years no attempt has been made to acquire or speak the language of the country.'[20] There is every indication

20. S. G. Williamson, *Akan Religion and the Christian Faith* (Ghana Universities Press 1965), p. 71.

that the early missionaries had expected English to supersede the local languages. The lack of urgency with which the need for working in the medium of the African languages was viewed accounted, at least in part, for the gap – often quite a long one – between the arrival of missionaries and the translation of the Bible into the local languages. Then, when the Bible came to be translated there was, generally speaking, a recognisable sequence of steps: the translation of selections from the Bible; the translation of the whole of the New Testament, then the preparation of the whole Bible; rarely was the Old Testament translated before other parts of the Bible.[21] On the basis of the evidence assembled by Phillips[22] the conclusion is unavoidable that the task of translating the Old Testament was put off in some places in Africa because of the observable affinity between it and African life and thought. In their preoccupation with inculcating a Western understanding of the Gospel, no investigative efforts were made to evaluate this affinity; after all there was a great distrust of African beliefs.

Training for the Ministry

Fourthly, the training of Africans for the ministry illustrates further the theological uncertainty being briefly surveyed. To use once again the story of Methodist missionary work in Ghana as illustration, the British Methodist Missionary Society was convinced, from the inception of its work in Ghana, of the necessity to raise an indigenous ministry, in accordance with its general policy on the subject;[23] it recognised that following the introduction of Christianity in Ghana the Church's continued prosecution of missions should be left in the hands of the native ministers. However, it soon became clear that this stated policy was hedged about with precautionary measures. The Ghanaian ministers were to be an

21. C. P. Groves, *The Planting of Christianity in Africa*, vol. IV (Guildford, Lutterworth, 1958), Appendix, pp. 357ff.
22. G. E. Phillips, *The Old Testament in the World Church*, Guildford, Lutterworth, 1942.
23. Dickson, 'The Minister – Then and Now', pp. 166ff.

auxiliary force; it was not readily envisaged that they would replace the European missionaries.[24]

This is an all-too-brief discussion of some of the facets of missionary activity as it was carried out in Ghana by missionaries from the British Methodist Missionary Society starting from 1835. It is for the sake of convenience that much of the discussion here has so far been limited to one missionary body and to practically one African country. As a matter of fact, however, the story of the Ghana Methodist Church is not in any way unique, for situations similar to that surveyed here prevailed in other African countries.

It is necessary now to raise the question of how matters stand today, now that the historic Churches in most African countries are independent. Has the situation of theological uncertainties been resolved?

Regrettably, to move from the era of the mission Church to the present is to encounter a familiar situation: on the whole the now independent and self-governing historic Churches in Africa have a pattern of life and thought which is not much different from that established by the missionaries. Worship style has not changed very much: in the churches founded by the British Methodist Missionary Society, Wesley's 'Abridgement of the Order of Morning Prayer' is still used on Sunday mornings. Williamson has commented, writing in the 1960s, that to enter any of the 'historic' churches in Ghana is to be mentally flung back to Europe (often Europe at the turn of this century), mostly because of their liturgical styles.[25] To be sure, attempts are being made to move away from these European patterns, but so far these have been mostly half-hearted and ineffec-

24. This explains why the ordained Ghanaian ministers were officially designated 'Native Assistants', and this despite the fact that their training was intended to make them, as much as possible, like the missionaries. The Ghanaian ministers were required to wear European clothing, and in a letter dated 30 July 1838, the head of the Methodist missionary unit in Ghana, T. B. Freeman, wrote that the Ghanaian ministers would acquire stature before their compatriots if they were sent to England to be 'improved'. It is interesting to note that when the British Methodist Missionary Society decided against adopting Freeman's suggestion, one of the first Ghanaian ministers tendered his letter of resignation. See Dickson, 'The Minister – Then and Now', pp. 168ff.

25. Williamson, op. cit., pp. 59–61.

tive. And, strangely enough, it does not seem to surprise the leaders of some of the more recent sects that they should be required to read to their Ghanaian congregations on Sunday mornings sermons written in, and sent from, America![26] Furthermore, the image of the African minister of religion is still modelled after the European 'original'. In the early days of Methodist missionary activity in Ghana the Ghanaian minister was among the best-educated in the country. Now the minister, generally speaking, does not by his training fit into the class of the best-educated; the setting up of universities[27] has meant that the minister has a much more critical congregation in the towns than was possible, say, thirty years ago. And yet the minister

> maintains the trappings of a social class with which we would normally associate the more affluent and the more highly educated. After all, he heads a Church many of whose members are highly literate, and for whose benefit he quite frequently preaches in both English and the local languages. He appears in the pulpit and at synods and Conferences dressed differently, because the Church's unwritten sartorial laws dictate that this should be the regulation attire, to be worn no matter how inclement the weather. They are used, by training, to offering the Holy Communion in the best silver, even in places where such wares would seem unreal.[28]

And he would have been trained in a seminary that is at the initial stages of adjusting its curricula towards training to fit the African situation. In 1967 Beetham observed:

> The curriculum [of African theological colleges] is in most cases too much tied to a traditional western pattern. Students can still come away from their lecture-room after studying the first two chapters of Mark's Gospel – with its account of the touch of Jesus of Nazareth on different kinds of illness, including mental sickness – without having come to grips either with the failure of their

26. The reference here is to the First Century Gospel Church.
27. Three in Ghana; Nigeria has about twenty in operation.
28. Dickson, 'The Minister – Then and Now', pp. 178–9.

own Church, despite its hospitals and clinics, to exercise a full ministry of healing or with the success of some Independent Churches in this respect.[29]

What all this amounts to is that the Church in Africa, by and large, retains much of its mission-days character, and this explains its present life-style, and what many would consider to be its weakness.

Social Concern

As an illustration of the Church's present character one might look at its social concern; here, once again, it will be with reference to Ghana. In March of 1978, after six years of increasingly incompetent and frantic rule by the military under the then military Head of State, Ignatius Kutu Acheampong, the Christian Council and the National Catholic Secretariat submitted a memorandum to the government decrying the use of force by the law enforcement authorities and various other groups to silence those whose views differed from the government's with respect to the system of government which would best promote the aspirations of Ghanaians; the memorandum asked the government, among other things, to ensure that 'a suitable atmosphere be created for the conduct of a fair and impartial referendum that will shape the future of our motherland'.[30]

Now the step taken by the Christian Council and the National Catholic Secretariat is one that has rarely been taken by the Church in post-colonial Africa which has seen much dictatorial rule, both

29. T. A. Beetham, *Christianity and the New Africa* (Pall Mall Press, 1967), pp. 106–7.

30. Memorandum submitted by the Christian Council of Ghana and the National Catholic Secretariat to the Government of Ghana, 7 March 1978, Accra. At about the same time as this memorandum was submitted, the Catholic hierarchy of Ghana caused a pastoral letter 'to be read in all Catholic Churches on Palm Sunday, 19 March, 1978.' In this letter, after affirming the conviction that the Church has the 'task of proclaiming the demands of God's reign in every arena of human existence,' the Bishops insisted that all Ghanaians must have the freedom to express opinions on government proposals regarding the kind of government under which they might live; such freedom could not be exercised where there was intimidation and where the media were manipulated by the government. See *Joint Pastoral Letter of the Catholic Hierarchy of Ghana on the Referendum*, Ghana, National Catholic Secretariat, 1978.

civilian and military. This is surprising considering that the Church, according to its own teaching, speaks in the name of all, Christians and non-Christians alike. The Church plays its true role when it preaches liberation from sin, death, the law and demonic powers, as well as liberation and justice in human relations. Thus the Ghana Churches were interpreting their role in society correctly when they sought to make the people aware of the dangers inherent in certain government attitudes and societal developments. But if so, how does one explain the unfavourable reaction to the Churches' stand by government officials and many of Ghana's citizens? The explanation lies in the fact that it was felt that the Church was abandoning its 'true' role of exercising spiritual oversight over its members, and was now taking on the state instead, thus playing a political role. Certain government officials in particular voiced this opinion loudly; in contrast to this the generality of the membership of the Churches seemed to have taken little notice of the happening: the stand taken by their leaders was to our knowledge not seriously discussed by the generality of the Church membership.

One could think of two main reasons for the unfavourable or passive reactions to the Church's stand. In the first place, the Christian Church today, in Ghana as in much of Africa, has the character of the Church as it was in the colonial situation. The Church in the colonial era often worked closely with the colonial government in various spheres, such as education. Indeed, the progress made by the Church then was often facilitated by the fact that the Church and the colonial administration had in part the common goal of bringing 'civilisation' to Africans; the two institutions often found themselves playing complementary roles. The main difference today is that there is a post-colonial situation in most of Africa, and most African countries have independent historic Churches led by African church leaders; in fact, however, there has been a tendency, consciously or unconsciously, to perpetuate something of that colonial era alignment between the Church and the ruling powers. For one thing the Church in Africa tends to have a middle-class image. The Church in some African countries, as indeed in countries in the 'First World', has a false sense of respectability which makes it more inclined to align itself with the rulers than with the ruled, especially where Heads of State make public avowals of an ostensibly Christian nature.

The question is: What are the consequences of such alignment for the Church's attitude to governmental policies and attitudes? Ghana's recent history gives at least one kind of answer to this question. The former head of the military government which was formed following the overthrow of Dr K. A. Busia's civilian government in 1972, I. K. Acheampong, aligned himself with the Christian Churches, historic and Independent, and was formally blessed at several worship services in more than one denominational church. It may perhaps be said that Acheampong needed all the blessing he could get, for he was never a leader; he continued to rule recklessly and irresponsibly. If the Church was uncomfortable about Acheampong parading his Christian affiliation – and from personal conversations with some Christian friends it became evident that his Christian protestations occasioned not a little unease in Christian circles – this was not publicly voiced. In the name of his military administration Acheampong donated a motor vehicle to Trinity College, a seminary run jointly by the Methodist, Presbyterian and Anglican Churches, and underwrote the cost of a new house for its principal. It is not an unrealistic assessment to suggest that the relation between the Church and Acheampong – and indeed between the Church and state since 1957, the year of Ghana's independence – was somewhat analogous to the relation between the colonial Church and the colonial government. The Ghana Church might not have been very happy with Acheampong (though there were several leaders of the Independent Churches who often proclaimed his virtues loudly and espoused his cause, often without any justification whatsoever), but it took the Church some time to take a *public* stand against political abuses.

The second reason for the surprise occasioned by the Church's public stand is simply that, considering the history of independent Ghana, the Church had kept quiet on socio-political issues for far too long. In the time of Dr Kwame Nkrumah, President of the First Republic of Ghana, the Church made attempts to get him to repeal the dreaded Preventive Detention Act. I myself got to know about the approaches made for this purpose by some church leaders at a very poorly attended public lecture given by Bishop Roseveare, the then Anglican Bishop of Accra, under the sponsorship of the United States Information Services; this lecture took place *after* Nkrumah's overthrow in 1960. As far as we know, that was the first time the Ghana Churches' efforts to influence the policies of Nkrumah were publicly dicussed by an ecclesiastical figure. It seems to us that the Church's membership should be made aware of what its leadership is doing in matters relating to the policies of the government, for these policies affect the lives of the people who are the Church's charge. Some argue that it would be inappropriate for church leaders who are engaged in discussions with government over matters of government policies to make known to the general membership of the Church what was going on even before a resolution of the matter had been achieved; such 'premature' public revelation, it is argued, could lead to the hardening of government's attitude. While I would not wish to argue that under no circumstances should discussions with government not proceed in secrecy, there should be some awareness of the risk involved in keeping members of the Church in the dark: the Church as a whole might not be helped to grow in theological awareness. This matter of theology and the Church will be taken up later.[31]

Of course, it is the government's duty to make arrangements for the security of the people being governed; it also has the responsibility of acting to ensure the freedom of the citizens. However, when government itself tramples upon the laws aimed at ensuring the individual's freedom, as many an African government has done, then the Church cannot but speak out and encourage people to be aware of their rights as Christians, and as citizens. Obstacles in the way of peoples' realising their humanity must not be tolerated by the Church. That the Church in Africa has sometimes displayed such tolerance is beyond doubt.[32]

31. See pp. 220–2 below.
32. There were many discerning Ghanaians who found I. K. Acheampong's very first broadcast as Head of State ominous; he said, among other things, that the ousting of K. A. Busia's civilian government had been motivated partly by the fact that under Busia the army had lost certain 'amenities' which it enjoyed in the colonial period! And this was at a time when Ghana was beginning to experience serious economic difficulties.

There are other aspects of the theological uncertainty plaguing the African Church to which I wish to refer. Sometimes incompatible situations arise unobserved and uncommented upon by the Church because of its less-than-authentic theological orientation. There is the matter of the solemnisation of matrimony, for example. In my article 'Christian and African Traditional Ceremonies'[33] comments were made on various aspects of the British Methodist Order (as authorised 'for use in the Methodist Church by the Conference at Newcastle-on-Tyne, July 1936') in the light of the Ghanaian matrilineal type of society. In this Order, which is still in use in those Methodist Churches in Africa which emanated from Britain, the principal actors in the wedding drama are, apart from the officiating minister, the prospective bride and bridegroom; the bride's father plays only a fleeting role when he says 'I do' to confirm that he is the one giving her away. The prospective bride and bridegroom are at the centre of the stage: they are the ones who make their vows. This contrasts with the African system of marriage in which two families, rather than two individuals, come together. Further, this Order refers to the 'causes for which matrimony was ordained': these are, the mutual comfort of the two in all situations, and the bringing up of children 'in the knowledge and love of God . . .' These causes emphasise the fact of the two being the principal actors. In African societies marriage has the primary aim of bringing forth children and perpetuating the family. Ceremonies in connection with the making of payments leading to marriage, seasonal festivals, and generally traditional ceremonies are incomplete without prayers being said to ask that the women might bear children. And, it needs to be remembered that before the church ceremony the two would have been legally married in accordance with traditional custom. This raises, among other things, the interesting question of whether or not it is pointless for the officiating minister to ask whether any one knows any just cause why the two may not be joined together. And speaking of the Order's pronouncement of the two having become one flesh, there is the matrilineal custom which prevents a child from inheriting the

33. In *Practical Anthropology*, vol. XVIII, no. 2, March-April 1967.

father's property; also, with the children issuing from the union belonging to the mother's family, it is less than meaningful for the Church Order to note simply that the bride and the bridegroom are one. Clearly there are unresolved incompatibilities here.

Now for a final illustration of the problem. The Methodist Church of Ghana, like all the historic Churches in Ghana and elsewhere in Africa frowns upon polygamy and does not admit those involved in polygamous marriages to the Lord's Table. A few years ago a member of the Methodist Church of Ghana who had been a polygamist died. In accordance with the Church's policy the body of the deceased was not taken to the church for the pre-burial service; it was taken direct to the cemetery, and at the graveside the story of his life was read by one of the five ministers present, though the account contained no mention of his having had two wives. Among the prayers read was one which featured the words, '. . . we have joy at this time in all who have faithfully lived, and all who have faithfully died . . .' It may be wondered why the deceased's body was not taken to the church if he had 'faithfully lived' and 'faithfully died'!

The theological contradictions which have been surveyed here arise from the Church in Africa having a bifocal view of reality. On the one hand, there is Christ whom the Church acknowledges and proclaims; on the other hand, since his worship in Africa is a reflection of its European origin, Christ wears a distinctly European aspect, and hence he is seen, more unconsciously than consciously perhaps, as relevant only in a circumscribed area of life – in the Church and generally in church circles. There does not appear to be a conscious awareness of the need to bring Christ into those other areas which seem to be reserved for the traditional spirit powers. This would explain why African Christians – lay-men/women and clergy alike – are able to live with such contradictions as have been cited without their being made uncomfortable by them.

The question has sometimes been asked: Is it not being more realistic to have such a bifocal view of reality? This question has sometimes been asked, more in jest, perhaps, by some African Christians; it needs to be taken seriously, however. If, as we have argued, religion is larger than Christianity, and the theologian is one who must know the structures of religion, then should not this bifocal attitude make sense? After all it would ensure that religion was brought into the totality of the African Christian's life. A cursory look at this view, however, reveals its inadequacy. Our concern is that there should be an inclusive view of Christian thought, for Christ's life did not place him in secluded, 'respectable' or 'proper' areas of life. He went into 'alien' situations, for there is nothing alien where the Son of God is concerned, contrary to what the adoption of the bifocal understanding of reality would imply.

For several decades now questions have been raised regarding the expression of the Christian faith in Africa, but either these have been swept under the rug, or ineffectual answers have been given. When in 1844 T. B. Freeman, that Methodist missionary, was criticised in the London *Times* mainly on the grounds that he was encouraging concubinage by his accommodating attitude to indigenous marriage customs, he wrote in rebuttal: '. . . wherever marriage is celebrated according to the law and usage of the country, even though the country be heathen, it is in substance or essence a valid marriage'.[34]

There is no evidence that the charges brought against Freeman, and his rejoinder, occasioned any serious discussion of questions of marriage either by the Wesleyan Methodist Missionary Society in London which had sent out Freeman, or by the fledgling Methodist Church in Ghana. When the question of marriage came up again, it was in 1938 when the Ghana delegation to the Tambaram Conference of the International Missionary Council was requested to raise questions regarding polygamy;[35] at that time the historic Churches in Ghana were run by Western missionaries who had taken a stand – and not a very informed one, at that – against polygamy. More

---

34. *The Wesleyan Missionary Notices*, New Series, vol. II (for the years 1842, 1843, 1844), p. 660. Freeman's attitude was echoed at Le Zoute in 1928 by Bishop Hening of the Moravians when he said that the Church has no right to consider as invalid conjugal unions contracted according to local laws and customs.

35. C. G. Baeta, 'Conflict in Mission: Historical and Separatist Churches' in G. H. Anderson (ed.), *The Theology of the Christian Mission* (New York, McGraw-Hill, 1961), p. 295.

THEOLOGICAL UNREALITY IN THE CHURCH IN AFRICA   107

recently this same issue came up in the Methodist Church in Rhodesia (now Zimbabwe) and was referred to the Methodist Missionary Society in London in 1971. A team consisting of British and African Methodist theologians was assembled, and after much discussion the predictable conclusion was arrived at that it did not make theological sense to view polygamy as one of the devil's devices; and, not only can monogamy not be incontrovertibly supported on the basis of the Scriptures, but also it would seem to reflect a Western cultural ethos which has been incorrectly labelled Christian. Mis-labelling and mis-typing have been among the factors in the creation of an unreal theological atmosphere in the Church in Africa.

It is a measure of the effectiveness of the Church in Africa that such issues as polygamy continue to be raised almost as if there were nothing to learn from past discussions. Serious self-evaluation has not been done by the Church, and there is a ready explanation for this: the historic Churches (and also sometimes the Independent Churches) tend to operate as if in the belief that it is in their interest to approximate as much as possible to church ethos as it obtains in the West. Generally speaking, the Church's leadership has not shown any real inclination to wrestle with the presuppositions underlying the theological stance inherited from the West.

5

Towards a Theological Expression

In recent years, an increasing number of Christians in Africa have been vocal on the subject of the need for the Church to think seriously through its faith in order to arrive at more relevant ways of witnessing to Christ. The more adventurous among these questioners have been theological educators at seminaries and universities, and their views have issued in a number of publications. If the leadership of the Church has not been seized of the urgency of the concerns being expressed by these questioners, it is mainly because no seriously sustained effort has been made by these questioners from *within* the Church through more vital participation and persuasion; the challenging questions raised have seldom been heard from within the worshipping community,[1] even though a number of Church-sponsored conferences and consultations have been held.[2] The question at issue, in all these discussions, has been: What kind of theological understanding should characterise the Church in Africa? Or, to put this in another way: In what should the theological stance of the Church consist if it is to be a genuine expression of selfhood?

Informal Theologising
If this question is taken to imply that hitherto the Church in Africa has had no theological interest whatsoever, then it must be pointed

1. See chapter 8 for comments on theology and the Christian community.
2. The most recent of such conferences was the Fourth Assembly of the All Africa Conference of Churches which met in Nairobi, Kenya, 1–12 August, 1981. One of the five sections of this Assembly dealt almost entirely with the subject of Christian theology in Africa.

out that this is not its intention, for in fact Christians in Africa have been theologising all along, even if not in any formal way; informal theologising is done in various ways, such as in song, prayer, and preaching. This is a point which cannot be made forcefully enough, for with the blossoming of theological exposition in recent years, particularly in the so-called Third World, there is the possibility – yea, a real danger – that Christians in Africa, and elsewhere, might come to associate theology solely with a systematic articulation of Christian belief.

As far as theologising through music is concerned, African Christians have for a long time been giving indication of what they would like to do in worship in the Church. In the Ghana Methodist Church the British Methodist Hymn Book, and translations from it, exist side by side with lyrics, especially in the Mfantse-speaking areas. The singing of lyrics is usually spontaneous and uncontrived. Like most types of African music the singing of lyrics calls for an initiator or cantor who not only must be very familiar with the story of the Bible and be able to relate it to the life-circumstances of his people, but also he or she must be sufficiently aware theologically to be able to fit the lyric into the preacher's message as it is being developed. The singing follows speech rhythm, as African singing usually does. The language is concrete and expresses the thought of a God who cares for the person in all life's situations, both spiritual and physical: he saves not only from sin but also from the dangers of childbirth, etc.

Williamson has listed the following as constituting, in his opinion, the main defects of lyrics: (1) their content lacks both variety and precision. He finds that certain concepts appear frequently which echo 'predominantly traditional thoughts'; (2) they make no mention of Christ.[3] There is reason to believe that Williamson's study is too limited to warrant these conclusions. After all he examined only eight of a considerable range of lyrics much of which is yet to be recorded and analysed; indeed, a collection made a few

3. S. G. Williamson, 'The Lyric in the Fante Methodist Church', in *Africa*, XXVIII, no. 2, April 1958.

years ago would lead one to set aside Williamson's criticisms.[4] Thus the criticism that lyrics contain such indigenous modes of expression as witness more to traditional religious belief than to Christian commitment does not seem to us to be soundly based, inasmuch as the lyrics do precisely what they should be expected to do as coming from a people with an indigenous faith in God: the singers praise God in the ways they know best through most meaningful expressions, even if they may sound formal to others. What needs to be underlined here is that in the lyrics Akan Christians express their understanding of the Christian faith, their theology; that is, our knowledge of these lyrics reveals that there is a great sense of gratefulness to God for the spiritual–physical salvation that he brings to mankind.

What of the Western type of music which features so prominently in churches in Africa? In Africa certain types of Western music have become part of the religious scene, especially in the urban areas, and our view is that they will continue to find a place in the Church's life, though the dangers attendant upon their indiscriminate use need to be recognised. In this connection three points may be made: (1) the way in which African Christians sometimes render Western hymns has not been lost upon discerning musicians. Quite often certain involuntary alterations are made to the music in accordance with tonal and other needs.[5] Thus the glissando technique is used by the Zulus of southern Africa to give a characteristic shape to Western hymns; and, as is well known, improvised congregational singing in African churches tends to be based upon tonal ideas which are different from those which Western hymn tunes, such as are mostly sung in the churches in Africa, are based; (2) the singing groups in the churches, by and large, are more at home singing songs which embody African traditional forms; (3) not enough awareness has been shown of the difficulties involved in translating Western hymns into African languages; quite often there is a clash

4. The Ghanaian Methodist minister, S. B. Essamuah, has been working on this project together with the musicologist, Dr A. Turkson of the School of Performing Arts, University of Ghana.

5. Henry Weman, *African Music and the Church in Africa* (Uppsala, Svenska Institutet För Missionsforskning, 1960), pp. 127ff.

between the rhythm of the African language and that of the Western tune, the reason being the African preference for speech rhythm, as already noted.[6]

If all this attention is being given to music here, it is for a good reason. Singing and dancing are a very important feature of life in Africa; these twin activities go on in joy and in sorrow, at worship and at play. Hence a service of worship would have much less meaning if it did not centre round a significant amount of the kind of stirring music that generates religious emotions. It is significant that in the African Independent Churches swaying or dancing is a regular feature.[7]

Mention of the Independent Churches provides us with the opportunity to comment on one significant characteristic of worship which the Church in Africa has inherited from the West – orderliness. In the historic Churches, everything is ordered from start to finish, so much so that some ministers in the Methodist Church in Ghana have been known to show impatience when a lyric has burst out in the course of a sermon. Worship patterns in African traditional religion, as well as the increasing appreciation being shown for the worship life of some of the Independent Churches, lead one to caution against allowing orderliness to stifle religious emotions. The spontaneous and less inhibited worship style of the Independent Churches has begun to have some influence on the worship style of some of the historic Churches; now some congregations are not averse to accompanying certain types of songs on the drums during worship. It may be added, however, that whatever experimentation has taken place in this connection has been done without the Church's executive fiat; it has depended almost entirely

6. Also, where a composition in an African language has been translated into English, often the rhythm of the English words clashes with that of the African music. Examples of this are to be found in *Asempa Hymns*, Asempa Publishers, 1980 – e.g. no. 394.

7. A few years ago I was privileged to witness a service of worship organised by one of the best-known of Ghana's Independent Churches, the Mozamo Disco Christo Church; the drumming and dancing on that occasion was a moving experience. In my judgement, however, not all Independent Churches are seriously engaged upon the exploration of the great variety of African music.

on the inclinations of individual clergy, or the leader of the singing group.

As the last paragraphs indicate, there is an important dimension of informal theologising in the contribution being made through the life and work of the Independent Churches to the African Christian's awakening to the fact that worship must be an authentic encounter with God. The number and variety of Independent Churches have increased considerably in Africa in recent decades, and there has been a steady growth in the volume of serious studies on their beliefs and life-style. Sprunger has listed the following facets of life and worship in these Churches as constituting their contribution to a 'relevant theology for Africa': the doctrine of the spirit; apostolic zeal and missionary power; the sense of belonging – a new community; the universality of the Church ('when Christ has really taken possession of a man and transformed his life, the prejudices, the inferiority complexes, the superior attitude, even paternalism have had it . . .'); tolerance – evangelical simplicity and love ('a readiness to accept a new approach; as long as it is Christocentric'); worship (the liturgy is flexible; 'what matters is to be there with Christ'); faith healing ('the physical needs of all members are catered for very effectively: and not only the physical aspect of sickness, but also the cause, the supernatural side of it'); counselling, prophetic advice – private and family prayers ('the daily problems of everyone are attended to by the community or by the prophet'); sacramental life and symbolism; and generosity – the art of joyful giving.[8]

Many discerning Christians would be prepared to admit that in several of these areas, such as faith healing, worship and apostolic zeal and missionary power, there is a great deal to be learnt from the Independent Churches; furthermore, it is a fact that the historic Churches have been slow to depart from the received Western forms. However, it would be dangerous thinking to assume – and this assumption is sometimes made – that an Independent Church

---

8. See A. R. Sprunger's 'The Contribution of the African Independent Churches to a Relevant Theology', in Hans-Jürgen Becken (ed.), *Relevant Theology for Africa* (Durban, Lutheran Publishing House, 1973), pp. 163ff.

is by definition a light to the historic Churches.[9] There is no question about the Independent Churches tending to have a more realistic appreciation of the Spirit and its working in a way that accords with both biblical ideas and African thought. Sprunger is certainly right when he observes that there is an 'acute sensitivity to the calls and to the directives of the Spirit'.[10] Nevertheless, it would be incorrect to say that all that happens in the Independent Churches is meaningful. Barrett goes so far as to say that the Independent Churches constitute an African Reformation and that it is out of this that 'an African theology' emerges.[11] Quite apart from the fact that the Bible is sometimes misinterpreted in some Independent Churches,[12] there is the issue of whether the facets of African culture adopted by these Churches are always the most meaningful in terms of their core value, or indeed, whether they are not so employed as to obscure the centrality of Christ. Barrett's claim is too sweeping, and it has justifiably elicited the critical comment: 'There is no necessary connexion between the fact that a community of believers develops who protest against the beliefs and practices of another group of believers, and the occurrence of reformation.'[13]

The logic of the criticism by Thomas quoted here is unimpeachable, though some of Thomas' own remarks on the life and thought of the Independent Churches are questionable, to say the least. He contends that the Independent Churches proceed on the assumption that 'the Word of God must be modified and adjusted to fit African thought'. When Thomas comes to explicate this assessment of the Independent Churches he makes sweeping and generally unfair indictments which are not always soundly based. Thus it cannot be said, as he does, that the Independent Churches as a class hold a 'strong belief in justification by works taken to the point where it

9. See Kwesi Dickson, *Aspects of Religion and Life in Africa* (Ghana Academy of Arts and Sciences 1977), pp. 24ff.

10. Ibid., p. 165.

11. D. B. Barrett, *Schism and Renewal in Africa* (Nairobi, Oxford University Press, 1968), pp. 169ff.

12. G. C. Oosthuizen, *Post-Christianity in Africa*, C. Hurst 1968; B. Sundkler, *Bantu Prophets in South Africa*, Oxford University Press, 2nd edn 1961.

13. J. C. Thomas, 'What is African Theology?' in *Ghana Bulletin of Theology*, vol. IV, no. 4 (June 1973), p. 18.

is thought that it is possible to bribe God';[14] nor can one take them to task as a class for being pro-polygamy: Thomas himself recognises that not all Independent Churches endorse polygamy; and, in any case, one cannot with any plausibility argue for monogamy against polygamy on the basis of Paul's 'Let each man have his own wife and each woman her own husband . . . equally, the husband cannot claim his body as his own; it is his wife's'.[15] It is true that compared with the Western ethos of the historic Churches what takes place in many of the Independent Churches would appear to be very unfamiliar, even bizarre, but this should not warrant the misleading conclusion that 'the Independent Churches are tending to move away from the Word of God to traditional African culture'.[16] As Andrew Walls has observed, '[The] concern for the Word has perhaps been the main "catholizing" factor for independents, giving them a point of reference (and thus a potential source of change) and a recognisable common ground with the other Churches.'[17]

The truth of the matter is that the Independent Churches tend either to draw unwarranted criticism, or to have every aspect of their life and thought held up as being eminently worthy of emulation. These Independent Churches are seekers, as much as the historic Churches, after ways to satisfy their people's spiritual longings. One cannot simply write off these Independent Churches as a spurious development. Some of their founders and leaders may turn out to have mixed motives, but then the inadequacies of some leaders of the historic Churches may not be readily discernible behind the facade of the Westernism that characterises their Churches' ethos. In short, no study of Christianity as it is developing in Africa would be complete without serious account being taken of the life and thought of the Independent Churches.

In some Churches in Africa – both historic and Independent – impromptu prayers are often offered by worshippers during public worship, usually at the invitation of the minister or whoever is

14. Ibid., p. 18.
15. Ibid., p. 19.
16. Ibid., p. 19.
17. *Occasional Bulletin of Missionary Research*, A quarterly publication of the Overseas Ministries Study Center, vol. III, no. 2 (April 1979), p. 50.

conducting the service. Regrettably, no collections of such prayers have, to our knowledge, been made. These prayers are made with much feeling, and they give indication of the offerers' understanding of the Christian faith. They generally consist in praising God; recalling his deeds of salvation, both ancient and present; petitions; and expressions of confidence in God's ability to save. These prayers are assented to most heartily by worshippers, and would seem to be found much more satisfying and uplifting than the prayers which feature in the Churches' orders of service and prayer books. Like prayer, preaching in the Church in Africa has not been given relevant consideration in theological education. As far as we know, instruction in preaching is usually based on books whose authors have had no African experience. No study has yet been made of sermons preached by those who have not received training in Western-type seminaries such as are operated by the Churches in Africa. Surely, the theologising being done by the semi-literate and literate non-seminary-trained preachers needs to be studied; it might yield useful ideas regarding what a sermon should consist in, judging by the enthusiasm with which congregations sometimes receive sermons constructed along lines which might not meet with a seminary-trained minister's approval.

So far it has been argued that theology has been, and is being done in the Church in Africa in an informal way. The question is, How is this informal theologising to be sustained and organised? From one point of view, this is hardly the right question since in a sense informal theologising cannot be organised, if by this is meant its being arranged or directed as to its shape or course, such theologising depending on the individual (and sometimes the congregation, as a whole), and also on a variety of spatial and temporal circumstances. However, theologising at this level should yield ideas which must be made to have an impact on theological training if the Church in Africa is not to be standing still in terms of theological awareness. It is clear, for example, that the Church must turn back the ever-creeping rigidity in worship style, and encourage experimentation and more spontaneity. There is a sense in which public worship needs to be directed, inasmuch as congregations are made up of individuals as well as an assortment of identifiable groups (such as the Singing Band, Women's Fellowship, etc.) which would sometimes be expected to make a group contribution, often through song, at some point or other in the course of the service. However, extreme formality tends to concentrate attention on form, to the neglect of content; that is, it creates the impression that worship is fully defined only in terms of what we do, when in fact it is first and foremost our response to what God has done, not simply for Christians but for all, in and outside the Church.[18] The point is that in worship there are two elements in tension – *receiving* from God, and *giving* to God. The spiritual and physical needs of man require that these two elements be held in a meaningful tension; otherwise unintelligibility, on the one hand, or a sense of contrivance, on the other, prevails – either would stultify meaningful theological expression.

Indigenisation

For some time now the issue has been not so much organising the informal theologising as encouraging a more active process of thinking and action in recognition of the need for the Church in Africa to teach and preach in an authentic way. Such expressions as adaptation,[19] indigenisation, translation, Africanisation, and naturalisation (often these terms are used interchangeably) have been pressed into service to describe the nature of the theological task; of these terms 'indigenisation' is perhaps the best known. The basic assumption underlying the concept of indigenisation is that there is a distinction between the 'core of the Gospel' and Christianity, the latter subsuming the former but including cultural elements which came with the Gospel through the missionaries. In other words, around the Gospel had been woven cultural vestments which the

18. Incidentally, this provides theological justification, if justification is needed, for bringing to God in worship what binds Christians to their fellows outside the Church.

19. J. S. Pobee, *Towards an African Theology* (Nashville, Abingdon Press, 1979), pp. 67ff.

missionaries considered to be of a piece with the Gospel message.[20]
The argument, then, is that the Western cultural elements should
give way to elements of African culture, thereby placing the gospel
message in a relevant setting.

Undoubtedly this procedure has provided a basis for much useful
discussion and action. In the area of music, for example, a number
of works have been created, such as: 'Missa Luba' (Joachim Ngoi
and Fr P. Guido Haazen), the 'Uganda Martyrs African Oratorio'
(Joseph Kyagambiddwa), 'Missa Zande' (Fr Giorggetti), 'Missa
Malawi' (Victor Chunga), and 'Missa Dagarti' (P. P. Dery of
Ghana);[21] these are settings of selected translations of the Mass in
local musical idioms. It is interesting to note that the Church in
Africa is not about to discard Western instruments, such as the
organ. Traditional drums have found their way, at last, into
churches and are being used to great advantage, but if artistes like
the Nigerian Fela Sowande had their way the organ would play a
very intriguing role side by side with the traditional drums.
Sowande, formerly musical director of Kingsway Hall, West
London Mission, has led the way in creating organ music based on
indigenous melodies, and there is no question about the impact
which his creations make.[22] The Ewondo of Cameroun sing the
'Bebela Mayebe', which is a rendering of the Apostles' Creed in
African musical idiom, to the accompaniment of the *balafons*, *mvots*
and other indigenous percussion instruments.

Apart from music, traditional religio-cultural symbols are beginning to be used to great effect in the Church. African artistic creations of various kinds are becoming familiar experiences in the
churches. The list of creations, alterations, modifications, etc. is

20. See, among others, Raimo Harjula, 'Towards a Theologia Africana' in *Svenska
    Missionstidskrift*, 1970, pp. 88–102 and Kwesi Dickson, 'Towards a Theologia
    Africana', in Mark Glasswell and E. Fasholé-Luke (eds.), *New Testament Christi-
    anity for Africa and the World* (S.P.C.K. 1974), pp. 198–208.
21. A. A. Mensah, 'Leadership Roles in Worship', AACC Consultation on African
    Church Music, 1976.
22. See Ayo Bankole, 'The Use of the Organ in African Church Music: the Nigerian
    Case', paper presented at the All Africa Conference of Churches Consultation
    on African Church Music, University of Ghana, 17–23 April 1976. Bankole,
    himself a gifted organist, died tragically within a year of giving that paper.

getting longer every year, and there is every reason to believe that this development will continue to be an essential element in the Church's search for identity. However, it is wondered whether this development, by itself, effectively counters the foreignness of the Church's theology. It is necessary to take a hard look at the indigenisation process as usually conceived, *viz*, replacing the Western cultural elements which surround the Gospel with African cultural elements, the assumption being that there is a core of the Gospel which is unchanging. The question surely arises: Is there a core of the Gospel which is not culturally coloured?

It may be remarked, to begin with, that there is some difficulty regarding the delineation of the 'core'. The expression, the 'core of the Gospel', has been used here to echo one way in which several African theologians have expressed the thought of the permanent as against the incidental. If by this core is meant, as it usually is, the salvation of God in Christ, then there cannot be much dispute about the adequacy of this characterisation, on the one hand; but, on the other, it will only serve to remind us once again of the limitations of our human understanding of God's salvation, for can we presume to know what God would do in any and every situation? In other words, are we in a position to claim to know fully what this core consists in?

It is in the light of this that Kraft's characterisation is to be preferred. He writes of the 'changeless, absolute truth that remains in the mind of God'. 'That divine truth,' he goes on, 'is beyond our reach in any total sense . . . , even though God has seen fit to reveal an adequate amount of insight into it via the Spirit-led perceptions of that truth recorded by the authors of Holy Scripture'.[23] Furthermore, given the fact that the Gospel was proclaimed in Africa in the era of modern missions by Western missionaries, it is to be expected that African converts should visualise and encounter the Gospel – or whatever of its truth had been vouchsafed to the missionary – through the missionary's eyes. It would be an illusion to claim that there is a 'core' of the Gospel which has not received a colouring from the missionary's life and thought. For the mission-

23. Charles H. Kraft, *Christianity in Culture* (Maryknoll, N.Y., Orbis Books, 1979), p. 294.

ary's belief in Christ receives a distinctive colouring through the traditions of confession, Church and forms of worship in which he has been brought up.[24] Thus merely eliminating the Western cultural attachments could still leave the Church in Africa with a Christ who wears an unauthentic countenance. It *is* important to be able to identify those cultural elements from the West that came with Christianity as it has been presented, but the indigenisation or Africanisation policy that proceeds solely along these lines to the exclusion of all other possible approaches assumes, quite wrongly, that there can be a proclamation of the Gospel that does not have a cultural particularity.

In this connection there is a further possibility of misunderstanding. To indigenise in the sense explained above, that is involving the drawing of a distinction between the so-called culturally uncoloured core of the Gospel and the Western cultural incidentals, has been taken by some to suggest a process of 'translation' whereby all that would need to be done in order to give the Church's theology authenticity in the context of Africa would be to examine the various Christian doctrines, as traditionally defined and stated in the West, and re-express them in ways which would make them acceptable in the light of African cultural traditions. Thus the various doctrines of God, man, redemption, etc. would provide the basis for a more culturally acceptable statement of Christian belief.[25] But, should the rethinking of Christian belief by the Church in Africa assume the inviolability of the traditional Western categories of doctrinal statement? The possibility of such a procedure becoming a limiting factor cannot be discounted, for the rethinking of Christian belief would then be done along the lines of areas of thought defined in the Western context. It is with considerable justification that Daniel von Allmen observes:

> Any authentic theology must start ever anew from the focal point of faith, which is the confession of the Lord Jesus Christ who

24. W. Anderson, *Law and Gospel* (Guildford, Lutterworth, 1961), p. 14.
25. E.g., see Donald R. Jacob's *Christian Theology in Africa*, 1966. The preparation of this document was funded by the Theological Education Fund; it is in private circulation.

died and was raised for us; and it must be built or rebuilt in a way which is both faithful to the inner thrust of the Christian revelation and also in harmony with the mentality of the person who formulates it. There is no short cut to be found by simply adapting an existing theology to contemporary or local taste.[26]

Of course, sometimes there might be good reason for attempting to relate fresh thinking to specific doctrines as traditionally defined, thus enabling discussion to proceed within reasonable limits; it would need to be recognised, however, that an uncritical resort to this procedure could very well stifle greater originality and result in confused thinking.

African Theology

In more recent years there has been much talk of an African theology, particularly in the last two decades or so. This development is, at any rate in part, in consequence of the recognition of the inadequacies of indigenisation as popularly conceived, though one suspects that for some indigenisation and African theology are interchangeable concepts. As a matter of fact, however, the quest for an African theology assumes that there is much more to be done than is implied by indigenisation which, by its very nature does not encourage original thinking and analysis; African theology is meant to involve a sustained articulation of faith which would bear the marks of an original African experience.

Already, however, the expression African theology has been the source of some confusion. The Nigerian theologian, Kato, has reacted most strongly to talk of an African theology.[27] While acknowledging the need for African theologians today, like their 'predecessors' among the Church Fathers such as Origen, Athanasius, Tertullian and Augustine, to 'make their own contribution to

26. 'The Birth of Theology', in *International Review of Missions*, vol. 44, pp. 37–55 (esp. p. 50).
27. Byang H. Kato died tragically a few years ago in Nairobi, Kenya. See his 'Black Theology and African Theology' in *Evangelical Review of Theology*, no. 1, Oct. 1977, pp. 35ff., and *Theological Pitfalls in Africa*, Evangel Publishing House, Kisumu, Kenya, 1975.

theology for the benefit of the Church universal',[28] he is unable to commend the efforts so far made because, as he puts it, 'many theologians spend their time defending African traditional religious practices that are incompatible with Biblical teaching'.[29] It seems to Kato that 'pagan practices'[30] are being urged by those who purport to be seeking the revival of the Church in Africa.

It is in view of this that Kato takes to task the Ghanaian theologian Agbeti; the latter had written that by the expression 'African theology' 'we should mean the interpretation of the pre-Christian and pre-Moslem African people's experience of God'.[31] Kato's criticism of Agbeti is instructive because it raises the question of how much care he exercised in getting to know precisely what had been said by those whom he was criticising. He manifestly misunderstands Agbeti when he takes the latter to be 'advocating a return to African traditional religions rather than expressing Christianity more meaningfully to the African'.[32] What Agbeti is in fact doing is questioning the suitability of the expression 'African theology' as used of Christian theology in Africa: in his opinion, the expression 'African theology' is misleading in the Christian context in which it is used since it properly characterises the articulation of African traditional religious thought, and not Christian thought.[33] Similarly, Turner has observed:

28. Kato, 'Black Theology and African Theology', p. 46.
29. Ibid., p. 45.
30. E.g., initiation rites.
31. J. K. Agbeti, in *Presence*, vol. V, no. 3, 1972, p. 6; Kato, 'Black Theology and African Theology', p. 46.
32. Ibid., p. 46. See S. U. Erivwo's review of Kato's *Theological Pitfalls in Africa*, in the Nigerian journal *Polycom*, vol. I, no. 1 (April 1978), pp. 62ff.
33. In a paper given at the 1975 Ibadan meeting of the West African Association of Theological Institutions entitled 'The Search for Theological Identity in West Africa' Agbeti said, '. . . the term African Theology does not accurately describe the spirit of our search for theological identity in Africa'. His preference would be for African Christian Theology (cf. A. Shorter's title *African Christian Theology*, Geoffrey Chapman 1975). In this connection it is interesting to observe that Kato's fellow evangelical and compatriot Tokunboh Adeyemo, in an article entitled 'Contemporary Issues in Africa and the Future of Evangelicals', in *Evangelical Review of Theology*, vol. 2, no. 1 (April 1978), heads a section dealing with works on African traditional religion as African Theology. See also S. P.

It does not seem to help much to speak of 'African Theology'. The term is viewed with suspicion because the interest in traditional religion associated with it calls up in the minds of many a return to paganism. The phrase 'an African theology' has about it, therefore, the quality of a slogan of vindication. It refers first to the attempt to find points of similarity between Christian notions and those drawn from the traditional religions of Africa. Secondly, it refers to the hope that a systematic theology expressed in the language and concepts of traditional religion and culture, may one day be written . . . The phrase implies in its popular usage an attempt to amalgamate elements of Christian and elements of traditional belief.[34]

Those who are talking of African theology and meaning by it African Christian theology may find Turner's description of their theological task unsatisfactory. Admittedly, the nature of the theological task facing the Church in Africa has not always been satisfactorily stated by the protagonists of African theology, especially when the task is so described as to echo the unsatisfactory indigenisation concept reviewed earlier. The expression African theology is not intended as a 'slogan of vindication', and whatever its 'popular' use might connote, it is not meant to be simply an 'amalgamation' of Christian and tradition belief elements; the aim of those involved in the quest is to arrive at a distinctive meditation upon faith in Christ that does justice to the life-circumstances of the African.

To return to Kato, one suspects he was confused by Agbeti's phrase 'pre-Christian and pre-Moslem African people's experience

---

Lediga's use of the expression in his 'A Relevant Theology in Africa' published in Hans-Jürgen Becken (ed.), *Relevant Theology for Africa*, Durban, Lutheran Publishing House, 1973. It is quite clear that the expression in question has been used in two different senses in recent literature. To use it as a description of African traditional religious thought is evidently justified, and yet it has justifiably been used by Christian theologians to mean an articulation of African Christian thought. Evidently it is essential that the use of the expression be clarified by its user. In this book, whenever it becomes necessary to use the expression, it will be in the sense of African Christian theology.

34. Philip Turner, in *Journal of Religion in Africa*, vol. IV (no. 1, 1971), pp. 64–5.

of their God', especially as Agbeti defines African theology as 'a theology which will critically systematise the traditional African experience of God and his relation with man . . .' Kato failed to realise what Agbeti meant by African theology because the use of 'God' was understood by him to point specifically to the Christian faith.

Now African theologians have not hesitated to proceed on the basis of the conviction that there is one God of the whole earth after whom all peoples in their differing religious particularities are seeking, so that all religions enshrine an encounter between God and man. This line of thinking, though not new, is found disturbing by some. Commenting on the readiness with which African theologians present at a Consultation in Ibadan, Nigeria,[35] took this theological position as their starting point, the German theological educator Hans Häselbarth has observed:

> I was surprised how unquestioningly the road in 'Catholic thought' was taken. It saddens me to see this. Everything I learned on this matter from my teachers – E. Käsemann, H. J. Iwand, E. Wolf, M. Fischer, H. Gollwitzer, W. Kreck, not to mention Barth's resounding 'No!' and the German Church struggle, including Barmen, is of no interest in this situation and seems not to fit into it.[36]

Häselbarth is clearly unconvinced, and he goes on to observe, somewhat condescendingly: 'These African efforts are still too diffident to be tackled with sledge-hammer criticism.' As a matter of fact, in adopting what Häselbarth calls 'Catholic thought' African theologians are doing no more than building upon certain strands in biblical teaching.[37] However, they are ready to acknowledge that the God of the whole earth, the God who is Father of our Lord Jesus Christ, has been imperfectly heard by Africans in their pre-Christian

35. This was the annual general meeting of the West African Association of Theological Institutions, August 1975.
36. 'Theology in the Context of West Africa', a paper prepared for the All Africa Lutheran Consultation on Theology in the African Context, 5–14 October 1978, at Gaborone, Botswana.
37. See pp. 18–19 above.

situation (and, indeed, no other religious group could justifiably claim to have perfectly heard him!). Thus from the point of view of African theologians, there can be a meaningful theology only when account is taken of the African religio-cultural situation as *one* of the source materials for theologising.

Liberation Theology

In the light of recent developments it is necessary to relate the discussion so far not only to what Black South African theologians are calling Black theology, but also to what may be broadly called Liberation theology: this expression is here used as a blanket description of Latin American Liberation theology,[38] Black theology,[39] Asian theology,[40] and Political theology.[41] The theological expressions which we have put into the umbrella category of Liberation theology are, of course, not identical in every detail, and the common characteristics we are about to specify may not apply in the same measure to all of them.

First, Liberation theology represents a disillusionment with theology as formulated in Europe and North America; indeed, it represents a disillusionment with all theologies which went before, because the latter are considered to be inadequate when it comes to their attitude to politics which, in the opinion of the proponents of Liberation theology, is at best deficient, and at worst non-existent. The concern of Liberation theologians is that theology should be experiential – it should place the concrete human situation in the forefront of the Church's thinking. In this connection 'Third World'

38. Among its exponents are J. Miguez Bonino, *Doing Theology in a Revolutionary Situation*, Philadelphia, Fortress Press, 1975, and Gustavo Gutierrez, *A Theology of Liberation*, Maryknoll, N.Y., Orbis Books, 1973.
39. James Cone, *Black Theology and Black Power*, Seabury Press, New York, 1969: and Deotis Roberts, 'Black Consciousness in Theological Perspective', in J. J. Gardiner and J. D. Roberts (eds.), *Quest for a Black Theology*, Philadelphia, Pilgrim Press, 1971.
40. Gerald H. Anderson (ed.), *Asian Voices in Christian Theology*, Maryknoll, N.Y., Orbis Books, 1976.
41. Dorothee Soelle, *Political Theology*, trans. and introd. by John Shelley, Philadelphia, Fortress Press, 1974.

Liberation theology has acquired a distinctive character: since the 'Third World' has suffered much from exploitation and domination at the hands of colonialists, Liberation theology sees this domination as the key element in 'Third World' theologising.

Secondly, for the exponents of Liberation theology the issue at stake is the function of theology: is theology merely an articulation of Christian thought with a view to providing spiritual edification as against physical and material well-being, or is its function to create awareness of the need for persons to have dignity? For Liberation theology the latter function is the true one. In line with its experiential basis Liberation theology places a great deal of emphasis on praxis or practical action as the primary reference of political thought: it advocates a shift from orthodoxy to orthopraxis, because it proceeds on the basis of the conviction that faith divorced from practice is not worth the name of faith.

Thirdly, as to the process by which one gives theology this orientation, in keeping with their intention to relate theology to the human situation the exponents of Liberation theology adopt methods of analysis which are usually employed by non-Christians. In fact some of them adopt mainly that method of analysis of reality which is historical and materialist, as inspired by the development of the thought of Karl Marx. As one would expect, therefore, Liberation theology would reject the view that faith transcends ideologies and cultures. And, lastly, a dialectical tension characterises Liberation theology, a tension between the biblical material, especially the oppression–salvation story of the exodus and that attitude of Jesus which issued in denunciation of the powers that be, on the one hand, and on the other the data and demands of practical politics.

Recent events and discussions necessitate our raising the question of the relation between Liberation theology as briefly outlined here and the theological quest going on in Africa.

In August 1976 theologians from Africa, Asia, Latin America and the Caribbean, and a Black American representative met at Dar-es-Salaam, Tanzania, and formed the Ecumenical Association of Third World Theologians with the aim of developing 'Third World Christian theologies which will serve the Church's mission in the world and witness to the new humanity in Christ expressed in the struggle for a just society'. The conference programme was as follows: (1) Socio-political and cultural analysis of the background of each continent; (2) An evaluation of the presence of the Church on the three continents; (3) Efforts toward a theological approach in the Third World.[42] At this meeting there was a detectable difference of approach between African theologians and theologians from Latin America, in particular; the final agreed statement does not adequately reflect this difference.[43] While Latin American theologians felt that African theologians seemed to be obsessed with matters of culture – and, indeed, it will have become evident in the foregoing that matters of culture are considered vital for the theologising process by many African theologians – in turn African theologians thought Latin American theologians were overly concerned with doing a doctrinaire analysis of society and making theology sound almost exclusively like political action. Both sides have a point. Our concern is not so much to comment on the Latin American approach as to explicate what Africans are doing in theology, and what the strengths and weaknesses of their approach might be.

To do this it is necessary to look at the two main theological strands emanating from Africa. To begin with, the theology emanating from Black South Africa has been critical of that theologising which considers Africa's religio-cultural traditions as being among the indispensable working materials. Black South African theologians speak of Black theology, some of the exponents of which are Tutu,[44] Boesak[45] and Buthelezi.[46] Tutu has observed, 'African theology has failed to produce a sufficiently sharp cutting edge. . . . It has seemed to advocate disengagement from the hectic business of life because very little has been offered that is pertinent, say,

42. See S. Torres and V. Fabella (eds.), *The Emergent Gospel* (Maryknoll, N.Y., Orbis Books, 1978), p. 272.
43. Ibid., p. 271.
44. See Desmond Tutu, 'Black Theology/African Theology: Soul Mates or Antagonists', *Journal of Religious Thought*, Fall-Winter, 1975.
45. See Allan Boesak, *A Farewell to Innocence*, Maryknoll, N.Y., Orbis Books, 1977, and 'Coming in out of the Wilderness' in Torres and Fabella (eds.), op. cit., pp. 76ff.
46. Manas Buthelezi, 'Toward Indigenous Theology in South Africa', in Torres and Fabella (eds.), op. cit., pp. 7ff.

about the theology of power in the face of the epidemic of coups
and military rule, about development, about poverty and disease
and other equally urgent present-day issues. I believe this is where
the abrasive Black theology may have a few lessons for African
theology.'[47] Arguing that it is insufficient to respond 'to the gospel
in terms of traditional culture' without taking into account 'the
gospel within the context of a given situation', Boesak expresses
the conviction that Black theology 'must not yield to uncritical
accommodation, becoming a "cultural theology" or a "religion of
culture". An authentic situational theology is prophetic, critical,
not merely excavating corpses of tradition, but taking critically
those traditions from the past that can play a humanising and
revolutionising role in our contemporary society.'[48]

Perhaps Buthelezi's 'Toward Indigenous Theology in South
Africa' states most succinctly the Black South African disen-
chantment with 'African theology'. In this paper Buthelezi takes a
critical look at what he describes as the 'ethnographic' approach to
theology in Africa which, as he sees it, proceeds by first ascertaining
what the African world view is, then translating the Gospel into
African thought-forms. Buthelezi finds this approach unsatisfactory,
for 'if indigenisation is thus conceived, it becomes a mechanical
program in which objectively identifiable motifs of the African
worldview are used to indigenise an already existing church which
is un-indigenised.'[49] He considers it significant that indigenisation,
according to him, has been encouraged by the European; in so
proceeding Africans are in effect being used to solve the psycho-
logical problems of the European who by this ruse is in reality
salving his own conscience. In effect, Buthelezi gives two reasons
why this approach is unsatisfactory: (1) it means doing a superficial
exercise of matching the already culturally-coloured Christian
teaching, and African thought, and this implies giving some kind
of legitimation to Western theology; (2) the emphasis that this
procedure places on African life and thought is not realistic since
it involves conjuring up the past which is not crucial to the African

47. Ibid., pp. 32–3.
48. Boesak, 'Coming in out of the Wilderness', pp. 82–3.
49. Buthelezi, 'Toward Indigenous Theology', p. 61.

in his present socio-economic and political circumstances. In view of these shortcomings Buthelezi prefers what he terms the 'anthropological' approach. Subscribing to the same Confessions as the European Christians is not a guarantee that the Europeans will accept Africans on the basis of the latter's integrity as human beings. What the African must do, in the circumstances, is to emphasise blackness which embraces the totality of the Black South African's existence: this blackness is the experiential starting point from which the African must seek to understand redemption in Christ.

Some of Buthelezi's critical comments are well conceived. Thus he has good reason to be critical of that kind of indigenisation which merely matches the received Christian teaching and African life and thought; he points out, with complete justification, that this would in effect be assuming the normative character of Western theology. The procedure being criticised by Buthelezi makes the erroneous assumption that Western theology is the given, and hence the basis for whatever cultural embellishments might be fancied. It is when Buthelezi comes to consider the place of African culture in theologising that his comments become, in my judgement, much less helpful, for though he argues for Christian thought taking account of the totality of the Black South African experience, he nevertheless rejects the bringing of culture into the discussion on the grounds that it would involve dredging up the past when, presumably, it might just be best to let sleeping dogs lie. On this basis, then, there is no meeting ground between South African Black theology and what has been called African (Christian) theology, the former rejecting the latter's basic premise that African culture has a part to play in theologising.[50]

50. Similarly some Black American theologians have expressed dissatisfaction with what they consider to be a cultural over-emphasis. In his 'A Black American Perspective on the Future of African Theology' in K. Appiah-Kubi and S. Torres (eds.), *African Theology En Route*, Maryknoll, N.Y., Orbis, 1979, James Cone takes a critical look at a statement made by the Kenyan theologian John Mbiti who had written as follows: 'The concerns of Black Theology differ considerably from those of African Theology. African Theology grows out of the joy in the experience of the Christian faith, whereas Black Theology emerges from the pains of oppression. African Theology is not so restricted in its concerns, nor does it have an ideology to propagate. Black Theology hardly knows the situation

However, it is essential that one should explore the reason behind Buthelezi's rejection of the African religio-cultural tradition as a valid element in the theologising process. Could he be saying that African culture has ceased to be an identifiable phenomenon? Or is he suggesting that it has nothing to contribute to the quest for a revelant Christian theology in Africa; that it has as much relevance as something which is dead and gone? It is difficult to believe that Buthelezi is saying that to speak of the African religio-cultural tradition is to speak of something which is no more a fact, for indeed works on the Black populations of southern Africa show clearly that indigenous traditions have not disappeared, and that as in the urban areas of West Africa, so in southern Africa the traditional values, the modern factors for change notwithstanding, play a role in life in the African communities.[51] It is more likely that Buthelezi is contending that this religio-cultural tradition has nothing to contribute to the quest for a relevant theology.

The Role of African Culture

There are indications that this view of the relevance of African culture is not universally held among Black South African theologians, even though references to the role it might play in Black theology have been somewhat less than sufficiently explicit. Boesak, for example, is prepared to acknowledge the usefulness of 'taking

---

of the Christian living in Africa, and therefore its direct relevance for Africa is either non-existent or only accidental' (*Worldview*, August 1974, p. 43). While acknowledging the value in African theology's concern with selfhood, Cone insists that there is a 'political ingredient in the gospel that cannot be ignored if one is to remain faithful to the biblical revelation'. After commending Desmond Tutu and Manas Buthelezi as 'prominent examples of this new theological perspective', Cone states further: 'If Theology is to be truly indigenised, its indigenisation must include in it a social analysis that takes seriously the human struggles against race, sex and class oppression.'

51. Some of the recent works of interest on southern Africa are : Monica Wilson, *Religion and the Transformation of Society*, Cambridge University Press 1971; M. L. Daneel, *Old and New in Southern Shona Independent Churches*, New York, Mouton Publishers, 1971; and Gabriel Setiloane, *Image of God Among the Sotho-Tswana*, Rotterdam, A. A. Balkema, 1976.

critically those traditions from the past that can play a humanizing and revolutionizing role in our contemporary society. It is taking from the past that which is positively good, thereby offering a critique of the present and opening perspectives for the future.'[52] However, this aspect of the matter is left undeveloped by Boesak. He does draw a distinction between 'corpses of tradition' and 'traditions from the past', disapproving of the former while approving of the latter by which he means, it must be presumed, those aspects of African life and thought which, coming from the past, remain part of a living tradition. The exact role of this living tradition, however, is not spelt out beyond the general acknowledgement of its usefulness.

This uncertainty regarding the role of African culture in the theologising process is further illustrated in an article by Goba, a Black South African theologian. In his 'The Task of Black Theological Education in South Africa'[53] Goba uses the term 'worldview' several times with evident reference to African life and thought. One of the fundamental points made in this article is that 'to discover from a black theological perspective the purpose of the ministry' it is necessary that serious attention should be given to 'the black/African worldview as well as the existential fact of oppression and therefore our quest for authentic liberation'.[54] We have described this point as fundamental because the author makes it several times; he evidently considers it a crucial element in his argument. Thus when he comes to question the relevance of the kind of theological training which he received in South Africa he makes the point that in the various theological disciplines which he studied

> . . . no clear attempt was made to relate these to the situation. A situation in which (1) the African worldview is pervasive, and (2) in which all black people are victims of oppression. The point is not how biblical studies or theology is taught, but the issue is

52. Boesak, 'Coming in out of the wilderness', p. 83.
53. Bonganjalo Goba, 'The Task of Black Theological Education in South Africa', in *Journal of Theology for Southern Africa*, no. 21 (March 1978), pp. 19ff.
54. Ibid., p. 20.

how the prevalent African worldview is taken seriously in the teaching of these subjects as well as the situation of oppression.[55]

When Goba turns his attention to the issue of religious pluralism he expresses the conviction that to combat this 'as a Church in the process of liberation, we need to retrieve the African worldview which blacks commonly share in South Africa'.[56]

It is evident from these references that Goba speaks of liberation in two senses which he considers to be concomitant: liberation in the socio-economic and political sphere, and liberation in the sense of the African's religio-cultural identity being recognised and made an aid in the teaching of the various theological disciplines. However, one does not gain from Goba's article any ideas, in more precise terms, as to the nature of this religio-cultural liberation to which he frequently refers; these references, like Boesak's, are lacking in any meaningful elaboration. Thus even though Goba would seem to go further than Buthelezi in his having a non-negative attitude to the African worldview, the modalities of the role which this worldview should play in theological education are not spelt out.

Hence, although some African theologians from outside South Africa have been known to give liberation a prominent place in their theologising,[57] there is no question about there being somewhat contrasting attitudes to the theologising process as envisaged in different parts of Africa. In a sense this is inevitable. Africa is a continent which presents a varied religious, social, economic, political, racial and cultural picture, and it should not be surprising that different theological emphases should exist. Thus it is true that, by and large, African theologians from outside South Africa have tended to keep socio-economic and political matters out of all discus-

---

55. Ibid., p. 20.
56. Ibid., p. 21.
57. The American exponent of Black Theology, James Cone, while being critical of John Mbiti, Edward Fasholé-Luke of Sierra Leone, and myself, speaks with approval of Jesse Mugambi of Kenya, Kofi Appiah-Kubi of Ghana, and Burgess Carr of Liberia (until recently General Secretary of the All Africa Conference of Churches); see his contribution in K. Appiah-Kubi and S. Torres, eds., *African Theology En Route* (Maryknoll, N.Y., Orbis, 1979), pp. 176ff.

sion of theology. There are two possible ways of accounting for this. Since for some doing theology is nothing more than indigenising in the sense of replacing the Western cultural incidentals with African cultural elements, the socio-economic and political concerns on which Black theology focusses so much does not strike 'indigenisers' as the kind of reality to which they could address themselves. It is interesting to recall that even when colonial rule was being experienced all over Africa, the 1955 Accra Conference on the relevance of Christian teaching as it was being done in Ghana did not concern itself with questions of colonial rule and liberation,[58] and socio-economic matters, generally. It may be argued that the Conference discussions were focussed in this way because the historic Churches in Ghana were at that time all run by Western missionaries who, evidently, would not be expected to raise socio-economic and political issues.[59] Also, if the Africans who took part in the Conference as representatives of the historic Churches in Ghana spoke, like the Western participants, entirely of the Ghanaian cultural awareness in the way reflected in the published report (that is, without reference to socio-economic and political matters), it was because they were members of Churches whose ethos encouraged having a limited perspective on the African scene in relation to Christianity. Of course, the situation of the historic Churches in Ghana has changed since the mid-fifties; they are now independent and self-supporting, and are run by Ghanaians. Despite this changed status, however, the historic Churches in Ghana, as in other parts of the continent of Africa, still have a Western ethos, as it is well known.

Incidentally, at first sight it would seem that what has been said here about the approach adopted at the 1955 Accra Conference lends support to Buthelezi's contention that the cultural approach has been adopted at the instigation of the European for the purpose of salving the European's conscience. As a matter of fact, however, the African cultural approach, properly understood, has its roots in the African reactions to Christianity from the time of its introduction

---

58. The publication which issued out of the Conference was entitled *Christianity and African Culture*, Accra 1955.

59. Incidentally, the Independent Churches were not invited to that Conference.

in Africa. That the early missionaries often adopted a high-handed attitude to African culture is generally acknowledged. What is not often realised, however, is that the hostility sometimes displayed by the African to the missionaries was often a reaction to this destructive attitude to African ways of life. It would be very surprising, indeed, if the high-handed attitude to the culture of the people had produced no reaction; and the reaction, such as there was, was often based upon a thoughtful assessment of this new faith as it was being encountered. Hence to say, as Buthelezi does, that the cultural emphasis in theologising in Africa is a European introduction is to ignore the long history of reactions, from the cultural standpoint, to Christian evangelism from the inception of missions in Africa. And there is every reason to believe that the Ghanaian situation was not unique.

Another reason why the present tendency among theologians from outside South Africa to have a preponderantly cultural approach to theologising is that most of Black Africa is ruled by Black Africans; the colonial situation exists in only a few African countries, notably South Africa, the great majority of African countries having achieved independence from their erstwhile colonial rulers, so that for the latter there is no question of Whites oppressing Blacks. Racial discrimination for reasons of colour, segregation into black areas, decisions as to what is good for Africans being taken almost entirely by a minority of Whites, etc.: these are well known ploys associated with White rule in southern Africa. In this sense one might sympathise with those who see the concerns of African theology as being different from those of Black theology.

Does this mean, given the fact that the Black South African awareness of the socio-economic and political situation in the country is important, that there can be nothing in common between South African Black theology and the culturally-based African theology? To answer this question further questions need to be asked: *What is the given situation to which the Church in Africa should address itself?* Are theologians outside South Africa right in seeing the situation as more or less fully defined by reference to culture? Would they have meaningfully defined the given situation by limiting the discussion to the area of culture? And, is the South African situation fully defined by reference to the socio-economic and political situation?

Now no one would deny that there is a cultural reality in Africa which colonial rule and the more recent influences of urbanisation, technology, etc. have not been able to destroy.[60] However, partly as a result of colonial rule, and partly in consequence of commercialisation, there is a pervasive defectiveness in the awareness of what constitutes African culture. For many foreigners, particularly those who have visited Africa, and also for some Africans in some urban situations, African culture appears to be nothing more than drumming and dancing. In a sense this is inevitable in a world in which mobility has become such a pronounced characteristic, for drumming and dancing are among the cultural characteristics most easily marketable and exportable; not only are visitors to African countries exposed to spectacles of traditional drumming and dancing,[61] but also African dance has made its way through cultural exchanges to North America and Europe. In consequence, this aspect of African culture has for some become the most significant aspect, if not the totality, of African traditional culture. Of course, the culture being portrayed in African countries is much more than this: culture is encountered in festivals, in drama and art, and in song, etc., and we do not wish to be understood to be saying that the Institutes of African Studies in African universities, and other bodies dedicated to the study and portrayal of African culture have such a myopic understanding of what culture consists in. Nevertheless, it is a fact that such university institutes and other cultural bodies are usually encountered by the public and visitors to Africa as the stagers of dancing spectacles.

There are in fact important cultural values which have far-reaching consequences for communal living, as we showed earlier. In African traditional society there is a great concern for the establishment of a good and just society,[62] which concern is demonstrated in various societal arrangements that ensure a secure place

60. See above, pp. 47f.
61. Many hotels in African cities have resident dance troupes.
62. T. Cullen Young, *African Ways and Wisdom* (United Society for Christian Literature 1937), *passim*.

for the individual within the context of the group. The point has been made that in describing African communalism the impression is often given of a mass of humanity within which the individual has no awareness of himself, and indeed does not have his individuality respected. In this connection I have observed: '. . . the individual is part of the community without which his self is not fully definable; on the other hand, one aspect of his relationship with the larger whole is the ensuring of his political rights as an individual, while another relates to his right to property'.[63] Any suggestion that in African traditional society the individual's existence was rendered of no account would amount to a misrepresentation of the reality of the cultural situation. Furthermore, to recall a point made earlier on,[64] African traditional society does not encourage excesses: extremes of poverty and wealth would not be accepted as the norm; and the traditional ruler who turned dictatorial would not be permitted to remain such for long. The view sometimes expressed that the African chief has unlimited powers, a view sadly encouraged in Ghana by its first President Kwame Nkrumah in his assumption of traditional chieftaincy titles *and* dictatorial powers, may have had its origin in the British policy, carried out in the former British colonies, by which the Chief was often the avenue by which British rule was exercised.[65] In traditional society the concern is for the kind of government that protects the individual as well as the community. Hence a situation of oppression and deprivation would be considered by the citizens as abnormal; it must therefore be ended, one way or the other. The point which we wish to underline is that African culture enshrines a whole range of values which regulate life in society.

This inevitably implies that if the cultural approach is to be a genuine effort at bringing about meaningful Christian teaching, then there should be an inclusive approach to the appropriation of traditional cultural reality. In this respect, then, the cultural

63. K. Dickson, *Aspects of Religion and Life in Africa*, (Ghana Academy of Arts and Sciences 1977), p. 35.
64. See above, p. 71.
65. S. G. Williamson, *Akan Religion and the Christian Faith* (Ghana Universities Press 1965), pp. 118ff.

approach would involve taking up issues in the socio-economic and political area, precisely those issues with which Black South African theologians are concerned. And there is no country in which poor and disadvantaged people are not to be found, whether the country be independent, or whether it be under an oppressive minority (such as in southern Africa), or whether it has the highest standard of living. African countries might be independent, but rule by Black leaders in these independent countries has not always taken into account the best interest of the ruled. To theologise without taking account of such iniquitous situations is not only to have a less than authentic cultural approach, but also to ignore the spirit of the Scriptures which demonstrate again and again God's concern for the poor and the oppressed. African theologians outside South Africa cannot legitimately ignore situations that affect the humanity of people adversely. In this sense, then, all theology in Africa (as indeed in every part of the world) has a common ground; as Nyamiti has observed: 'this [Black South African theological] movement essentially belongs to all African theology, and deserves respect, interest, and support not only on the part of African theologians, but of all those who are interested in human liberty and other rights'.[66]

While socio-economic and political issues must be given the attention they deserve, it is a fact, however, that *misrule and mismanagement do not constitute the totality of the situation prevailing in Africa*. It has been said, with complete justification, that 'true development recognises that civil, political, economic, social and cultural human rights are inseparable'.[67] In adopting the cultural emphasis we wish to be understood to be giving recognition to the need for Christian theology to address itself to the *totality* of the African existence. Theology *judges*, but that can only be part of its task, for it also *affirms*, and what it affirms ranges from the African humanity to the Christ; and there is much in the religio-cultural reality which could

---

66. C. Nyamiti, 'Approaches to African Theology', in S. Torres and V. Fabella, op. cit., p. 43.

67. Hans Thoolen, in *Development* (published by the United Nations University and the Division of Economic and Social Information/DPI), vol. IX, no. 6 (July–August 1981), p. 14.

facilitate the actualisation of the twin roles of judgement and affirmation. Black South African awareness of the socio-economic and
political factors is important. However, can it be said that these
factors, glaring and challenging though they be, *fully* define the
South African situation, as some would seem to argue? This is the
point at which to go back to the question asked earlier about what
the African situation consists in; after all it should first be determined what the situational reality is if theology is to be meaningful.
That this may not have always been satisfactorily done is the
assumption underlying the raising of the issue.

Some would say that it is more accurate to speak of situations
given the lack of uniformity which characterises Africa in the
political, economic, social, racial, religious and cultural spheres. In
response, one may say that though there is indeed a certain lack of
uniformity in the picture which Africa presents, there is a sense in
which Africa's *basic* contradiction is cultural. The contradictions in
African societies are not exhausted by reference to the presence of
oppression, such as is to be encountered in South Africa, and also
in some Black African countries which have African leadership. To
remove socio-economic and political contradictions is not to have
eliminated all the problems facing Africa, for socio-economic and
political freedom may not necessarily ensure the perpetuation of
that basic freedom which can only be guaranteed by a reaffirmation
of Africanness. Social issues are extremely important; no one would
deny that it is of the utmost importance that human freedom in the
socio-political sense should be established, but it is being contended
here that such freedom should be seen to belong to a wider freedom,
which is cultural.

As argued earlier, there has been a cultural dislocation, the result
of contact with the European world, and this dislocation has not
perhaps been recognised for what it is – certainly not by the Church
in Africa which continues to function in blissful ignorance, by and
large, of the serious cultural handicap under which it labours. While
the feeling that African culture cannot be relevant in the present
situation may arise from a misunderstanding about, or even ignorance of, what the cultural reality is, there is also the possibility
that the thought of giving recognition to this reality is a source of

uneasiness arising from the feeling – unarticulated, and perhaps unrecognised – that in the order of things African culture is inferior to Western culture, aspects of which are to be encountered in the urban areas in Africa, in the educational institutions, in governmental systems and in the Church. In this connection it has been observed:

> [Anthropologists] have concluded that cultures are to be regarded not as assignable to some level of overall superiority or inferiority with respect to other cultures but, rather, as more or less equal to each other in their overall ability to meet the needs felt by their members. In this sense it is felt that any given culture shapes a way of life that must be seen as valid for those immersed in it. Cultures are therefore both as good as each other in shaping that way of life. None is anywhere near perfect, since all are shaped and operated by sinful human beings. But none in its healthy state is to be considered invalid, inadequate, or unusable by God and humankind.[68]

African culture is admittedly not in a very healthy state given the influences, often deleterious, which have acted, and continue to act, upon it. Changes have occurred, some good, others not so good; there is definitely some cultural confusion, the result of many decades of a cultural double-mindedness. However, African ways are increasingly resorted to; the increasing tempo of discussions on 'African theology' is a witness to this. And this is where one would argue, against Buthelezi and Boesak, for having a more positive attitude to the African religio-cultural tradition. Surely the traditional religio-cultural ideas and values have a part to play in establishing the humanity of the African population in South Africa; they could provide a booster to the determination of the African population to seek an end to the iniquitous system under which they live.

This is not to reduce the African situation to a uniformity. The situation prevailing in South Africa is not the same as the situation in independent African countries. The circumstances differ from

68. Kraft, op. cit., p. 49.

one country to another. Thus, while oppression *is* a painful reality in many an African country outside South Africa, it is not of the same kind as the oppression being experienced by the Africans in South Africa where the feeling of racial superiority underlies the policies of the ruling Whites. On this basis, then, it might be argued that Black South African theology cannot but assume its present character. Our argument, however, is that such a theology should properly be part of a larger theology. Theology will make a greater impact where it addresses itself to the situation in such a way as to underline the *fullness* of a people's humanity. The emphasis on culture adopted in this study arises from the conviction that the realisation of the African's full humanity would come from not only the winning of the socio-economic and political freedom, but also – and more importantly – the winning of the cultural battle, for it is the latter which defines, more fundamentally, the humanity of a people. What this amounts to is that a more *inclusive* theological approach would be preferable as being more likely to ensure a more permanent change – what we have called the wider freedom.

But there is an additional reason why this inclusive approach is to be preferred. The effectiveness of the struggle for a just society is often blunted by the fact that the Church in whose name, or from within which, African theologians speak is often a symbol of all that may be considered wrong with society. We have already referred to the middle-class image of the Church in Africa which makes it identify itself more readily with the ruler than with the ruled; there is a false sense of respectability which arises from the European origin of the historic Churches, and after which the Independent Churches sooner or later hanker, with predictable results. The Church can only claim the right to speak in the name of society when it is fully identified with it. A religio-cultural awareness should help shake the Church out of its middle-class fastness and reinforce Christian conviction regarding the just society. A rekindling of the awareness of the meaning of life as enshrined in African religio-cultural values should underpin the quest for selfhood.

Selfhood means *conscious existence*, an expression which aptly characterises the goal of Christian preaching. Christ calls us to *live*, which implies having a personality, and all that it involves. The

Church in Africa needs to live, as also do the people in whose name it speaks. Should the phrase 'a new life' or 'a new creature' be preferred as a description of what Christ seeks to make of us, we would say that if by this were understood the abrogation of selfhood, then this would be a contradiction in terms, for new life can only be such if it comes to a distinct personality, to make the recipient realise his full potential as one whom God in his wisdom and goodness has created. Looked at in this way, the cultural emphasis becomes unavoidable.

6

Cultural Continuity with the Bible

In the light of the cultural approach being argued for in this study the theological task facing the Church in Africa assumes even greater complexity. For one thing, this approach calls for a broader understanding of culture, an appreciation of its scope as it shapes life's pursuits and defines societal interrelationships; for another, if the Scriptures constitute a factor in theological formation, then the question arises of how the centrality of the Scriptures, the source to which Christians go in matters of faith, is to be viewed in relation to African life and thought. The latter is a rather large subject, with many ramifications with which we cannot hope to deal in detail here. It will be sufficient to highlight certain aspects of it.

But, first, a reminder that the methods of biblical study and interpretation inherited from the West were developed in a specific cultural context. With the Enlightenment certain developments in the study of the Bible became apparent; three of these are relevant to our purpose. First, it was considered essential that the Bible should be recognised as a distinctive Jewish phenomenon arising out of a faith-encounter which ancient Israel had with God. It is a particular story, that of a people that believed itself to have been called by God to play a particular role in the world, that of bringing true religion to the nations.[1] Then, secondly, with the application of reason and critical detachment questions began to be raised, for example, about those who composed the biblical books: had they so expressed the divine revelation as to illumine or obscure it? Thirdly, critical detachment did not mean that the exegete should

1. See the so-called Servant Songs in Isaiah.

approach the text of the Bible without any presuppositions whatsoever; one must come to the Bible armed with questions arising out of one's time and circumstances. Thus in the West the critical study of the Old Testament was to a large extent influenced by the prevailing modes of thought and philosophical interests associated with the Enlightenment. The Graf–Wellhausen documentary hypothesis, with its developmental basis, fitted into the belief in progress which was characteristic of such eighteenth-century Western writers as the Scottish philosopher David Hume and the French philosopher Jean-Jacques Rousseau.

The developments just surveyed in such brief terms are of interest, for they reveal two unavoidable guidelines for the study of the Bible: it is important to know the biblical story *as it is*; and, the exegete should come to the Bible armed with questions relevant to his circumstances. Further comments on these guidelines are necessary, especially as some of their implications may not be readily recognised.

To see the Bible as a distinctive Jewish phenomenon is to come up against the fact, among others, that the experience reflected in it gives a certain definition of what is 'orthodox' religious thinking. It is by this understanding of 'orthodoxy' that Scripture judges people, ideas and events which feature in the story. This 'orthodoxy' needs to be respected, of course, but its limitations and possible repercussions with respect to the interpretation of the text also need to be recognised. Biblical exegesis in our time has often assumed, consciously or unconsciously, the inviolability of this 'orthodoxy', sometimes with unsatisfactory consequences. Just one example will suffice to illustrate this. The story of the healing of Naaman, the Syrian warrior,[2] contains the request by Naaman for a quantity of Israelite soil on which he might perform his acts of acknowledgement of the sovereignty of Israel's God back in his own country. Now the Old Testament contains passages which illustrate the concept of the localisation of deity as held in the ancient world;[3]

2. 2 Kings 5.
3. E.g. 1 Kings 20:23; in the belief that deities were localised the Syrians were not anxious to take on the Israelites on the hills where the Syrians presumed Yahweh to dwell, the northern Kingdom's capital, Samaria, being situated on a hill!

according to the construction usually put on Naaman's request, then, he considered Yahweh to be localised (this conception, incidentally, is denied in several biblical passages[4]). When one has decided that Naaman's request is merely an illustration of that defective concept of localised deities, it becomes almost inevitable to conclude, as modern commentators usually do, that Naaman's declaration of monotheism in 2 Kings 5:15 is at best suspect; as one commentator has expressed it, Naaman's 'striking confession of monotheism . . . is the more striking as coming from an Aramaean, yet is naively inconsistent with this request for two mules' burden of earth so that he might worship Yahweh in Damascus. His reason consented to monotheism but convention bound him practically to monolatry.'[5]

It is possible, however, to look at the incident differently, and with greater realism, from the point of view of Naaman himself. When one concedes that the declaration of monotheism must have been made in all seriousness – and there is no reason why this concession should not be made – the mules' burden of soil could then be seen as being meant by Naaman simply as a *symbol* of the presence of God, much as an Akan (Ghana) might have as a symbol of God's presence the *Nyamedua* (God's tree), that three-forked branch which carries a pot.[6] In other words, *Naaman's expressed way of recognising the greatness of Yahweh was as valid for him as Israel's traditions were for her.* And this is where one might recall the incident of Jesus' meeting with the Samaritan woman at Jacob's well,[7] in the course of which Jesus said, in effect, that no one could presume to have arrived at a definitive understanding of what worshipping God should consist in.[8] This is only one aspect of what may be called 'relevant reading' of the Bible.

To seek the historical past is not to have exhausted the methods by which the Bible might be approached. There are in each generation, and in each set of circumstances, questions which pose a

4. E.g. Jer. 29:4f.
5. John Gray, *I and II Kings* (S.C.M. 1979), p. 507.
6. See p. 53 above.
7. John 4:1ff.
8. John 4.21.

challenge to the exegete. A message has been given in the Bible, and this must be encountered *authentically* (by living beings in their own particular circumstances) for its true import to be realised. The question to be asked is: What enlightenment may be derived from the Bible *here and now*, its distinctive cultural origin notwithstanding?

Up till now the study and interpretation of the Bible as done in theological colleges in Africa have simply been a regurgitation of Western methods and insights; it is often taken for granted that the task of theological education in Africa is merely to pass on Western theological scholarship to succeeding generations of African students. There is undoubtedly a great deal to be learnt from the researches done by Western theologians; it would be foolish to fail to recognise the importance of the contributions that Western theologians have made. However, should theological education in Africa simply assume the inviolability of Western patterns and insights? Should not the Church in Africa evolve ways of studying the Bible that would underscore its character as an expression, through particular historical circumstances, of God's dealings with *mankind*? Are not the peoples of Africa to be reckoned among those whose fathers have been the avenue of God's self-disclosure?[9]

It is for good reason that it has been urged:

What is needed now is for Africans . . . to start afresh, beginning with the direct interaction of their cultures with the Scriptures rather than tagging along at the tail end of the long history of western embroidery, and to restate the Christian faith in answer to . . . African questions, with . . . African methodologies and terminologies.[10]

And,

Any effort to arrive at a view of the relevance of Scripture to a specific society and culture involves a two-directional task of hermeneutical translation: the human mediator of the message must understand the Scripture itself and translate it into appro-

9. Heb. 1:1–2.
10. Charles R. Taber, *Gospel in Context*, vol. 1, no. 1 (January 1978), p. 10.

priate terms in the receptor culture, and also understand the culture (a hermeneutical task) and translate it back into categories which he can compare with Scripture.[11]

This, then, is the task to be tackled with a view to aiding the quest for Christian theology in Africa, in general, and the development of distinctive methods of biblical study and interpretation, in particular.

In the first chapter the point was made that the Scriptures contain an important strand which teaches that there is a theological continuity between Israel and other peoples. This theological position is of particular interest in the context of this study in view of the observation, made by a number of writers, that there is what amounts to a cultural continuity between Israel and Africa. In the present chapter, then, we propose to explore the African predilection for the Old Testament,[12] and to note what theological developments might issue out of this predilection.

Phillips has devoted some attention to this predilection for the Old Testament. He relates how this was remarked upon by missionaries working in Africa, and quotes the following passage from a letter by a European missionary:

> I am often struck with astonishment, when I hear F. reading to those people the Old Testament stories, at the resemblance between the manners of the Israelites and other primitive nations and the Basutos. Could you have watched their faces the other day as they listened to the story of Abraham, Eleazar, and Rebekah; every word seemed so telling; she, though so rich, at

11. Ibid., pp. 7–8.
12. At various times in the history of the Church feelings of dissatisfaction with the Old Testament have been expressed. In the second century Marcion argued for getting rid of the Hebrew Scriptures, and though his views were attacked by many of the Church Fathers (e.g. Irenaeus, Tertullian and Origen), they have been revived in a number of forms again and again. Thus neo-Marcionist views have been expressed by Schleiermacher and Harnack, to name just these; also neo-Marcionist was the view expressed by some in India that the Old Testament should give way to the ancient religious and philosophical Hindu traditions, so that the New Testament becomes the fulfilment of India's religious aspirations. Generally speaking, African attitudes have not been in the Marcionist tradition.

the well drawing water; indeed every detail comes home here with a force which dwellers in cities can never know.[13]

Indeed, he reports that some African Christian leaders were against making the Old Testament the starting point for the instruction of converts since the latter, finding the Old Testament atmosphere very congenial, might not want to go any further: 'The whole emphasis of their reply to many questions was on the need for caution in the use of the Old Testament, lest the Church should be more Jewish than Christian.'[14] Some of these same African leaders, Phillips recounts, went on an evangelistic journey in the course of which a new church building was dedicated; at this dedication ceremony each of the four African preachers took his text from the Old Testament.[15]

More recently the African predilection for the Old Testament has been documented by a number of writers. Sundkler finds that in many of the Independent Churches in South Africa the Bible plays a key role in preaching and teaching; the Old Testament in particular, especially in the Zionist Churches (these originated in America), enjoys considerable authority. 'A common argument in all *materia theologica* is: The truth is to be found in "uDutelonom" or "uLevi" (Deuteronomy or Leviticus).'[16] Then Sundkler adds, significantly, 'in some quarters, the differences between the Old and New Testament standards are felt as a problem, and where this is so the Old Testament standard is generally accepted.'[17] Also, the Old Testament is often so interpreted as to make it conform to Bantu practices. This, notes Sundkler, explains the interest shown in John the Baptist since he is not only Elijah but also stands for much that is held to be valuable in traditional African life: purification rites and ancestral cults.

Writing from that same part of Africa Oosthuizen endorses Sund-

---

13. G. E. Phillips, *The Old Testament in the World Church* (Guildford, Lutterworth, 1942), p. 6.
14. Ibid., p. 9.
15. Ibid., pp. 9–10.
16. Bengt Sundkler, *Bantu Prophets in South Africa* (Oxford University Press 1961), p. 277.
17. Ibid.

kler's findings, stating: 'The young Churches in Africa do not discard the Old Testament or give it a secondary place – not this but its misinterpretation is the problem of Africa.'[18] He states, further, that since the Old Testament did not enjoy a prominent place in Western theology, a serious study of it in Africa was considered unnecessary. Oosthuizen's interest in this subject leads him to survey the life-style of some Independent Churches outside South Africa; though references to these are scanty and do not add up to a realistic picture of those Churches, they do underline a close interest in the Old Testament, generally.

After studying the texts used for sermons in the very popular Aladura Church of Nigeria, Turner comes to the conclusion: 'If there is any truth in the common statement that the Independent Churches rely much more heavily on the Old Testament, here is one measure of how far this is true'; that is, in the Aladura Church there are many more sermons based on the New Testament than on the Old Testament:[19] '. . . no single Old Testament book, not even among the shorter ones, can compete with any one of sixteen from the New Testament'.[20] Fully aware that in so concluding he might be said to be contradicting the views of Sundkler and others, Turner remarks that he is not contradicting the view that 'the Independents have an Old Testament interpretation of the whole Bible'. The point is that often Church ethos and Scriptural interpretation suggest an inclination to rely on the Jewish springs of Christianity, even though the citation of biblical texts may suggest otherwise. This may be illustrated by reference to one of Ghana's Independent Churches, the Apostolic Revelation Society, founded in 1945/46 by Charles Kobla Nutonuti (now Prophet Wovenu). A few years ago a student of ours at the University of Ghana spent some time studying this Church with the aim of discovering whether or not it demonstrates a predilection for the Old Testament. He concluded, on the basis of the biblical texts cited by the Prophet, that there was no indication of a preference for the Old Testament. This is essentially the finding made by Turner with respect to the

18. G. C. Oosthuizen, *Post-Christianity in Africa* (C. Hurst 1968), p. 163.
19. H. W. Turner, *Profile Through Preaching* (Edinburgh House Press 1965), p. 21.
20. Ibid.

Aladura Church. However, a detailed look at the life of the Apostolic Revelation Society does give indication of a tendency to model the Church's ethos along lines indicated in certain Old Testament institutions and practices. Thus this Church celebrates three festivals each year;[21] the most conspicuous of these is the week-long Missionary Anniversary, the activities during which include 'sacrifices, vowing, ordination and "meeting God in the wilderness" '.[22] Even though sacrifice and vowing are encountered in the New Testament, the main activities of the Festival have a distinctly Old Testament flavour. Thus on the first day of the Anniversary the 'Passover' feast is commemorated. While each worshipper places his hands upon the head of a sacrificial victim (usually a sheep), the Prophet leads the congregation in prayer, and then asks his ministers to slaughter the animals. The worshippers then take the slaughtered animals home, but not before the Prophet has instructed that the flesh should be consumed before midnight of the same day.[23] Indications of an Old Testament atmosphere are also found outside this annual celebration. Baeta refers to food taboos observed by members of this Church which are 'those stated in the Old Testament';[24] he also observes of Prophet Wovenu's own account of his call: 'The phraseology of these utterances is assimilated as much as possible to that of Old Testament prophecies.'[25]

Several reasons have been given for this partiality for the Old Testament. One of these is the Old Testament's political appeal.[26] That the Old Testament has this appeal, especially for the underprivileged and the disadvantaged, has for long been recognised and given dramatic statement, especially by Black American preachers. The story of the exodus, with its oppression–salvation motif, has in America inspired sermon and song for some three centuries. It

21. Exod. 23:17.
22. S. S. Nyomi, *The Old Testament in an Independent Church* (a research project, 1978), p. 10.
23. Cf. Exodus 12:8, 10. Nyomi was told by a member of this Church that the historic Churches were wrong in neglecting the Old Testament sacrificial system.
24. C. G. Baeta, *Prophetism in Ghana* (S.C.M. 1962), p. 82.
25. Ibid., p. 93, note 2.
26. Oosthuizen, op. cit., p. 164; Sundkler, op. cit., p. 277.

should occasion no surprise that Africans in South Africa were not long in discovering this appeal. In a country where racial laws relegate them to the backyard of society, the story of a slave people who triumphed against great odds is bound to have a special appeal.

Thus it is that for the Independent Churches in South Africa the central figure is 'Moses, leader, liberator, lawgiver; Moses overcoming the dangerous waters of the Red Sea'.[27] Oosthuizen has a significant statement of this: 'Moses is seen as greater than Abraham, the father of the believers . . .'[28] Not surprisingly, a good number of leaders of Independent Churches in South Africa have been regarded as Moses.[29] Two hymns by Isaiah Shembe, one of the African church leaders, well illustrate the centrality of Moses in the thinking of his Church; these hymns do not in fact mention Moses by name, but there is no mistaking the implied reference:

> Today you are the laughing-stock of all the Nations.
> So wake up Africa
> Seek thy Saviour.
> Today our men and women
> Are slaves.[30]

and,

> We ourselves are saved,
> We all Nazaretha (i.e. Nazirites)
> We shall drink at that rock
> Of Sinai's mountain.[31]

As a matter of fact, the oppression–salvation theme is to be found not only in the life and work of Moses; the whole story of ancient Israel, from slavery in Egypt to Roman times, is an illustration, again and again, of this theme. Israel served one nation after another: Egypt, Assyria, Babylonia, Persia, Greece and Rome. In

27. Sundkler, op. cit., p. 277.
28. Oosthuizen, op. cit., p. 164.
29. Sundkler, op. cit., p. 334.
30. Ibid., Hymn no. 46.
31. Ibid., Hymn no. 63.

the confrontation with these nations the Israelites were released from slavery, they came from exile, they violently resisted oppression under Greece, and while they smarted under subjection to Rome, they were nevertheless the only Roman subjects who were exempted from having the image of the Roman emperor on their coins. A casual acquaintance with the Old Testament surely shows that it is impossible for any oppressed people not to find solace in the Israelite story. Indeed, the uncritical reader might even find support for hatred and retaliation for wrongs done to the oppressed.[32]

It has sometimes been remarked that the Israelite story is likely to have this kind of appeal only for Africans in southern Africa where racist policies prevail: South Africa and Namibia. It is true that the situation in that part of the continent most clearly illustrates that hopelessness which would make the downtrodden look forward to the kind of relief that Moses brought to his people. The question is whether the Old Testament, or indeed the Bible as a whole, could have played a role in bringing an end to colonial rule in former African colonies. While some would answer this in the affirmative, others argue that the colonial rule itself exerted an important influence in the development of independency in Africa. The latter view is contested with some justification by Barrett who has stated: '. . . while colonialism has been a cause contributing to independency, the latter cannot be correctly described as a reaction to colonialism – it is primarily a reaction to mission . . .'[33] Several other writers have noted that with the production of Bible translations African converts could read the Bible for themselves, and, as Ayandele has observed in connection with Nigeria: 'Unrestricted access to the Bible, with its notions of equality, justice and non-racialism, provided the early converts with a valid weapon which they were not reluctant to employ against the missionaries who brushed these ideals aside in church administration and in their relations with the converts.'[34] In other words, the Bible became the

32. E.g. Isa. 14:1–2.
33. D. B. Barrett, *Schism and Renewal in Africa* (Nairobi, Oxford University Press 1968), p. 126.
34. E. A. Ayandele, *The Missionary Impact on Modern Nigeria, 1842–1914* (Longman 1966), p. 176.

instrument of self-awareness, that quality the possession of which led to the sounding of the call for freedom from colonial rule. The truth of the matter is that colonial rule was such as to engender awareness of the political appeal of the Bible when the latter was made available to African converts by the missionaries.

A second reason for the decided preference for the Old Testament is the legalistic approach to the Gospel adopted by the early missionaries to Africa, an approach which often led to the Gospel being received as law rather than as grace. The European missionary saw his task as being two-fold: to get his audience to take the Gospel message seriously, and also to pass on to his converts his own mode of belief and life, believing this to be worthy of emulation. Andersen's words on the subject are worth quoting:

The sending Churches . . . must provide the Christians who have been won by their preaching and gathered into Churches with a model both of doctrine and of Christian life in the Church. They cannot simply throw them on their own resources. They are pledged to carry out a task of Christian education in the widest sense of that word. Part of this consists of an introduction to the study of the Bible, and in this the missionary is guided by the principles of interpretation favoured by the Church to which he belongs. He naturally introduces his converts to the confession of faith which is current in his own Church, to his own way of saying prayers, to his practices of piety. He must give the converts certain indications as to the common life of Christians in the Church, and as to the kind of relations in which they may engage with their non-Christian neighbours. But such instruction at once carries with it the danger of legalism. If the missionary allows himself to be imitated, if he is concerned to fashion the converts after his own image and not after the image of Christ, law and not Gospel is in command.[35]

35. Wilhelm Andersen, *Law and Gospel* (Guildford, Lutterworth, 1961), pp. 15–16. The missionary who considered it essential to fashion converts after his own image would not be in a position at the same time to fashion converts after the image of Christ; his understanding of Christ would have been coloured by presuppositions which had nothing to do with Christian discipleship.

When in the 1860s a group of Methodist converts broke away from the main Church in the Gold Coast (now Ghana), it was mainly on the grounds that the missionaries had failed to apply stringently the rules they themselves had promulgated against the taking and selling of alcoholic beverages by members of the Church; they wanted to be on their own so as to apply the rules strictly! A contemporary observer notes that this group soon developed a number of prohibitions which they expected those who joined with them to observe, even though these could not be said to have anything to do with Christian discipleship.[36] For members of this group the Church's rules had taken precedence over its faith; they had become more conscious of a growing institutionalism than of a faith. With considerable frequency and regularity the early Methodist missionaries to Ghana found it necessary to discipline their converts for a variety of offences. These offences are not always described in detail, but they mostly had to do with marital matters, the taking of alcoholic beverages, drumming and dancing. Disciplinary measures involved mainly expulsion, suspension, or exclusion from participation in the Holy Communion.[37] This preoccupation with rules and regulations persists in this Church whose *Standing Orders* still contain clauses which clearly demonstrate that the Church came into being through the efforts of European missionaries.[38]

The prominence given to rules and regulations by the early missionaries, and in our time by the leaders of self-supporting historic and Independent Churches, takes the African to his pre-Christian background: traditional religion places considerable emphasis on the following of ritual and other regulations. Thus there

36. Kwesi Dickson, 'The Methodist Society: A Sect', in *Ghana Bulletin of Theology*, vol. 2, no. 6 (1964), and *Aspects of Religion and Life in Africa*, p. 17.
37. This particular sanction persisted until recently. Some fourteen years ago the Church asked one of its committees to examine the theological implications of this sanction. The committee members, with few exceptions, felt that this sanction assumed that man could direct or control the course of God's grace.
38. E.g. Standing Order 548/2 stipulates: 'There shall be no drumming at a member's wake-keeping.' See Kwesi Dickson, 'The Methodist Minister – Then and Now' in J. S. Pobee (ed.), *Religion in a Pluralistic Society* (Leiden, E. J. Brill, 1976), note 34, pp. 177–8.

are totemistic taboos which may not be broken: certain animals may not be eaten; should this prohibition be inadvertently or unavoidably disregarded, certain precautions must be taken in order to avoid dire consequences coming upon the culprit, and indeed upon the society at large.[39] Again, as Parrinder notes, 'great care . . . is taken in the disposal of all cuttings and secretions from the body. Women who swear a pact of loyalty to their husband, promise not to remove part of his sponge, mat or other personal belongings. Hunters and priests have taboos of cutting their hair, which has a virtue (as in the story of Samson and the Nazirites).'[40] The prevalence of taboos in African culture is so well known that it is hardly necessary to give further examples.

Thus African converts, coming from a background of traditional religion, with its many prohibitions and rules and regulations, are likely to see the insistence by the Church on rules and regulations as a familiar matter. The idea might develop that the 'perfect Christian is the man who keeps all the ritual and moral rules'.[41] Furthermore, it would then not come as a surprise for the African convert to see in the Old Testament a kindred atmosphere since the latter contains bodies of rules and regulations which were meant to govern the ritual and moral life of the ancient Israelites.[42] Indeed, ritual and other regulations are to be found scattered throughout much of the Old Testament, and some of these have their counterparts in African usages. Two examples will suffice to demonstrate this. First, there are such taboo situations as arise when a woman gives birth. Leviticus notes that a woman who gets a male child shall be unclean for seven days, or if the child is female the period of uncleanness lasts a fortnight.[43] Most African peoples observe taboos in connection with childbirth: the mother may be forbidden to eat salt for a certain number of days;[44] she may not leave the

---

39. G. Parrinder, *West African Religion* (Epworth 1949), pp. 187ff.

40. Ibid., p. 201.

41. Andersen, op. cit., p. 16.

42. Exod. 20:1–17; also Deut. 5:6–21; Exod. 20:22–3; Lev. 17–26.

43. Lev. 12:2f.

44. E.g., among the Gu and the Peda of Ouida; Parrinder, op. cit., p. 110.

house for several days, and should she be forced by circumstances to go out she may not respond to the greetings of the public.[45]

The reasons for these and other taboos are varied, but among the Akan of Ghana the woman who has just given birth would be regarded as unclean mainly because of the blood shed during childbirth; and the child would share the mother's seclusion because it would be regarded, until the expiration of eight days, to be properly a citizen of the spirit world, on loan to its earthly parents, so that the eight-day period of seclusion would afford the family the opportunity of discovering whether or not the child had come to stay. A second example of taboo situations relates to sexual relations with a woman during her period. This is being cited here for the simple reason that as late as the sixth century B.C. Ezekiel defines a righteous man as one who among other things, does not 'approach a woman in her time of impurity'.[46] It has been suggested that this stipulation in Ezekiel 18:6 is an addition since it is not included in the lists in verses 11 and 15 where, as in v. 6, defiling a neighbour's wife is noted as an evil act. However, not only does this reference occur again in Ezekiel 22:10, but also Leviticus mentions it twice, once in that section of Leviticus which shows unmistakable signs of its being based upon ancient material.[47] Similarly, intercourse during the period of menstruation is deprecated among the Kono of Sierra Leone who consider it to have the effect of either preventing pregnancy or making the woman leprous.[48] Many African peoples place a ban on sexual relations under these conditions because of the taboos surrounding blood, that mysterious life force that both cleanses and contaminates; it is clear from Leviticus 15:19ff. that as in African traditional thought so in the Old Testament it is this mysterious quality in the blood that explains this kind of prohibition.

A third reason why the African might be more inclined towards the Old Testament is that in Africa, as in ancient Israel, religion pervades life.

45. Ibid.; this is also the practice of the Wassaw of Ghana.
46. Ezek. 18:6.
47. Lev. 15:24; also 18:19.
48. R. T. Parsons, *Religion in an African Society* (Leiden, E. J. Brill, 1964), p. 34.

Societies differ in the degree to which they recognise sacred values. Where science and technology have acquired a high degree of visibility and there is therefore a greater inclination to apply methods of efficiency to human concerns, the secularising trend is accelerated, and religious beliefs and practices are increasingly confined to certain segments of the life of the community. In such a society – and the United States of America may be cited in illustration – no religious organisation can lay claim to the allegiance of the total population, and no official tie exists between religion and the secular government.[49] The point is that the tendency in technologically advanced societies is towards giving religion a reduced visibility even though religion, often in a great variety of forms, may claim the allegiance of many. There is the other kind of society in which there is a greater inclination to see life in its totality as informed by religion.

In the rural communities in Africa every member shares in the religious presuppositions of his community, and is expected to live in accordance with traditional customs. True, much of Africa has come under the influence of many forces, with the result that the life of Africans has been tinged to a greater or lesser degree. Even so, there is a sense in which African society has not completely shed its basic, monolithic simplicity, as observed earlier; even where Christianity, Islam and other religious institutions have been whole-heartedly embraced by sizeable sections of the population, traditional religious values and ideals still exercise considerable influence on many. In other words, the traditional religion enjoys considerable visibility.[50]

49. The American President opens his Inaugural with a prayer, but the injection of religion into such areas as primary education in the public sector has sometimes been successfully contested in American courts.

50. It has already been observed that there is no thought of a natural world in which the unseen powers do not operate. It is in this connection that Mbiti has observed, 'Wherever the African is, there is his religion.' J. S. Mbiti, *African Religions and Philosophy* (Heinemann 1969), p. 277. And, significantly, when Mbiti comes to spell out this assertion, he lists the examination room, the university and the parliament house as being among the *loci* where traditional religion is brought into play, precisely those *loci* which are associated with Western influence.

Birth, puberty and marriage, death: these are events which are held to be full of meaning because of their sacred associations; not only do these life-stages involve, as it is believed, the working of invisible and irresistible forces, but also they remind society constantly of its obligations to the spirit powers – God, the divinities, the ancestors, etc. Agricultural pursuits bring the African face to face not only with the God who gives rain and sunshine, but also with the Goddess of the earth. It is hardly necessary to go into any greater detail about how religion and life are inseparable in African life and thought.

Similarly, in ancient Israel religion was not divorced from life. The expression 'monolithic simplicity' used above of African society could be applied with justification to ancient Israelite society. Of course, there were many influences upon Israel – Canaanite baalism, Assyrian religion, Hellenism, to name just these; but though not all Israelites successfully resisted these influences, the message of the Old Testament is clear, as in the Great Shema: 'Hear, O Israel: the Lord our God is one Lord'.[51] Life was held to be what was in consonance with God's wishes. It is because of this that Egyptian wisdom is given a peculiar Israelite treatment, with the fear of the Lord being held as the beginning of wisdom; Manasseh is severely criticised by the biblical writers for adopting Assyrian religious practices;[52] and the Jews rose up against the Greek kings in order to preserve their faith which Antiochus Epiphanes had proscribed.

Right at the beginning of the formation of Israel as a people we encounter the thought of the involvement of Yahweh in human affairs:

Then the Lord said to Moses, 'Go in to Pharaoh; for I have hardened his heart and the heart of his servants, that I may show these signs of mine among them, and that you may tell in the hearing of your son and your son's son how I have made sport

51. Deut. 6:4.
52. 2 Kings 21:2f.

of the Egyptians and what signs I have done among them; that you may know that I am the Lord.'[53]

When Israel defeated the Canaanites under their chieftain Sisera, the turning of the ground into a muddy trap following a torrential downpour was seen by the Israelite leaders as the work of Yahweh.[54]

The conviction that religion pervades life is expressed in other ways in the Old Testament. There are the frequent references to sin and sickness as being inseparable – sin has both spiritual and physical consequences.[55] David's murder of Uriah was to have evil consequences for him – as well as for an innocent child;[56] in Genesis the pains of childbirth are accounted for by reference to sin;[57] the prophet Ezekiel was commissioned to speak 'words of lamentation and mourning and woe'[58] because of the sins of Israel; and, Job and his friends argued passionately that if Job had not sinned he would not be in the distressing situation in which he found himself.

Three more passages might be cited in further explication of the point being made.[59] First, the practice of tampering with someone else's established rights of property. Jewish law forbade this in no uncertain terms,[60] as also does the Book of Proverbs which gives this legislation a significant twist:

Do not remove an ancient landmark
    or enter the fields of the fatherless;
For their redeemer is strong;
    he will plead their cause against you.[61]

Here a religious sanction is added to a regulation which every

53. Exod. 10:1–2; for a poetic version see Ps. 114.
54. Judg. 5:4–5, 20.
55. William D. Reyburn, 'Sickness, Sin, and the Curse: The Old Testament and the African Church – II' in *Practical Anthropology*, vol. VII, no. 5 (Sept.–Oct. 1960), pp. 217f.
56. 2 Sam. 12:10f.
57. Gen. 3:16.
58. Ezek. 2:10.
59. See Kwesi Dickson, 'The Old Testament and African Theology' in *Ghana Bulletin of Theology*, vol. IV, no. 4 (June 1973), pp. 31ff.
60. Deut. 19:14; also 27:17.
61. Prov. 23:10–11.

society would consider as making for peace and good relations. In the second passage the skilled craftsman is spoken of as being such through God's guidance:

> And you shall speak to all who have ability, whom I have endowed with an able mind, that they make Aaron's garments to consecrate him for my priesthood.[62]

It is only the occasional Bible commentary that considers it necessary to bring out of this verse its significance for understanding the ancient Israelite – indeed, the Ancient Near Eastern – view of human skills being made possible by God. Particular crafts and trades might be learnt through family and guild traditions, but they were nevertheless seen as God's gifts to man. The third reference is to Isaiah's statement of the farmer's manual labours:

> Does he who ploughs for sowing plough continually?
>   does he continually open and harrow his ground?
> When he has levelled its surface,
>   does he not scatter dill, sow cummin,
> and put in wheat in rows
>   and barley in its proper place,
>   and spelt as the border?
> For he is instructed aright;
>   his God teaches him. . . .
> Does one crush bread grain?
>   No, he does not thresh it for ever;
> When he drives his cart wheel over it
>   with his horses, he does not crush it.
> This also comes from the Lord of hosts.[63]

The conviction being expressed here by the prophet is that it is God whose wisdom makes the farmer adopt the procedures needed for the production of food.[64]

What all this amounts to is that there is much in the Old Testa-

---

62. Exod. 28:3.
63. Isa. 28:24f.
64. See Otto Kaiser, *Isaiah 13–39* (S.C.M. 1974), *ad loc.*

ment to make the African sense in it a kindred atmosphere.[65] Indeed comparisons between the Old Testament and African life and thought have been undertaken in the past, though the efforts made have hardly kindled any interest in theological circles. The reasons for this are varied: the canons of Old Testament study would seem to rule out such a comparison; usually those who undertake this comparison provide no valid justification for it; and African theological institutions, which might be expected to show interest in this kind of comparison, are usually so closely modelled after theological institutions in the West in constitution and curricula that such an area of study would seem ruled out. There is a fourth reason; comparisons are sometimes such as to make one wonder what the essential realities in the Old Testament and African life and thought are.

The writer whose work most clearly illustrates this last-mentioned weakness is J. J. Williams whose book, *Hebrewisms of West Africa*, was published in 1930.[66] As I have reviewed this book in some detail elsewhere, it will suffice here to note briefly the main weaknesses in his analysis.[67] One of these becomes immediately evident when Williams writes: 'We have in Ashanti [Ghana] exactly that "mixed religion" which we find among the Israelites of old. They worshipped Jehovah, but they worshipped the gods as well.'[68] Such a statement evidently raises the issue of what Judaism consisted in, for it ignores the questionings that are recorded for us in the Old Testament regarding the attitude to be adopted to what Williams refers to as 'mixed religion'. What Williams has done is to cite what is an aberration, and by putting this in the place of the authentic Hebrew religion he provides no authentic basis for comparison with Asante (Ashanti) religion. Moreover, African religion may be

65. W. D. Reyburn, 'The Message of the Old Testament and the African Church – I' in *Practical Anthropology*, vol. VII, no. 4 (July–Aug. 1960), pp. 152ff.

66. J. J. Williams, *Hebrewisms of West Africa*, Allen and Unwin 1930.

67. See Kwesi Dickson, 'Hebrewisms of West Africa – The Old Testament and African Life and Thought', in *Legon Journal of Humanities*, vol. I (Ghana Publishing Corporation 1974), pp. 23ff.; also 'African Traditional Religions and the Bible' in E. Mveng and R. J. Z. Werblowsky (eds.), *Black Africa and the Bible* (the Jerusalem Congress on Black Africa and the Bible, 1972), pp. 155f.

68. Williams, op. cit., p. 72.

'mixed', but it has features which such a description suppresses, as our earlier analysis of it shows. In addition to this basic weakness, Williams makes comparisons between certain Hebrew and Asante words apparently on the basically misleading principle of similarity in sound; to equate the Asante *ntorɔ*[69] and the Hebrew *torah*,[70] the Asante *ɔbayi*[71] and the Hebrew *'obh*,[72] etc., amounts to exhibiting doubtful ingenuity, for the significance of the terms in their respective contexts is obscured thereby, to say the least. Furthermore, any student of Asante religion would look in vain for meaningful reference to the ancestors and their importance; and, the analysis of the Hebrew and the Asante languages undertaken by Williams provides no real help towards using the Asante language as a means of approaching the study of the Hebrew language.

With all these shortcomings it comes as no surprise that Williams' book has excited so little interest among those committed to the development of Christian theology in Africa; it has provided little or no encouragement for further exploration of the subject. It is our conviction that, when the proper safeguards have been applied, a comparison between the Old Testament and African life and thought can have very useful consequences. One could compare a considerable number of customs and societal arrangements found in the Old Testament and African life and thought, but given the limits of space it will be sufficient to look briefly at three areas where useful comparisons could be made; this will provide additional basis for evaluating what may be described as a cultural continuity.

The Theology of Nature[73]

To begin with, a few preliminary remarks on the word Nature. In both the Old Testament and the African languages best known to

69. The male principle.
70. Instruction, the law.
71. Witch.
72. *'Asa 'obh* = to practise necromancy.
73. See my 'The Old Testament and African Life and Thought', in K. Appiah-Kubi and S. Torres, *African Theology En Route* (Maryknoll, N.Y., Orbis, 1979), esp. pp. 102–3.

me there is no word corresponding to Nature. The Old Testament speaks of Creation, a word whose connotations are quite different from those usually associated with the word Nature, for the word 'creation' implies that the world has been created; in Genesis it is made clear the creation is the product of divine will, as well as being subordinate to man.[74] Similarly in the Akan (Ghana) language, for example, the equivalent of what is meant by Nature is *Nyame n'abɔdze* (God's created things). Hence it is to be understood from the outset that we are here concerned with Nature which God has created.

African religion adumbrates, as essential to its understanding, a theology of Nature. It has already been observed that the African believes himself to share kinship with Nature, and relates to it in a way that is basically alien to the Westerner. The description of the gods of Africa as 'nature gods' is accurate only if it is understood to mean that various aspects of Nature are held to be the means whereby reality is experienced: the stone, the sea, the tree and generally the various elements in the human environment are mean-ingful to the African because they point to something beyond them-selves. Man is in concert with Nature; not only is he subject to Nature's fierce wrath, but also he is sustained by Nature's bounty and shares kinship with the things that make up Nature. The African relies on the Supreme Being as well as the Earth Goddess.

The Old Testament (as well as the New) retains much that is in accord with practices such as have been outlined in this study so far as representing the African approach to religion. That the belief that man could by the use of magical arts and practices control gods and demons existed to a late age in Israel is shown by the fact that as late as the seventh century B.C. Deuteronomy finds it neces-sary to legislate against it; the compilers of this book forbid the community to resort to or to shelter 'any one who practices divin-ation, a soothsayer, or an augur, or a sorcerer, or a charmer, or a medium, or a wizard, or a necromancer'.[75] That such practitioners

---

74. John Macquarrie, 'The Idea of a Theology of Nature', in *Union Seminary Quarterly Review*, vol. XXX, nos. 2–4 (Winter–Summer 1975).
75. Deut. 18:10f.

of the magical arts should be condemned is indication that they were resorted to in the community.

More specifically, in ancient Israel certain natural objects were regarded as sacred. One might cite the Oak of Moreh which stood in a Canaanite sanctuary appropriated by Abraham as the site of an altar to God;[76] it was under this oak that Jacob buried the idols belonging to his family.[77] The well at Beersheba is said to have been named by Abraham when he made a covenant there with Abimelech;[78] Abraham called on the name of God at this place.[79] This was also the place where Isaac set up an altar to God following a theophany.[80] The conjecture might be made that this well was used as sacred water. It is interesting to observe that Beersheba means either the Well of an Oath or the Well of Seven; with respect to the latter meaning it only has to be realised that seven was regarded as a sacred number in the ancient world for the possible sacred associations of the well to become apparent. The spring at Gihon, where Solomon was consecrated, was quite possibly a sacred spring.[81] There is a possibility that the Serpent's stone at which Adonijah made sacrifices in pursuance of his desire to sit on the throne of David had some sacred significance.[82] The stone used as a threshing floor by Araunah which David was advised to acquire in order to make it the base of an altar to God probably had similar significance, as one might conclude from the pointed advice given to David to purchase it.[83] Sinai (or Horeb), and probably also Carmel, were sacred mountains; and Mount Zion was the mountain which 'God desired for his abode, yea, where the Lord will dwell for

76. Gen. 12:6.
77. Gen. 35:2–4.
78. Gen. 21:25f.
79. Gen. 21:33.
80. Gen. 26:23–5.
81. 1 Kings 1:38–40. Roland de Vaux has argued that Solomon's consecration took place at Gihon simply because the ark was there, and not because the spring had any special significance – see his *Ancient Israel* (Darton, Longman and Todd 1973), p. 102; however, it is not easy to rule out the possibility of this spring having some kind of special significance.
82. 1 Kings 1:9.
83. 2 Sam. 24:18–25.

ever'.[84] As de Vaux notes, '. . . Yahweh appropriated the mountains formerly consecrated to the old gods'.[85]

Indeed, Yahweh himself was sometimes conceived as a Nature deity. As late as the time of Elijah, the prophet fled from Carmel to Sinai, the mountain with which Yahweh was specially associated. God revealed himself to Moses in the Burning Bush, and according to tradition the 'Lord went before [the Israelites] by day in a pillar of cloud to lead them along the way, and by night in a pillar of fire to give them light, that they might travel by day and by night'.[86] Even if it is argued that this kind of language is not meant to be taken literally, it is still significant that God's leadership should have been so described. Also, Yahweh is conceived as a storm God; the poetic account of the victory of Barak and Deborah over Sisera on Mount Tabor describes how Yahweh came to his people's aid in a storm which resulted in the enemy's chariots being bogged down in the mud.[87] Thunder is Yahweh's voice.[88] It was Elijah's purpose, in his challenge to the priests of Baal at Carmel, to assert that it was Yahweh alone who could send rain; and the significance of this trial of strength is not merely that fire consumed Elijah's sacrifice, but that the prophetic act of pouring water issued in the coming down of rain to break the three-year drought.

Thus a considerable amount of detail can be assembled to support the view that Yahweh was seen, not merely as controlling Nature, but as revealed through it. When in the thirteenth century B.C. the Israelites settled in Palestine, a new issue was raised of Baal versus Yahweh; some Israelites were so influenced by the sensuous religion of the Canaanites that they called Yahweh Baal. Nevertheless, it may not be doubted that from the beginning Yahweh was something more than a Nature deity. That Yahweh was conceived as a God of the wilderness, resident in a sacred mountain, revealing his power through storm and fire, is plainly true, but something more was present. It is just as wrong to deny that to ancient Israel Nature

84. Ps. 68:16.
85. R. de Vaux, op. cit., p. 281.
86. Exod. 13:21.
87. Judg. 5:4ff.
88. Ps. 29:3–9.

had some sacred significance as it is not to recognise that the essential characteristic of Israelite religion, and that which forms the basis of the New Testament faith, is the belief in a God who reveals himself through history. To whatever extent at one time, or even throughout Israelite history in Old Testament times, the faith of Israel exhibited or was intermixed with elements of Canaanite religion, the faith which was handed on to posterity was in a God who was essentially something other than a God of Nature. This may be illustrated by reference to the Deuteronomic theology of Israel's right to the land.

Deuteronomy makes it abundantly clear that the people of ancient Israel came to possess the land of Canaan in the course of a divinely-directed history. It was not because of any special characteristics Israel might have had that made her deserve the land;[89] it was God who so directed the course of human movements as to result in Israel's possession of it. The land being God-given, therefore, the people of Israel were to act appropriately in at least four respects: first, they were to enjoy the fruit of the land,[90] and since the fruit was made possible only by God's bounty, the first fruit should be presented in the sanctuary before God;[91] second, since the fruit reflects God's goodness, it should be shared with the poor, the widows, the fatherless and the Levites;[92] third, the people of Israel were to desist from copying the pagan practices of the people among whom they lived, or they would themselves also perish; that is, God was prepared to rid himself of Israel in the interest of the preservation of righteousness;[93] fourth, the land should not be violated in any way. Thus a hanged body 'shall not remain all night upon the tree, but you shall bury him the same day, for a hanged man is accursed by God; you shall not defile your land which the Lord your God gives you for an inheritance'.[94]

89. Deut. 9:4–5.
90. Deut. 11:13–15.
91. Deut. 26:1ff.
92. Deut. 18:1ff; also 14:28–9, 15:7–8 and 16:13–15; it is in line with this attitude to the underprivileged that Deuteronomy gives a law of release which emphasises more than ever the humanity of the slave – Deut. 15:12ff; contrast Exod. 21:1ff.
93. Deut. 8:19–20.
94. Deut. 21:23.

The land, then, was the basis of the people's identity. There is no thought of the land *itself* being divine, or having divinity in it. It is simply the land that God gave them. Thus God and Nature are not confused; Nature, like man, is created by God. 'The heavens are the Lord's heavens';[95] Yahweh is above and apart from Nature.

Now to pursue further the question of whether the ancient Israelites found in Nature itself any significant revelation of God. On the one hand, Nature yields to Yahweh's control, and Yahweh calls forth upon Egypt the ten plagues, or sends famine and pestilence upon his people;[96] on the other hand, these manifestations of Yahweh are meaningful only to the person of faith. The Israelites believed that it was to the person who was aware of God in his personal life that the signs of the divine in the created order would be plain. It is along such lines that the revelation of God to Job is to be understood. Western Christians might be puzzled by the answer given Job in the last chapters of the book of that name. Job, it will be recalled, is confronted by the power and wisdom of God in Nature, and this satisfies him. George Bernard Shaw misunderstands when he says that God did not answer Job, but merely sneered at his insignificance. Shaw could not have been more wrong. For Job the awe-inspiring manifestation of the divine attributes through Nature is a solace because Job passionately believed in God. Without the prerequisite of faith, Nature does not reveal God in a manner that brings solace and spiritual healing. For unless we abstract from Nature, and set store only by its bounty and magnificence, neglecting its ugly and harsh elements, it reveals only the Creator's incomprehensibility and man's insignificance. It is only when man has sound reasons of another kind for believing in God that he finds in Nature the handiwork of God. The ancient Israelites understood this.

One might thus sum up the Old Testament view of Nature: (1) The Old Testament does not deny a revelation in Nature. God is creator. The marks of the creator are visible in his creation; (2) It is asserted in the Old Testament that God sustains the created

95. Ps. 115:16.
96. Amos 4:4–13.

order, and controls his purpose for his redeemed. This involves the possibility of miracle. The Old Testament attributes the plagues in Egypt to Yahweh's almighty hand; (3) Nature itself will, in the fulfilment of God's purposes, be perfected. This view is frequently expressed in apocalyptic passages. Many an Israelite thinker was unable to conceive the blessedness of the time to come with Yahweh reigning without a transformation of the natural order.[97]

To bring all this back to African life and thought we might first contrast briefly Canaanite and Israelite ideas on the land. The Canaanites believed that the land was infused with divinity. Baal, the real owner of the land and whose manifestations were acknowledged as local deities, was in Canaanite myth killed by Mot, the god of death; subsequently Baal was revived by his sister Anath. The death of Baal represented the time of the year when there was little vegetation, and his revival the appearance of vegetation and the maturing of grain and fruit. The land, then, was considered by the Canaanites to have divinity in it. The African understanding of the nature of the land is closer to this Canaanite view than to the Israelites' in that Africans consider the land to be a divinity.[98] However, the African view shares something with the Israelite conception: the land, in African as well as Israelite thought, is the basis of group consciousness. Not only is the land not to be defiled,[99] but also it plays a part in the African's awareness of group interrelatedness.

Spirit possession[100]

On the basis of the Old Testament, spirit possession may be described as God acting in such a way as to put a person in a position whereby he or she acts as God's instrument. A person who is put in that kind of position has no alternative but to do God's

97. E.g. Isa. 51:3; 55:12f.
98. See pp. 58–9.
99. African festivals of renewal invariably include ritual for cleansing the land.
100. Much of the material here is owed to Mr Ofosu-Adutwum's M.A. thesis entitled *Hebrew Prophetism and Spirit Possession in Africa – A Comparative Study of Inspiration in Two Religions*, University of Ghana, 1977.

bidding, which is, to speak God's word to others; this was the usual activity attendant upon the spirit of God coming upon a prophet. Sometimes, however, as Ezekiel's life illustrates, the person is incapacitated by the inrush of God's spirit.[101] Ezekiel's paralysis was not a form of punishment; it was for the purpose of dramatising the rebelliousness of Israel.[102] The prophets' consciousness of their possession emanating from God comes out in the way they usually introduced their message: 'Thus says the Lord' – they saw themselves as the representatives of God. However, they did not merely utter God's word without being involved in a most fundamental way in that message. It is true that they were compelled by the call, but not to the extent that they had no consciousness of what they said while in the state of possession, or that they were uttering messages that did not touch them in any significant way. The sense of compulsion and commitment is easily illustrated: Isaiah could not get out of the mission being entrusted to him by pleading that he was unclean,[103] and Jeremiah pleaded in vain that he was inexperienced.[104] Ezekiel was asked by God to swallow a roll on which was written the message he was to proclaim – he was, in other words, to work the message into his very being.[105] There was no question of hiding under a cloak of semi-consciousness; this was why there was a sense of dismay when the call came to the prophets. And believing as they did that they stood in the council of Yahweh,[106] there was no question of their serving the interests of the lesser spirit powers. Jeremiah was horrified because

> In the prophets of Samaria
>   I saw an unsavoury thing:
> They prophesied by Baal
>   and led my people Israel astray.[107]

101. Ezek. 3:24f.
102. Ezek. 3:26.
103. Isa. 6:1–8.
104. Jer. 1:1ff.
105. Ezek. 2:8–3:3.
106. I Kings 22:19–22.
107. Jer. 23:13.

The national God was believed to be the source of true inspiration.

With respect to Africa, seldom does possession originate from God;[108] it is usually the lesser divinities and other spirit powers which possess. While usually the possessed person passes on messages to the people around him, sometimes there is no such outreach, at least not through the spoken word; the message may be in the madness or death which a spirit might bring upon a person through possession as a punishment, inasmuch as the unexpected development might serve as a warning. The person possessed by a spirit power is under obligation to do the spirit's bidding. The Nuer of the Sudan speak of the spirit 'laying hold of' or 'taking hold of' a person, much as the Hebrews did. Possession also does often bring with it a sense of dismay, but this dismay arises less from a feeling of inadequacy or unpreparedness before the spirit power than from the burden of the body of prohibitions which the person who becomes the agent of a spirit power invariably has to observe.

With respect to induced possession African practice has much in common with the Old Testament: in both the ecstatic state may be induced through the use of music,[109] though unexpected possession is perhaps more characteristic of the Old Testament; 'the hand of the Lord' is suddenly laid upon a person, and he cannot but prophesy. There is no incontrovertible evidence of deliberate inducement.[110]

The Old Testament prophets were conscious of their having been

108. M. J. McVeigh, *God in Africa* (Boston, Claud Stark, 1974), pp. 73–4.
109. In the Old Testament dancing is not specifically mentioned, but it may reasonably be assumed that it formed part of the prophetic activity.
110. In this connection two passages may be referred to, Jeremiah 42:1–22 and Habakkuk 2:1. The former deals with the request made to the prophet for a word from God regarding the intention of Ishmael and his associates to go to Egypt in a bid to escape the wrath of the Babylonian king following the murder of Babylon's envoy Gedaliah. According to the account Jeremiah waited for ten days before responding to the inquiry. What exactly is the significance of this ten-day wait? Does it suggest a conscious putting of oneself in a position to receive God's word? Then there is Habakkuk's declaration: 'I will take my stand to watch, and station myself on the tower, and look forth to see what he will say to me.' Is there here a suggestion of a conscious preparation of oneself for possession? The evidence, it must be admitted, is not clear.

called to bring back the erring people to God. They saw themselves as the conscience of their people, charged with the responsibility of waking them up to spiritual realities and sharpening their conscience with respect to social inequities. They lived for their people and felt deeply about their condition: Elisha weeps,[111] and Ezekiel eats bread and drinks water with quaking because the stability of the nation is about to be shattered.[112] Of course, not all of Israel's prophets were so dedicated and committed; Jeremiah speaks of prophets who 'commit adultery and walk in lies; they strengthen the hands of evil-doers, so that no one turns from his wickedness; all of them have become like Sodom to me, and its inhabitants like Gomorrah'.[113] This critical observation indicates the dedication with which Jeremiah and other prophets approached their task as God's spokesmen.

African prophets are also conscious of having been called to serve the people. However, their oracles are mainly aimed at maintaining the religio-cultural heritage on which society's equilibrium is believed to rest. This contrasts with the messages of such as Jeremiah who spoke against maintaining the religious traditions.[114] In this connection Edwin Smith has asserted that Jeremiah's teaching that religion is the business, not of the group but of the individual and his God, has no equivalent in African prophetic pronouncements.[115] This way of distinguishing between Hebrew and African prophetic teaching, though it has some truth in it, needs to be qualified, however. Prophets speak to concrete situations; to be aware of this is to press distinctions with caution, for situations differ. Furthermore, it needs to be kept in mind that though Jeremiah spelt out individual religion, he did not jettison the concept of community.[116]

As far as the attitude adopted to the prophets is concerned, it

111. 2 Kings 8:11–12.
112. Ezek. 12:18.
113. Jer. 23:14.
114. Jer. 7:1–15.
115. Edwin Smith argues that close parallels do exist between the Old Testament and African life and thought; see his *The Shrine of a People's Soul*, S.C.M. 1929, and *The Christian Mission in Africa*, London and New York, International Mission Council, 1926.
116. See p. 175 below, note 152.

can be said that in both the Old Testament and African traditions the attitude is more or less ambivalent. The Old Testament prophets were often respected and reverenced, but they were not beyond being feared and hated and persecuted. Obadiah, the head of Ahab's household, addressed Elijah as 'my lord'[117]; Nathan the prophet fearlessly criticised David, and the latter did not challenge Nathan's right to censure him.[118] And yet Ahab had Micaiah imprisoned for daring to speak what God had given him for Ahab.[119] One of the signs of a true prophet, according to popular belief in Israel, was that his prophecy should come true; by this canon Jeremiah himself was found wanting; there were those who despised him on the grounds that his prophecies went unfulfilled.

It remains a fact, finally, that Israelite prophecy was able to be critical of Israelite institutions in a way that prophecy in Africa has not been of African traditions. Also, prophecy in the Old Testament embraced non-Israelite peoples, so that the inexperienced Jeremiah would shudder at the thought of prophesying to the nations.

The Individual and the Community

The concept of corporate personality, or the solidarity of the group, played an important role in the life of Israel. This is not to say, however, that in Israel the individuality of a person was not defined, or that the individual was not aware of his individuality, as some would seem to suggest.[120] What is true of the Old Testament is that it witnesses to a person's life being closely bound up with that of the group – the social group was a most important factor. Thus a son who married would continue to live, with his wife, in the father's house: this was considered 'good and pleasant' for it meant the

117. 1 Kings 18:7.
118. 2 Sam. 12:1–15.
119. 1 Kings 22:26.
120. See especially the views of Wheeler Robinson *The Christian Doctrine of Man*, T. and T. Clark, 3rd edn 1926, and a critique of them by J. W. Rogerson, 'The Hebrew Conception of Corporate Personality: A Re-examination', in *The Journal of Theological Studies*, new series vol. XXI, 1970, pp. 1ff.

dwelling together of 'brothers' in unity, thus perpetuating the name of the family.[121]

The basic group to which every Israelite belonged was the family or 'house'. This was much more than the nuclear family of a man, his wife and children. The 'house' being one's father's 'house', it was traced through the father; in other words, it was patriarchal. The family consisted of more than one generation; for example, Achan's family was headed by his grandfather.[122] Widows, orphans, resident aliens and illegitimate children may all belong to a family.[123] The family head had considerable authority in ordering the family affairs. The sense of solidarity was demonstrated also in the institutions of blood revenge[124] and Levirite marriage;[125] also, a member of a family may be protected against having to be sold into slavery to repay a debt.[126] Regarding religious observances the members of a family had opportunity, especially in earlier days, to act as one; until the Passover was made into a national celebration based at Jerusalem it was a family celebration.[127]

A larger group than the family was the clan which consisted of several families; thus David belonged to the family of Jesse which, together with other families, made up the clan of Ephrathah whose members lived in Bethlehem.[128] The heads of families formed a

---

121. Ps. 133. When Heber's wife, Jael, treacherously killed the Canaanite chieftain, Sisera, to whom she had extended hospitality, the biblical record does not remark upon her treachery; on the contrary, she is praised (Judges 5:24f.) because by disposing of Israel's enemy she had removed the threat to Israel's equilibrium.

122. Josh. 7:1.

123. Judg. 11:1–7.

124. This was the practice by which a near kinsman of the slain person avenged his death by eliminating either the slayer or someone else from the slayer's family (Gen. 4:23–4; 2 Sam. 3:22–7, 30). Israelite law recognised that not all murders would have been committed with intent; hence it made provision for the person who had killed without premeditation to take refuge in special cities set aside for the purpose (Num. 35:9–34; Josh. 20).

125. According to this practice a near kinsman to the deceased would marry his widow in order to raise a son to the deceased (Ruth 4:4–10; Deut. 25:5ff.).

126. Lev. 25:47–9.

127. Exod. 12:3–4, 46.

128. Micah 5:2.

group of elders who organised the affairs of the clan as a whole; they ensured, for example, that in time of war the clan raised a contingent of a thousand troops. The clan, like the individual family, would from time to time gather for religious festivals.[129] The institution of blood revenge to which reference has already been made operated also at the clan level. Like the family, then, the clan recognised and actively promoted its oneness.

Then there was the tribe which was a collection of clans. Each tribe had its own territory and enjoyed a considerable measure of autonomy; at least this was more so in the early days, before the establishment of the monarchy. Each tribe had its own leader who was its spokesman. There must have been some kind of tribal organisation, though the exact nature of this is disputed.[130] There were times in the course of the settlement when several tribes would come together to fight a common enemy,[131] though individual tribes often acted alone.[132] All the same, there was a common allegiance to Yahweh[133] – this was the one common characteristic which operated throughout the sweep of Israelite history; in view of this it is not surprising that in the post-exilic times Israel was constituted as a religious community headed by a high priest.[134]

Corporateness, then, whether in the family, or the clan or the tribe, or the nation was a fact, even though this did not prevent Israel from being torn in two by internal dissension. It now needs to be asked whether this group consciousness embraced only the living, or whether it included the unborn and the dead.

There are suggestions in the Old Testament that the ancient Israelites considered the unborn as part of the group. Genesis 17:7ff., which speaks of the blessing by God of Abraham and his descendants after him, would seem to imply that Abraham's 'house'

129. I Sam. 20:6, 29; here several translations have 'family' though the Hebrew is *mishpachah*, clan.
130. See J. Maxwell Miller, *The Old Testament and the Historian* (S.P.C.K. 1976), pp. 63–9.
131. Judg. 5:12f.
132. Judg. 1:9–15.
133. Shechem (Josh. 8:30–5), Bethel (Judg. 20:18), Shiloh (I Sam. 1:1ff.) were among the sanctuaries in Israel.
134. Hagg. 1:1.

consisted of the unborn as well: the covenant relationship with Abraham would not be complete without its having embraced generations yet to be born. In this connection the so-called Zion covenant spelt out in 2 Samuel 7:1ff. is of interest; this passage which shares certain characteristics with the Abrahamic covenant, has a similar perspective: the succeeding generations are unalterably part of the covenant with David. These two passages do have a specific character in that they deal with special situations and specific personalities; to what extent one may legitimately draw a general conclusion from passages which have such specificity may be debated, even though these passages are clearly suggestive.[135]

When it comes to rites in connection with the dead, there is interesting material in the Old Testament, even if it is not plentiful. To the ancient Israelites, as to most Africans today, a proper burial was considered most essential; an Israelite would be horrified at the prospect of his bones being exposed to the birds and the beasts.[136] There was some kind of belief that the dead continued to have some existence in the grave.[137] The ancient Israelite desired to be buried in the family grave;[138] it was a terrible disgrace when Uriah the prophet's body was cast 'into the burial place of the common people'.[139]

Israelite thought went beyond the idea of mere survival to one of life after death. One expression of the latter idea is seen in the concept of She'ol, the place to which the dead were believed to go,

135. One New Testament passage seems to add to this suggestiveness. In Hebrews 7:4–10 the author speaks of the superiority of Melchizedek to the Levitical priests; the explanation is that Abraham gave tithes to Melchizedek who in turn gave Abraham his priestly blessing. In both cases the priestly descendants of Levi yet to be born through Abraham are included with him. In the words of 7:9–10, 'One might even say that Levi himself, who receives tithes, paid tithes through Abraham, for he was still in the loins of his ancestor when Melchizedek met him.'
136. Jer. 8:1f.; 16:4; 22:1–9.
137. Isa. 22:16.
138. Judg. 8:32; 2 Sam. 17:23.
139. Jer. 26:23.

and where they had some kind of existence.[140] Though it was a shadowy place, certain Old Testament passages speak of life there as being modelled after life on earth.[141] Popular religion invested death with a great deal of power. The dead were consulted; this is illustrated not only by the calling up from the dead of Samuel by the medium of Endor,[142] but also by Isaiah's question: '. . . should not a people consult their God? Should they consult the dead on behalf of the living?'[143] Also, there is some evidence that at some time in ancient Israel food was placed on the tombs of the departed.[144] However, there is in the Old Testament and other Jewish literature a rejection of various cult practices in connection with the dead, such as offering food to the dead,[145] and shaving the hair and making cuts on the body as signs of mourning;[146] and, with respect to the medium of Endor episode, it is noteworthy that when Samuel was conjured up he did not give Saul any information which the latter did not already know, as if to say that it is futile to depend on the dead. All the same the dead were owed certain duties which the ancient Israelite took seriously as acts of piety,[147] and from that point of view it may be said that the dead were honoured in a religious spirit. That the living were conscious of the dead may be deduced from that proverb quoted by both Jeremiah and Ezekiel: 'The fathers have eaten sour grapes, and the children's teeth are set on edge.'[148] It would be fair to say, even if the evidence is not overwhelming, that in ancient Israel the dead were part of the community in the consciousness of the living.[149]

140. *She'ol* was considered to be a place of darkness (Job 10:21; Ps. 88:12); no worship of God took place in She'ol, whose inhabitants are referred to as *repha'im*, shades (Ps. 6:5, 88:10; Isa. 38:18).
141. Isa. 14:9f.
142. 1 Sam. 28:3ff.
143. Isa. 8:19.
144. De Vaux, op. cit., p. 60.
145. Ecclus. 30:18.
146. Deut. 14:1; Lev. 21:1f.
147. 1 Sam. 31:12; 2 Sam. 21:13–14, etc.
148. Jer. 31:29; Ezek. 18:2.
149. De Vaux observes that such expressions as 'to sleep with one's fathers' and 'to be reunited with one's own' emphasised that 'the ties of blood reached beyond the grave' (De Vaux, op. cit., p. 59). It is true that one reads in the Old

Group consciousness had several positive elements. The theological reality of the one God gave Israel a fairly homogeneous belief system, and consequently helped to weld her into a political unit. Thus the commandment '. . . you shall love your neighbour'[150] was feasible only because the Israelites recognised their common origin in Yahweh. It is not accidental that the word 'brother' (*'ach*) was given such a wide connotation in Old Testament times; thus in Lev. 19:17 it is used in parallel with 'neighbour'. It is in keeping with this that Leviticus enjoins loving the neighbour and the stranger as oneself.[151] The sense of community required the Israelite to be a responsible citizen, responsible for the individual as well as for the group; so that a person may be held responsible not only as an individual but also as a member of the community. Thus it would be unwise to speak of individual responsibility as distinct from the sense of community; the two were complementary concepts, reinforcing each other.[152]

Did this sense of corporateness embrace the enemy? Certain passages show an awareness of the need to act in love toward the enemy.[153] Also, though the Old Testament does not speak against slavery as an institution, it does teach that love should operate in the master–servant relationship,[154] and the prophetic indictments against injustice witness to their conviction that man was destined

Testament that the dead do not know what happens to the family members in the living (Job 14:21–2) for after all the dead 'know nothing' (Eccles. 9:5), but this kind of language is best regarded as exaggerated metaphor, for the Old Testament clearly admits a link between the living and the dead.

150. Lev. 19:18.

151. Lev. 19:34.

152. Even as Jeremiah announces the new covenant whose laws would be written on each individual heart (Jer. 31:31–4), he foresees the restoration of the people of God; similarly Ezekiel says, '. . . the soul that sins shall die' (Ezek. 18:4), as well as, 'Then the nations will know that I the Lord sanctify Israel, when my sanctuary is in the midst of them for evermore' (37:28).

153. E.g. Prov. 25:21–2, and Exod. 23:4f.; with respect to the latter passage the centre of concern is an animal, but inasmuch as the animal's plight results in its owner being put to some physical and mental inconvenience, the owner stands to benefit by the help that goes primarily to the beast.

154. Deut. 15:12–18, 23:15f.

to love rather than to hate. All this notwithstanding, the attitude to the wicked is often characterised by a lack of love. It is particularly in the field of international relations that the lack of humaneness becomes even more glaring. Where the nationhood of Israel was at stake, then the admonition to love seemed to be suppressed. It is true that in the eighth century Isaiah could paint a picture of the nations having ceased from learning the techniques of war and coming to Jerusalem;[155] however, the real facts of life, in particular the possibility of hostile nations seeking to end Israel's sovereignty and her corporate life through hostile acts, made Israel adopt a hard attitude.[156] Thus when the Judaean exiles returned to Palestine from Babylonia, the recollection of the circumstances that had menaced their collective existence led some into extreme attitudes towards non-Israelite peoples.[157]

It is evident, from what has already been said about the African religio-cultural tradition, that there is much in common between the Old Testament and African life and thought in the matter of the sense of community. As in ancient Israel, so in Africa the concept is exemplified in the family (which is extended, and includes 'illegitimate' children), the clan and the tribe. Of course, with urbanisation and other developments triggered off by forces from outside Africa it is increasingly becoming a rarity to have a family or clan living as an identifiable group in its own locality. However, family reunions take place from time to time, especially at important festivals, and clan members, no matter how widely dispersed, recognise their oneness, so that a clan member who moved to another locality would, under normal circumstances, be expected to introduce himself to the local clan group; indeed, it is not unusual to find in the cities and towns of Ghana clan 'chiefs', elected as leaders

155. Isa. 2:2–4.
156. Hence the regularity with which Deuteronomy enjoins the destruction of the inhabitants of Canaan (7:2, 16–24, etc.), and Isaiah pours withering scorn upon the Babylonian tyrant who has fallen (13:1–14:23); the author of that introductory piece, Isaiah 14:1–4, goes to the extent of envisaging a time when Israel would rule over her captors – as if there were any real virtue in being a captor!
157. See such passages as Jer. 49:1–6; Ezek. 25:8–11; Ezek. 25:12–14; and Neh. 7:5–6.

by the local clansmen and hence the reference points for local and visiting clansmen.

In the African context also the community is made up of the unborn, the living and the dead. The child is believed to be one of the departed members of the family who has been reborn, and until the spirit was reborn it was a member of the spirit world, a world which, it is believed, overlaps very significantly with the physical world. In connection with the place of the dead in the community it will suffice to state here briefly the values associated with ancestral cults: (1) They give a sense of solidarity and security; (2) The ancestors integrate for the African his world-view, seeing that they are believed to mediate between God and man; and (3) The ancestral cults serve to remind the living of those virtues which define the morally good life.

It would be untrue to say, in view of the strong sense of community in Africa, that the individual has no self-awareness. It is true that the individual would hesitate to act against what custom has laid down, and from that point of view it may be said that the African concept of community is a limiting factor upon the individual's self-expression. However, not enough caution has always been exercised in stating this concept. Thus Shorter has argued that communalism poses two dangers: 'the risk of infantilism under a superior father-figure or mother-figure, who takes decisions for the children and who sees the superior's task as testing the subject's obedience and imposing a common pattern of life on them'.[158] In the light of what was said earlier on the African religio-cultural reality Shorter's analysis is one-sided, for African societies know how to deal with totalitarianism, whether in the family, or clan or tribe. It is not without justification that Nyerere has said: 'In our traditional African society we were individuals within a community.'[159]

A great deal of evidence could thus be adduced in support of the view that there is a certain similarity in outlook between the Old Testament and African life and thought. Of course, it may be

158. Aylward Shorter, *African Culture and the Christian Church* (G. Chapman 1973), pp. 204–5.
159. Quoted by Shorter, op. cit., p. 197.

argued that since Africa does not belong to the milieu whose peoples interacted with the ancient Israelites no meaningful comparison could be made between the Old Testament and African life and thought. Isaac has in fact stated: 'It is evident immediately that there is weakness in a methodology which compares contemporary practices with ancient ones which are, moreover, from a separate area.'[160] This cannot be considered to be the final word, however, for not only are the canons of Old Testament comparative study often one-sidely stated, but also demonstrably there is much in the Old Testament that is recalled in African life and thought. While the canons[161] may be respected, some of them must be so stated as to take account of other parameters. Thus one of the canons of the comparative study of the Old Testament is that, in such comparison, sight should not be lost of the relation between the Old and New Testaments. If this should be taken to imply, as is sometimes done, that the Old Testament has no independent value except as it is linked to the New Testament, then serious doubt is cast upon any comparison involving the Old Testament by itself.

However, the unity of the two Testaments should not be pressed to such an extent that it becomes inevitable to deny that the Old Testament has any independent value.[162] There are some religious ideas which have greater visibility in the Old Testament than in

160. Erich Isaac, 'Relations Between the Hebrew Bible and Africa', in *Jewish Social Studies*, vol. XXVI, no. 2 (April 1964), p. 93. It must be added that though Isaac thus cautions, he nevertheless details some areas in which there is common understanding between the Old Testament and African life and thought. Contrast P. E. S. Thompson, 'The Approach to the Old Testament in an African Setting', in *Ghana Bulletin of Theology*, vol. II, no. 3 (December 1962), pp. 1ff.

161. For a concise statement of these canons see Th. C. Vriezen, 'The Study of the Old Testament and the History of Religion', in Supplements to *Vetus Testamentum*, vol. XVII (Congress volume, Rome, 1968, E. J. Brill), pp. 1–24.

162. Some would, out of exasperation, say that all talk of the unity of the Bible should be abandoned. It is Bruegemann's opinion that such talk may have contributed to theology's inability to adapt to new situations. It could, for example, according to Bruegemann, make us unaware of the contemporary character of the Old Testament wisdom literature, with its concerns in the area of concrete living; Walter Bruegemann, 'The Triumphalistic Tendency in Exegetical History', in *Journal of the American Academy of Religion*, 38, 1970,

the New. No reader of the account of Isaiah's call[163] would fail to be struck by the picture painted of the majesty of God. It is hardly necessary to give another Old Testament illustration of this for, indeed, prophet after prophet pictures Yahweh as having incomparable majesty and as the only one who deserves to be so recognised. Then, in the Old Testament a clear reminder is given of the fact that salvation has both spiritual and material dimensions,[164] a thought which underlies the contemporary statements of Liberation theology. In connection with this there is the frequent statement of Yahweh's involvement in world events and world politics. He is involved with Israel as he is with Syria, the Ammonites, etc.[165] The prophets and the psalmists alike point out again and again the danger of a dead, formal religion: what, for example, is sacrifice if it does not express inward penitence? What is of the utmost importance, according to these religious stalwarts, is righteousness – God is righteous, and he requires that human beings should be righteous also. These and other important religious values are prominently displayed in the Old Testament, thus underlining its importance as a religious document in itself. It is not without justification that Anderson has observed:

In many ways the Old Testament, with its healthy this-worldliness, its sensuous taste for the goodness of life God has given us, its grappling with the meaning of faith in the context of the political sphere, its portrayal of the anguish of a Jeremiah in the midst of his people's suffering and tragedy, is much closer to modern man in a post-Christian age than the literature of the

---

pp. 367–80. Of course, the unity of the Bible forces itself upon one, mainly because the Bible tells one story, the story of a people united and motivated by their conviction of the Lordship of God to whom worship was due. See B. W. Anderson, 'The New Crisis in Biblical Theology' in Charles Courtney, Olin M. Ivey and Gordon E. Michaelson (eds.), *Hermeneutics and the Worldliness of Faith* (*The Drew Gateway*), vol. XLV, nos. 1, 2, 3 (1974–5).

163. Isa. 6.
164. Isa. 40:1ff., etc.
165. Amos 1:1ff., Jer. 1:1ff.; Jeremiah was to prophesy to 'the nations'.

New Testament which is freighted with categories that are alien, or seemingly alien, to our experience.[166]

The African theologian would see even more in the Old Testament than has been spelt out here by Anderson, for many aspects of life and thought in ancient Israel are for the African a present reality.

Gaster, whose enormous effort, *Myth, Legend, and Custom in the Old Testament*,[167] draws upon the traditions of a great number of peoples, including African peoples and others whose home lies outside the Ancient Near East, has reacted thus to the opinion that 'it is methodologically frail to institute parallels between Biblical beliefs and practices and other peoples who lived (or live) much later and in quite other environments':

> . . . such comparisons are never intended to imply direct cultural contacts or borrowings but merely to illustrate patterns of thought and feelings, to show the variety with which certain basic notions have been expressed in different times and places, and to suggest, on the strength of cumulative analogues, the true (or original) significance of things which may now be seen only in a distorting mirror. In precisely the same way, *semantic* parallels between diverse languages are no less valid and instructive because those languages themselves are unrelated. Indeed, in both cases the diversity enhances, rather than diminishes, the significance of the comparison. Moreover, in *interpreting* any one or other particular custom I have generally used the control of *context*, choosing that explanation which best accords with the acknowledged tenor and meaning of other usages with which it is ceremonially associated. True, some of the explanations may even then be incorrect, but this seems a calculated risk worth taking, for while, on the one hand, some things in the Old Testament may thus become distorted, on the other hand, some may otherwise be missed.[168]

166. Anderson, 'The New Crisis in Biblical Theology'.
167. Theodor H. Gaster, *Myth, Legend and Custom in the Old Testament*, Duckworth 1970.
168. Ibid., Preface.

Gaster's statement adequately explains the grounds upon which the Old Testament and African life and thought may be looked at together, as is done in this study. Not only could such a procedure provide African students with a vital pedagogical tool for the study of the Old Testament, but also the development of a distinctive Christian theology in Africa may thereby be facilitated.

The validity of such a comparison, then, is beyond question, and what has been said above about ancient Israelite and African traditions shows that there is a sense in which one could speak of a religio-cultural continuity; and when it is realised that the New Testament shares the same cultural presuppositions with the Old Testament, then this continuity embraces the Bible as a whole.

However, to speak of a continuity is not to imply a convergence of ideas, for there is also a discontinuity between the two traditions; this dialectical relationship must be recognised if the facile adoption of Old Testament institutions is to be avoided.[169] Failure to realise the nature of the relationship accounts, at least in part, for the misinterpretation of the Old Testament by some Independent Churches, as Sundkler and Oosthuizen report. Sometimes the desire to adopt a traditional practice has dictated the kind of interpretation to be put on a biblical passage. Thus, as Sundkler notes, 'because this Bantu standard for testing Bible interpretation is accepted as self-evident . . . it is possible for the Zionists to quote Micah 4:13 in support of *isangoma* – divination.'[170] Similarly, Phillips notes that in 'both East and West Africa there are secessionist Churches which encourage polygamy, insisting it is permitted "in the bible" '.[171]

The way to counteract this misuse of the Old Testament is not to keep it away from converts, or to keep down to a minimum the references to the Old Testament in the Church's teaching. The great need of the Church in Africa is for a biblical hermeneutic

169. Some of the differences have been noted above, but one could cite the Old Testament and African ideas on death and the hereafter; here the Old Testament takes a distinctive turn with the development of the view that the dead shall rise – Daniel 12:2.

170. Sundkler, op. cit., p. 277.

171. Phillips, *The Old Testament in the World Church*, p. 7; see also Jomo Kenyatta, *Facing Mount Kenya* (Secker and Warburg 1938), p. 271.

which will take seriously the biblical story's Ancient Near Eastern background, as well as the particularity of the African situation. Biblical commentaries by African theologians could have a distinctive character; for, in addition to the relevant critical tools, they could utilise the continuity–discontinuity relationship to achieve interpretative realism. This is an essential aspect of the quest for an authentic Christian theology.

In this connection it is essential that attention should be given to the question of Bible translation in Africa. Only brief remarks will be made on this here, for the subject has been treated extensively, and with considerable perception, by other writers.[172] The Bible has been translated into an impressive number of African languages,[173] but our experience of Bible translation in Ghana in recent years suggests to us the possibility of there being much translation work that seems to be aimed at emphasising the 'outdatedness' of Scripture![174] A bad translation will only succeed in preventing a 'relevant reading' of the Bible, for it will have imposed a barrier between the text and its meaning for the reader; not only would the particularity of the story have been obscured, but also the introduction of existential questions would become either impossible or unrealistic. Where the full import of the text has not been realised, the reader wallows in uncertainties.

Besides the matter of translation there is another even more fundamental matter, one which would almost certainly be considered controversial. The formation of the canon of the New Testament which came about in the course of the development of Christian tradition was influenced, at least in part, by the desire to present a standard of conduct or belief by which Christians were to live.[175] But before the appearance of the Gospels the standard

172. See, e.g., Kraft, op. cit.
173. C. P. Groves, *The Planting of Christianity in Africa*, vol. IV (Guildford, Lutterworth, 1958), pp. 357ff.
174. On problems of translation in general see, among many others, Chaim Rabin's 'The Uniqueness of Bible Translation' in E. Mveng and R. J. Z. Werblowsky (eds.), pp. 108ff.
175. The word *kanon* was used in several senses, the two most relevant to our purpose being: (i) a list or catalogue; (ii) a rule of conduct or belief. Though the first

was derived from the teachings of Jesus which his disciples had cherished even before his death and resurrection. Indeed, that contemporary of Marcion, Bishop Papias of Hierapolis, testifies that though there were written Gospels in his time there was a decided preference for oral tradition.[176] Thus by the time the Gospels appeared there was already a well defined picture of Christ on the basis of oral tradition, and the selection of the Gospels was influenced by a consideration of their conformity or otherwise with the understanding already gained as to the life and work of Christ. In formulating the canon the Church had before it a number of works some of which were deemed to be unacceptable in terms of how the picture of Christ painted by them related to the picture already formed of him.

Without wishing to be understood to be denying that in many ways the Church had from its inception been guided by the Spirit, we deem it necessary to raise the question of whether, in the circumstances of the Church in Africa, this selection of sources of life and work of Christ is the best that could be made. Perhaps in the light of the questions the African Christian asks of Christ, questions to which the institutionalised Church in Africa, given its present inherited traditions, is not equipped to address itself meaningfully, there may very well be other sources of the life and work of Christ deemed unworthy of being canonised by the early Church which could be found more satisfying spiritually in the light of the African's religio-cultural and other circumstances.

A suggestion of this nature is likely to evoke immediately the response of its being an invitation for the dismantling of the great wealth of Christian tradition which has been assembled in the New Testament. Such a reaction could be a hasty one, however; for in the light of what the whole Church understands today of its nature and task, given the increased consciousness of the impact of social circumstances, such re-examination of the canon of Scripture could result in a clearer expression of the Church's oneness. Of course, it

---

meaning is much older, the latter sense evidently coloured the thinking of the early Church.

176. Eusebius, *Church History*, III. 39.3.

must be conceded that here we are operating in the realm of conjecture, but it is a conjecture that one is justified in making considering that throughout the centuries the Church has sought to see, with sometimes clear, and at other times warped, vision the possibilities of the Gospel of Christ. The cultural approach being urged in this study necessitates the raising of such an issue.

7

The Theology of the Cross in Context

To conclude this second part of the book consideration will be given to one crucial area of Christian belief, the cross of Christ. No matter what the cultural perspective of the Christian might be, the matter of Christ's death and its significance cannot but be considered most central; Christians everywhere, from whatever cultural background, must react to this central belief. And yet, it has been argued that the cross being such a radical event all talk of culture not only loses its significance but also it amounts to setting man's pride over and against the Gospel;[1] according to this line of argument, the cross underlines the seriousness of sin which permeates human life and thought. This cannot be the last word, however, for as long as it is only flesh and blood which will stand beneath the cross, the question of meaning and significance, in relation to human or cultural identities, arises. Indeed, the annals of the Church reveal that the cross has been seen from different perspectives in accordance with prevailing cultural circumstances.[2]

1. For a discussion of views of this kind see H. R. Niebuhr, *Christ and Culture* (New York, Harper and Row, 1951).
2. According to the Ransom theory, to get mankind out of the clutches of the Devil a ransom was paid through Christ's blood. This theory fitted into the social conditions of the patristic age in which it originated, an age of unrest, conflict and brigandage, of capturing and ransoming. In the 12th century Anselm of Canterbury rejected this conception of the work of Christ as a lawsuit with the Devil and put forward the Satisfaction theory according to which Christ's death was a satisfaction paid to God whose honour had been violated through human sin, a theory which was of a piece with the conditions prevailing in the mediaeval age, an age of feudalism and chivalry, and hence one in which concepts of honour and satisfaction featured prominently. The Forensic or Penal Substitution theory

New Testament Teaching

What is important is that there should be a genuine wrestling with this Event. The New Testament plainly invites people to undertake this.

Thus it is appropriate, in dealing here with theological experimentation, that an attempt should be made to look at the cross from the African perspective. To do so, however, it is necessary first to examine the New Testament material on the subject, and then, given the history of the Church in Africa, to raise the question of the relevance of the theological understanding of the cross which the Church in Africa has inherited.

In studying the New Testament material on the cross we shall confine ourselves to the teaching of Paul. This procedure does not mean constricting the discussion unreasonably, for Paul's letters contain the greatest concentration of biblical references to the death of Christ.

The basic theme of Paul's preaching may be stated thus, using Paul's own words: 'For the word of the cross is folly to those who are perishing, but to us who are being saved it is the power of God.'[3] For Paul God was in the crucifixion carrying out his plans for the ultimate good of the human race. The Corinthian situation which forms the background to this declaration has been admirably described thus by Küng:

[The Corinthians] regard the wretched earthly Jesus as belonging to the past and prefer to invoke the exalted Lord and victory over the powers of fate. From the fact of possession of the Spirit and from their 'superior' knowledge they deduce a self-assured freedom which permits them to indulge in all kinds of self glorification, arrogance, uncharitableness, self-opinionatedness, violence, even drinking bouts and intercourse with sacred prostitutes . . . Paul refers these extravagant, utopian, Libertinist, resur-

---

issued out of the post-Reformation period which was dominated by ideas of law and jurisprudence, hence the conviction that Christ underwent the punishment due to man for his sin, made amends for sin and by his blood purchased man's forgiveness.

3. 1 Cor. 1:18.

rection fantasts, who want to anticipate heaven on earth, to the Crucified.[4]

Paul is at pains to point not simply to the death but to the cross of Christ, as we see in Philippians 2:8: 'And being found in human form he humbled himself and became obedient unto death, even death on a cross.' Paul must have had good reason for emphasising the fact of Christ's death on the cross; he was not prepared to modify his preaching simply because the cross was 'a stumbling block to Jews and folly to Gentiles'.[5] Jewish tradition would make it sound foolhardy to preach to Jews about salvation through the cross; for 'a hanged man is accursed by God; you shall not defile your land which the Lord your God gives you for an inheritance'.[6]

There is more to Paul's use of the kind of language that underlines the importance of the cross. Sacrificial language evidently appealed to him. Christ is the Passover victim,[7] and by dying for us as a sacrifice he wrought salvation for us since we were incapable of working out our own salvation.[8] The cross is full of power, a power which lays bare our powerlessness; we could not possibly have done by ourselves what the cross has done for us. Thus Christ's sacrifice is 'the sacrifice by which God reconciled the world to himself, the sacrifice in which he took responsibility for evil, accepted us as we

4. Hans Küng, *On Being a Christian* (New York, Pocket Books, 1978), p. 399.

5. 1 Cor. 1:23.

6. Deut. 21:23. In this connection it may be recalled that the author of the Letter to the Hebrews notes pointedly that Christ 'suffered outside the gate' (Heb. 13:12); this language recalls Old Testament sacrificial legislation which stipulates that the carcasses of certain victims for sacrifice were to be taken 'outside the camp' and burnt at the end of the main ritual (Lev. 4:21, 16:27, etc.), the clear implication being that the victim would have acquired a contagion that would make the carcass dangerous; hence the law's insistence on a cleansing ritual for the attendant who carried out the carcass for burning. Christ, then, died outside the sacred precincts, according to Hebrews. Paul and the author of Hebrews must have known what they were doing when they described Christ's death using this kind of imagery. The language was such as could alienate a Jew seeking to become a Christian; for to the Jew the cross was a criminal's death, as well as being the death of a person forsaken by God. To the Greek it was sheer stupidity to say that death could be part of a divine plan for the salvation of man.

7. 1 Cor. 5:7, 10:16; Rom. 3:25, 5:9, etc.

8. 1 Cor. 15:3.

are, and accepted in himself the consequences of evil and sin; for in the light of his death, men recognise the inadequacy of their attempts to justify themselves, or expiate their own sin'.[9]

Furthermore, unlike those of us who resist God and seek in vain to work out our own salvation, Christ proved to be the obedient One, and in his death on the cross there is a great lesson for mankind. Christ's death on the cross, as Käsemann has expressed it, 'declares that God is only "for us" if he destroys our illusions, and new obedience characterises the man who foregoes his autonomy in order to await his salvation from God alone'.[10] We are thus reconciled with God,[11] sharing a common life with Christ and with one another.[12]

It is clear that Paul felt very strongly about the cross. He categorically states that the cross accomplished our salvation. He is not about to keep himself at a distance from the cross simply because it excites ridicule and bewilderment in certain quarters because of its associations. To the Corinthians he states his preoccupation in words which adequately sum up this brief survey of Paul's convictions regarding the cross: 'For I decided to know nothing among you except Jesus Christ and him crucified.'[13]

In view of this it becomes somewhat disconcerting, at first, to discover that Paul uses quite forceful language about the resurrection also. Paul would be bewildered by such views as have been expressed in our time that no significance should be attached to the references to the resurrection.[14] It is generally felt that the New Testament evidence for the resurrection should be taken seriously, and to do so is to become aware of the urgency of Paul's language which leaves no room for doubt that he considered the resurrection to be a crucial element of faith in Christ: '. . . if Christ has not been

9. Frances Young, *Sacrifice and the Death of Christ* (Philadelphia, The Westminster Press, 1975), p. 137.
10. Ernst Käsemann, 'The Pauline Theology of the Cross' in *Interpretation*, vol. XXIV, no. 2 (April 1970), pp. 151ff.
11. Rom. 5:10.
12. 1 Cor. 10:14ff.
13. 1 Cor. 2:2.
14. R. Robert Bater, 'Towards a More Biblical View of the Resurrection', in *Interpretation*, vol. XXIII, no. 1 (1969), p. 64.

raised, then our preaching is in vain and your faith is in vain.'[15] From this and other passages it becomes evident that the resurrection meant a great deal to Paul; Paul appears to be as much resurrection-conscious as he is cross-conscious.

Though some of the passages which refer to the resurrection do so only in the course of Paul's dealing with matters of controversy, the references are no less significant, if for no other reason than that Paul considered it necessary to use the resurrection fact in that way. Thus we have 1 Corinthians 6:14: 'And God raised the Lord and will also raise us up by his power.' In this section of 1 Corinthians Paul is dealing with the issue of prostitution, and he makes the point that prostitution is wrong – how could one practise immorality when we are members of the Christ who has been raised? Our human personality may have been shaped by its physical existence on earth, but we are to be restored to life. Similarly, Paul's words in 1 Corinthians 15:14, to which we referred above, came up in connection with a controversy; apparently the view was held by some that there would not be a resurrection of the dead.[16] This verse occurs in 15:12–19 where Paul points out the impossible and ridiculous conclusions which logically follow from a denial that there is any resurrection of the dead. If, Paul argues, the dead are incapable of being restored to life, then Christ was not raised; after all Christ was a human being. If the dead are not raised, the resurrection of Jesus cannot have occurred; this would negate what is already known about the life of Christ. Even if one allows that some of these passages do not set out to relate the resurrection to salvation primarily, and that the resurrection comes in as Paul addresses himself to particular issues, it still is quite clear that Paul set much store by the fact of the resurrection.

When one has allowed all that, it still is a fact that the tone of the references to the cross and the resurrection cannot be said to indicate that Paul sets up the resurrection in such a way as to diminish the importance of the cross. On the contrary, the cross remains for Paul the great challenge. It would not do to put the

15. 1 Cor. 15:14.
16. 1 Cor. 15:12.

cross in the shadow of the resurrection; to do so would be to do injury to the Pauline material. It is in fact possible to see in Paul's letters a distinction between the cross and the resurrection as they relate to the Christian's life, even if sometimes he speaks of the two in such a way as to suggest that they constitute one reality. The variety of imagery Paul uses serves to underline his conviction that the cross was the event that worked our salvation, bringing us into a new life with Christ. The resurrection, the event which brought living people into physical contact with Christ, becomes the visible symbol of that newness of life which the cross accomplished for humanity. The language of the cross is such as to suggest that, for Paul, far from its being merely a 'transit station' on the way to the resurrection, it is the foundation of the story of man's salvation. As Küng has put it, the cross puts 'in question a false conception of the resurrection'.[17]

Western Thought

In the light of all this, those statements by some Western theologians which put the cross in the shadow of the resurrection need to be questioned; the cross gets to be overshadowed in significance, it becomes a disaster, a regrettable prelude to Easter.[18] Thus it has been asserted:

> So far as the death went, and if that were the end or consumm-
> ation of His work – in the way that traditional Christian teaching,
> with its emphasis on the significance of Christ's saving work on
> earth culminating in His death as consisting in the placating or
> reconciling of a holy God to sinful men, and thus obtaining
> forgiveness for them, too much tended to present – there would
> have been no Christian Gospel or Christian Church.[19]

---

17. Küng, op. cit., p. 400.
18. In West Africa, after over a century of Christian activity, Good Friday, by its mode of celebration (this often includes the singing of mournful hymns by the Church Choir and congregation as they process slowly from one end of the town to the other) seems to be viewed as a regrettable interlude.
19. J. M. Shaw, *Christian Doctrine* (Guildford, Lutterworth, 1953), p. 219.

Here is a firm statement of the conviction that without the resurrection the cross could not have provided the basis for a community of believers. Pannenberg has expressed the same opinion more succintly: 'Without his resurrection his message would have turned out to be a fanatical audacity.'[20]

I suspect very strongly that such views of the cross and its relation to the resurrection arise essentially out of a Western understanding of death; the New Testament does not permit one to say, as categorically as the scholars just quoted do, that the cross had so much significance and no more.

With the growing complexity of life in the West death is fast ceasing to be a public event.[21] Häselbarth has observed:

> Until recently, to use an example, death in a German village used to be an affair that affected all the inhabitants. Work had to stop, people came together for condolences and thereafter formed the procession from the dead man's home to the Church. Bells rang and the choir sang. In the local inn people ate and drank together. The deceased was laid to rest in the centre of the village, that is in the graveyard surrounding the Church.

In other words, death was an affair which involved the community as a whole. Häselbarth goes on to comment on the role of today's 'commercial burial-institutes': These 'do for the family what formerly relatives, neighbours and brotherhoods used to do. They relieve the gravity of death by camouflaging it with flowers, wreaths, taped music, lighting-effects, expensive dress and caskets.' In the circumstances, 'Dying, as well as living through a time of mourning, becomes the private experience of the individual. Read what the printed announcements of death say: "The funeral within the small

---

20. Wolfhart Pannenberg, 'The Revelation of God in Jesus of Nazareth', in *Theology as History* (New York, Harper and Row, 1967), p. 116.

21. For this brief statement of how death is viewed in the West we are depending almost entirely on a paper by the German scholar Hans Häselbarth entitled 'The Concept of Death in African and Western Societies'; it was presented at the 1975 meeting of the West African Association of Theological Institutions at Ibadan, Nigeria. See also Häselbarth's *Die Auferstehung der Toten in Afrika*, Gütersloher Verlagshaus Gerd Mohn, 1972.

circle of his loved ones has taken place in all quietness", or: "We kindly ask you not to pay any personal visits" – sentences which in an African context would sound outrageous.' Death would seem to be an embarrassment which must be passed over as quickly as possible, a goal which morticians (to use the American term) have made possible for people in the West to realise, generally speaking. In the circumstances the average Westerner is not likely to see death as a meaningful end. 'Death', notes Häselbarth, 'does not fit into a world-view guided by the ideas of activism, progress, success, optimism, rationalism and youthfulness.' It has been commercialised out of all meaningfulness.

African Thought

In these days there are signs of death becoming commercialised in the urban centres in Africa, but to a very large extent death is celebrated in the traditional ways, even in the larger towns and cities. The following are some of the significant ideas in the celebration of death:

Death is caused by evil. The African understanding of causation is of relevance here: nothing happens which will not have been *purposefully* caused. Death invariably receives something more than a physical explanation. To be sure, physical explanations are understood, but the African would go beyond the physical to seek a theological explanation. Thus the death of a centenarian may very well raise questions of why he died at that particular time, and not earlier, or later; and a religious explanation stands ready at hand: some agency or other with evil designs might have caused the death. In the event of sickness or death there is resort to ritual specialists to try and find out the *real* cause of change in the person's physical state even where such a change might have been physically caused, such as by snake-bite. The spirit world not being separate from the physical world, according to the African conception, all that brings suffering and deprivation is ultimately traceable to other than physical causes. 'The religious beliefs of the people are used to offer the explanation, and Africans turn to their relationship with God, fellow members of the community, ancestors and spirits.'[22]

Death does not end life. The occurrence of death is not considered to mark the cessation of life. The dead are believed to be going on a journey, one which is described in such physical terms as crossing a river in a boat, and which involves having the wherewithal to pay one's way;[23] since he might become thirsty on the way, he would need water.[24] Then, once on the other side, in the land of the dead, he lives a physical existence which is patterned after his earthly existence. He may become a revered ancestor, called upon as a member of the living group in various situations. Some of the death ceremonies might appear to imply a denial of the dead being alive; thus in some widowhood ceremonies ritual activity is undertaken to sever the relationship between the widow and the dead husband. In fact, however, it is because the dead are believed to be alive that it becomes necessary to perform such rites which have as one of their aims to prepare the widow for possible remarriage. To use Mbiti's terminology, the dead remain the 'living-dead', revered and communed with. Indeed, it might be said that in African thought death leads into life. The Asante of Ghana, for example, carry out special rites on the sixth day following the death;[25] on this day, known as 'the day of rising'[26] one of the ceremonies performed signifies that 'death had gone back and life forward'.[27]

Death does not sever the bond between the living and the dead. In most African societies there is great concern for giving the dead proper burial so that they arrive safely in the land of the dead. Death rituals may take weeks, or months, or even years, especially where

22. J. Mugambi and N. Kirima, *The African Religious Heritage* (Nairobi, Oxford University Press, 1976), p. 94.
23. Hence money may be put in the lifeless hand of the dead before the burial.
24. Water may be poured into the mouth of the deceased as part of the death ceremonies.
25. I.e., the third day following the burial.
26. Not rising from the dead.
27. R. S. Rattray, *Religion and Art in Ashanti* (Oxford University Press 1959), pp. 164f.

there is the custom of a second burial, as among the Igbo of Nigeria. This second burial takes place some time after the initial rites, and its purpose is to ensure that every proper procedure has been followed to ensure the arrival of the dead in the other world, as the belief goes.[28] However – and paradoxically – installing the dead properly on the other side ensures that they remain members of the living as well. In other words, the rites have the effect of strengthening the bond between the living and the dead, especially as the latter are recognised as a source of reference for an ethically acceptable life.

Death is an occasion for seeking more life. Since death makes people into spirits and thus members of the spirit world, the dead are believed to be in a position to grant boons. At death messages may be given to the fledgling spirit to take to the world of the dead. These messages are illustrative of the African concern for life: they are concerned with health, children, and generally those things which would strengthen the effectiveness of the petitioners as contributors to the maintenance of society's equilibrium. Where reincarnation beliefs are held, prayers may be said petitioning the spirits to ensure that when the dead person returns to this existence he would be more successful in life. In any case, death becomes an occasion for seeking greater life.

Death does not negate natural self-expression. Death does imply loss, but it does not end man's self-expression. Loss may have occurred, but there is on-going life, and this is symbolised in various ways. In the last century one Methodist missionary serving in Ghana commented, in a report to his superiors in London, on the Ghanaian woman's propensity for dancing in public: '. . . often have I been grieved while seeing their children joining with them imitating their example, perhaps the very day in which a near relation, Father, Brother, Sister, has been called into the eternal world.'[29] The dancing is a powerful affirmation of life, from the African point of

28. Kwesi Dickson and Paul Ellingworth (eds.), *Biblical Revelation and African Beliefs* (Guildford, Lutterworth, 1969), p. 45.
29. Thomas Birch Freeman's Report of 30 July 1838.

view. One of Nottingham's observations is apt here: 'Without death the eliminator, there could be no continuing life. But even when this positive affirmation is obscure, in many societies the termination of the death rituals, which furnish occasion for the gathering of a group of otherwise scattered individuals, is marked by discreet feasting and circumspect conviviality.'[30] This affirmation of life is widespread in Africa as part of death rites; it has the effect of saying, very eloquently, that life must go on.[31]

Death affects the whole community. In African societies death affects a much wider social group than the deceased's immediate family. The ritual in connection with death serves to reaffirm the sense of solidarity of the larger group, and to place the latter's support at the disposal of the bereaved. Relatives, friends, neighbours, and even those who only knew others who had known the deceased – all these would flock around, taking part in wakes, visiting the bereaved and at the appropriate moment making donations to them. Throughout the period of the rites there will be a concourse of people, coming and going. There is identification with the family of the deceased. Quite often the number of people present at a funeral is not in direct proportion to the social importance of the deceased when he was alive. Death, whether of the high or the low, brings about a great deal of community interaction.

In the light of this understanding of death in Africa, and also considering the New Testament understanding of the significance of Christ's death, how would the Church in Africa see the cross if it felt free, as it should, to re-examine the received theology from the West?

It is evident, to begin with, that it would not speak in muted tones but in glorious affirmation of the cross as that which is the basis of the Christian hope. The South African theologian, Gabriel Setiloane, has anticipated this in his 'liturgical statement' entitled 'I am an African' in which he writes:

30. Elizabeth Nottingham, *Religion and Society* (New York, Random House, 1962), p. 32.
31. Mugambi and Kirima, op. cit., p. 102.

And yet for us it is when he is on the cross,
This Jesus of Nazareth, with holed hands
   and open side, like a beast at a sacrifice:
When he is stripped, naked like us,
Browned and sweating water and blood in
   the heat of the sun,
   Yet silent,
That we cannot resist Him.

The context of this statement is, of course, South Africa where Africans suffer humiliation and die both in their homes and in prison, but it is a picture that could be viewed against the background of many an African country outside South Africa. The cross demonstrates human degradation and evil, but it also demonstrates triumph. However, a more detailed answer is needed to the question of why Africans cannot 'resist' the Christ on the cross. Instead of going through the six characteristic ideas arising from the celebration of death in Africa, we shall note three ways in which African life and thought could be recalled to great advantage, having in mind the teaching of the New Testament on the significance of the cross.

1. The African believes that death binds up relationships in society, revitalising the living and underscoring their sense of community. Paul's language about the cross clearly adumbrates this kind of understanding. He writes:

> The cup of blessing which we bless, is it not a participation in the blood of Christ? The bread which we break, is it not a participation in the body of Christ? Because there is one bread, we who are many are one body, for we all partake of the one bread. Consider the people of Israel; are not those who eat the sacrifices partners in the altar?[32]

What Paul is saying here is that eating and drinking at the Lord's Table is sharing in the death of Christ, and also sharing in life one with the other. The reference to Israelite sacrifice here is instructive.

---

32. 1 Cor. 10:16–18.

It is evident in 1 Corinthians 10:18 that Paul had in mind the peace offering,[33] the most significant characteristic of which was the communal meal which took place as part of its ritual: the worshipper would invite kinsmen to a meal made from the flesh of the victim. This sacred meal had the dual effect of uniting with God[34] those who participated in the eating, and strengthening the bond binding them together as a community. It is evident that the kind of language Paul is using here relates his ideas very closely to African experience and the goal of life. Not only is this kind of common meal as a sacred act widely known in African ritual,[35] but also one of life's goals, as already noted, is to maintain the social solidarity, and hence society's equilibrium.

2. It has just been pointed out that one of the implications of the communal meal in Israelite sacrifice (as in sacrifice in African traditional religion) was that the worshipper and kinsmen had fellowship with God. Now the cross is the supreme sacrifice in which Christ is both the initiator and the victim, so that in a singular sense by his death on the cross Christ is linked to us. One very important piece of Old Testament legislation on sacrifice may be recalled: the victim for sacrifice was to be without blemish.[36] Christ

33. *Zevach shelamim*, or simply *zevach*, *shelem* and their plural forms. It is significant that the Septuagint translates *shelem* in the Pentateuch on quite a number of occasions as *soterion*, which indicates safety or health. See N. Snaith, 'Sacrifices in the Old Testament', in *Vetus Testamentum*, vol. VIII, no. 3 (July 1957).

34. It was evidently not understood in ancient Israel that God took part in the eating, notwithstanding the appearance in the ritual legislation of such a phrase as 'food for God' – Lev. 3:16; 21:6, 8, 17, etc.; after all meat was excluded from his due. The phrase in question is a carry-over from an earlier understanding which did not become characteristic of the authentic Hebrew religion.

35. J. Omoṣade Awolalu, *Yoruba Beliefs and Sacrificial Rites* (Longman 1979), pp. 143ff. Among the Haya of Tanzania the clan head would distribute such sacred meat to members of the clan. Such communal sharing, in other societies in Africa, takes place with respect to the libation drink which, after it has been partly poured on the ground to the ancestors, is then shared by the living present on the occasion.

36. The Old Testament makes an exception with regard to the freewill offering, this being an offering that might be made just when the animal available might not be without blemish – Lev. 7:16–17; this exception serves to underline the concern that the victim for a sacrifice to God should be unblemished.

was the perfect victim; by his death he merits, to use an African image, to be looked upon as Ancestor,[37] the greatest of ancestors, who never ceases to be one of the 'living-dead', because there always will be people alive who *knew* him, whose lives were irreversibly affected by his life and work. He becomes the one with whom the African Christian lives intimately (as well as with the other living-dead), on whom he calls, and to whom he offers prayer. The physical cross, like the staffs and stools looked upon as material representations symbolising the presence of the ancestors, becomes the symbol of Christ's being *the ever-living*.

3. The cross does not deny our human identities and the life-characteristics which go with them. Paul himself is an illustration of the truth of this assertion. He was a Jew who treasured his Jewish identity; the New Testament documents leave us in no doubt about this. Indeed, he found the Jewish national characteristics most helpful to him in his attempt to state Christian realities; hence the extent to which his language recalls institutions belonging to the 'old Israel'. He describes the death of Christ using the language of the Passover, that great feast which his fathers had celebrated in Egypt and which was still celebrated in his time by Jews and Jewish Christians alike; it was indeed understood that every celebration was a participation in the first Passover. Paul needed his Jewish background in order to express most vitally the significance of the death of Christ; that was the only way in which he could speak meaningfully about something that meant so much to him. When he says that he was determined to preach nothing but the cross, the language in which to do this was part of the cultural tradition in which he had been born. To be sure, he was aware that there was a limit beyond which he could not go to employ his Jewish traditions; thus he rejected the view that one could gain salvation by way of the law. Nevertheless, for him there was no alternative to expressing his faith using the resources of his cultural heritage.

That Paul's position is not without its dangers must be acknowl-

37. In African thought those who become ancestors must have lived exemplary lives; it is not every one who dies who becomes an ancestor, so that the cult of the dead is not to be equated with that of the ancestors.

edged; thus, because of his attachment to his background, Paul seems to have an uncertain attitude to *other* peoples' traditions,[38] when his attitude to his own tradition should have meant for him the corollary of his having respect for others' attachment to *their* own traditions. This, however, is not to question the wisdom of his relying on his Jewish traditions as a way of reacting to what God in Christ has done for him.

In adopting a critical attitude to certain Western formulations of the significance of the death of Christ it is not being suggested that the Church in the West is to be denied the right being pressed here for the African Church, that is, to interpret the Scriptures to suit its circumstances. What has been pointed out here, among other things, is that while certain Western formulations of the significance of the cross may correctly reflect Western social circumstances, they may not be in full accord with biblical teaching. Herein is a danger which must not be taken lightly in expressing the Gospel in a given cultural situation.

Thus it can hardly be argued that the cross renders of no account all cultural assertion. Indeed, as we have observed elsewhere, 'the radical nature of the cross serves to underline the extent to which God would go to identify himself with mankind in the totality of human circumstances'.[39]

38. See p. 89, note 1.
39. Kwesi Dickson, 'Continuity and Discontinuity Between the Old Testament and African Life and Thought' in K. Appiah-Kubi and S. Torres, *African Theology En Route* (Maryknoll, N.Y., Orbis, 1979), p. 107.

Part Three

Implications for Theological Education

8

Theology and the Seminary, the Congregation and the Community

All that has been said in the preceding chapters must have some consequences for theological education in Africa, to which subject we now turn in this concluding chapter, first raising the issue of the purpose of such education.

At a consultation attended by lecturers from Lutheran institutions in southern Africa which took place at Grahamstown in 1972, the following statement of purpose was adopted:

> The purpose of theological education is to further in Church and society Christ's mission through persons who by their education are better enabled to serve and minister to all people in the various relationships in which they live – in family, community, congregation and Church – nurturing and challenging them with the Gospel to be the people of God, developing and using their full potentials, thinking and acting responsibly and serving in congregation and culture.
>
> To this end theological education, taking into account and furthering the various charismatic gifts, special talents and interests of the theological student seeks to help the student:
>
> > To live and help others to live Christ-reconciled lives through acceptance and understanding of the Gospel both as an historic reality and as a living word of life in all its relationships, guiding and freeing both person, Church and society;
> >
> > to interpret Scripture relevantly and together with others design practical plans for individual and common action accordingly, thereby enabling people to be conscious of their

situation, possibilities and mission and involving them in the same;

to serve in the Church and its congregations as one who having been firmly grounded in its faith, traditions and practice, including the ecumenical and denominational aspects, works together with his fellow workers and congregational members for the furtherance of the mission of the Church as proclaimer of God's Word, functioning in such various capacities – leader and enabler, servant, etc. as his calling, the gifts of the Holy Spirit and his situation require;

to understand people and society in the context of their social, cultural and religious tradition and the present situations of change (increasingly pluralistic and industrial) in which they live, in order that he may serve them according to their needs, participating responsibly in bringing about a just and equitable society;

to be involved in the kind of education which will enable him to develop the theological understanding, critical thinking and disciplined life of prayer and service necessary for his ministry, and which will also provide opportunity for specialisation in particular fields of service.

All this in the power and under the guidance of the Holy Spirit.[1]

It is a somewhat wordy statement, couched in the sort of language theologians and churchmen seem to reserve for such formulations, but its main point is clear: theology is done in specific contexts – it is not an esoteric exercise, unrelated to the practicalities of life; on the contrary, it expresses the Christian's commitment to the society in which he finds himself. However, that this statement displays a certain bias is quite evident: it highlights the theological student – the one who serves the Christian congregation, guiding it and interpreting the Scriptures. Whether or not this was intended by those who drew up the statement we cannot say, but certainly the

1. *Ghana Bulletin of Theology*, vol. IV, no. 4 (June 1973), Appendix.

statement as it stands does not relate theology and the Church in any vital way, beyond noting that the Church is the arena in which the theologically trained person serves in the various ways indicated; whatever role is given the Church in theology is in consequence of its being served and led by the theologically trained servant of the Word. It seems to us that this matter of the relation between theology and the Church as a whole needs to be given a great deal of attention if the polarisation of the Church into theologians (the specialists) and the rest of the Christian body is to be avoided. That this polarisation is to be encountered in Africa should give no cause for surprise; while at one time all theological direction was given by the missionaries, and therefore from *their* home Churches, now whatever direction there is emanates from the African leadership, but this leadership has its springs in the Church's missionary past. Of course, such polarisation is not a peculiarly African pheno-menon, for it is to be found in Europe and America as well. What makes its presence in Africa of so much concern is that not only does it mean that the Church in Africa is living in the colonial past, but also – and consequently – it is indicative of the Church's powerlessness with respect to giving authentic theological direction in a continent where social, economic, political and cultural experi-mentation, consolidation, and not inconsiderable misjudgement are taking place. Goba, the Black South African theologian, addresses himself, perhaps consciously, to this polarisation when he observes: '. . . the context of theological education is the Church as it exists in any contemporary situation.'[2] Whether this matter of the relation-ship between theology and the Church is made sufficiently clear by such a statement is another matter, however. It is not unusual to see a connection established between formal theological training and theological activism (theology in the dynamics of the community) without the Church, *qua* Church, a community of believers, being involved in any way in this kind of theological outreach. Is it not essential that things should be such that the Church should be able to recognise itself in the theologian's theology which may have

2. Bonganjalo Goba, 'The Task of Black Theological Education in South Africa', *Journal of Theology for Southern Africa*, no. 21 (March 1978), p. 21.

repercussions for the society for which the Church prays and in whose name it claims to speak?

At an All Africa Lutheran Consultation which took place at Gaborone, Botswana, 5–14 October 1978, it was agreed that a 'new mode of theological education should be devised which will:

(a) be contextual and action-reflected orientated;
(b) eschew confessionalism/denominationalism;
(c) try new methods, e.g. tent-making ministry, Theological Education by Extension;
(d) proceed with the study of the theology of other religions (Islam, etc.), so as to provide viable strategies for dialogue and to produce informed emissaries;
(e) evaluate our present teaching/preaching materials.[3]

This somewhat laconic statement of the concerns and content of theological education does bring up issues some of which are not raised in the Grahamstown statement. The Gaborone and Grahamstown statements agree on the need for a 'contextual' kind of theological education, one which is 'action-reflected orientated', to quote this rather cumbersome description of the sharpening, through theological education, of the Christian conscience in relation to human situations (of oppression, poverty, etc.). The reference to 'confessionalism/denominationalism' is of interest as reflecting a sense of frustration arising from the Churches in Africa being bound – initially in consequence of their mission-Church status, and now apparently by choice – by historical circumstances having to do with the West. It is a concern which has been raised from time to time, in muted tones, by various individuals. Some acquaintance with the deliberations of the Ghana Church Union Committee,[4] and the Nigerian Church Union efforts which were aborted just when the attainment of union was in sight,[5] reveals the extent to which leaders of the historic Churches in Africa appear

3. Alison Bareš (ed.), *Christian Theology and Theological Education in the African Context*, pp. 6–7.
4. It is hoped the united Church, the Church of Christ in Ghana, will be inaugurated sometime in the 1980s.
5. O. U. Kalu, *Divided Children of God*, New York, NOK Publishers, 1978.

to be hide-bound by denominational traditions. It may be wondered whether this attachment to traditions emanating from the West may not hamper the kind of contextual, innovative thinking which the Gaborone Consultation hoped for, even after union has been achieved.[6]

The Gaborone statement's reference to 'new methods' is an important reminder, especially in view of the fact that much of the resources of the Churches in Africa seems to go into the traditional form of theological training which has resulted in the turning out of generation after generation of clergy who seldom fit into the social background into which they had been born and in which they work. Some new approaches are being tried; thus 'Theological Education by Extension' is already going on in Nigeria, Ethiopia, Tanzania, Botswana and South Africa.[7] This type of theological education is given through afternoon, evening and weekend classes (non-residential) organised by a team of teachers; it was devised partly in reaction to the unwillingness sometimes displayed by those trained in seminaries (usually located in the urban areas) to work in rural areas. Studying the theology of other religions is, as indicated in the first chapter of this study, a matter of great importance. It was argued then that the theologian needs to have some understanding of what *religion* is all about; knowledge of only one religion, Christianity, does not provide a sufficient basis for understanding God's approach to man. In most African cities three important religions may be encountered – Christianity, Islam and African traditional religion – and until a decade or two ago most African university Departments of Religion and seminaries studied theology without sufficient account being taken of these other religions which are practised by considerable numbers of Africans. While acknowledging the importance of the Gaborone statement in this connection, it is my judgement that it does not go far enough. Dialogue can be very useful, and much understanding has been achieved thereby; it

6. During the early stages of the Ghana Church Union talks, when the present writer was a member of the Church Union Committee, on several occasions the solutions arrived at by other Union Committees abroad were invoked to solve problems encountered by the Ghana Committee.

7. Bareš, op. cit., p. 9–10.

might in fact lead to the adoption of an inclusive theological position,[8] such as we have argued for in this study, or it might not. Christians in Africa have every opportunity, through living encounters, to gain a greater insight into God's relations with man. The importance of the last point made in the Gaborone statement is not always recognised. The need to use the right resources to teach and preach is a pressing one; we shall return to this matter in subsequent comments.

In the discussion which follows we shall consider theological education from three angles: *Theology and the Seminary* (and University Departments of Religion), *Theology and the Congregation*, and *Theology and the Community*.

Theology and the seminary

In many African countries, as in the West, theological education takes place both in the seminary and in the Departments of Religion in the secular universities. Seminaries (and Bible colleges) in Africa, of course, have Church affiliation; some of them are in association with more than one denominational Church. The majority of seminaries work at the sub-undergraduate level. Until recently, most seminary entrants in West Africa did not have the West African School Certificate or an adequate number of Ordinary Level passes; now about half the entrants come with the School Certificate or equivalent qualification.[9] Usually this pre-seminary educational preparation would not qualify the entrants for admission to the universities, which usually require a certain number of passes at the Advanced Level; the exception to this will presently be noted. Rarely do graduates enter the seminary,[10] and when they do they

---

8. W. Cantwell Smith has written: '. . . in dialogue one's understanding changes including one's understanding of God. That is what dialogue is all about. Thus even our faith may change (grow, develop). (Unless we are open to that, the dialogue is hardly serious.) Yet the object of our faith does not change, since He is God.' See *Religion*, vol. 3 (Autumn 1973), p. 113.

9. Roman Catholic seminarians on the whole have a higher percentage of Ordinary and Advanced Level qualifications.

10. Contrast seminaries in the United States of America which invariably are graduate institutions of theology.

are usually given a short period of training (often not more than a year), with emphasis on what are known as 'practical' subjects (church administration, preaching, etc.).

West African seminaries do not as a rule prepare their students for degrees. Some seminaries have established links with universities and seminaries abroad in order to present their students for degrees offered by those institutions. As far as we know, only some Baptist seminaries in Nigeria are involved in this kind of relationship (with Baptist colleges in America). At the 1975 Ibadan meeting of the West African Association of Theological Institutions (WAATI) a decision was taken against seeking accreditation from universities and seminaries outside Africa; as much as possible, the meeting decided, seminaries should seek to establish links with local universities for accreditation purposes. Nothing much has come out of this, for the West African universities have tended to insist that the granting of accreditation would require as a precondition that seminary entrants should have the same qualifications as prospective undergraduates.[11] Well before the accreditation discussion took place some West African seminaries had already established links with the local universities whereby the seminaries would present students for the universities' sub-degree Diploma in Theology/Religious Studies examinations.[12] Also, since some West African universities make it possible for holders of the Diploma qualification to do university residential degree work without their having first obtained the requisite Ordinary and Advanced Level passes, seminary students who have obtained that qualification have in many cases been admitted to the universities to study full-time for a degree.[13]

11. WAATI went ahead and set up an Examinations Board which has already presided over several degree and diploma examinations. It remains to be seen whether African universities will give recognition to the WAATI diplomas.

12. In Ghana the two major Catholic seminaries, as well as the main Protestant seminary, Trinity College, are in this kind of relationship with the University of Ghana. A similar relationship has existed for an even longer period between some East African seminaries and Uganda's Makerere University.

13. Until recently this was particularly true of the University of Ghana. Owing to certain constraints, this university is reconsidering this programme.

The university Departments of Religion are, of course, within secular universities, and do not therefore have to seek ecclesiastical direction as to the kind of courses they might mount. As a rule they do not offer the 'practical' courses. With respect to the teaching of theological subjects, however, the university Departments of Religion have so far turned out to be more innovative. Innovations with a distinctly cultural bias have been made for some time, though the efforts made to date have hardly been thorough-going; certainly the break-through that would establish a distinctive pattern of theological education in terms of the kinds of theological disciplines taught and their content is yet to be achieved. A beginning has been made, all the same. It may be noted in this connection that the study of African traditional religion as a theological discipline was pioneered at the university Departments of Religion in contrast to which the seminaries may, with considerable justification, be described as bastions of Western orthodoxy, their systems being usually modelled after Western systems with respect to the kinds of courses offered and their content. In recent years, however, some effort has been made to relate seminary work as much as possible to the African background of the entrants, but the seminaries have a much longer way to go than the universities to provide relevant theological education. Indeed, given the Church's goals, the seminaries should consider themselves to be under a greater obligation to develop new approaches to theological education; that this compulsion has not been felt to any appreciable degree explains the seminaries' uncertain character. The Church's 'colonial' character has prevented it from seeing with any clarity the magnitude of the task facing it with respect to the training of its clergy. Moreover, the paucity of clergy, in comparison with the increasing numbers of Christians, has predisposed the Church to thinking simply in terms of producing ordained personnel, after the existing pattern, to take charge of congregations; the question of what kind of clergy would be most suitable in these days, and in this particular cultural context has not, in the circumstances, been seen as a pressing one. Questions of this kind need to be raised and given serious consideration, at least by the seminary Boards of Governors and teaching staff;

unfortunately, members of governing boards are seldom chosen for their theological innovativeness, and seminary teachers are usually so harassed by heavy teaching schedules that they have little or no time to do any serious innovative thinking.

This is only a brief review of the present situation with regard to theological education in Africa. Its defectiveness in various directions has not gone without comment by some theological educators in Africa, but even though in recent years some critical assessments of the seminaries' effectiveness have appeared in writing, these have not, to our knowledge, been seriously discussed by seminary boards.

Agbeti, a former member of staff of Ghana's main Protestant seminary, Trinity College, has made some public comments with respect to theological education in Africa out of which the following three suggestions may be distilled: (1) The seminary should be headed by an African who is concerned about 'the spiritual, material and intellectual relevance of ministerial training in the context of contemporary needs of . . . Africa in general'. An African is more likely to 'initiate and perpetuate any future plans for the institution's enfranchisement and transformation';[14] (2) the teaching staff should be predominantly African;[15] and, (3) the view that the university Departments of Religion 'are clearly crucial places for a serious academic engagement, and no doubt any so-called African Theology must come through them'[16] should not be given credence, for basically three reasons: the secular universities of which the Departments of Religion are part are not likely to want to foster the Church's aspirations; then, the university lecturers and professors are not in regular touch with congregations, and also they may not have interest in the Church's converting mission; thirdly, the university teacher may have only a limited knowledge of traditional religious beliefs and practices, while a Christian university when set up would, among other things, expose students 'to critical and

14. J. K. Agbeti, 'Theological Education in Ghana', in *Ghana Bulletin of Theology*, vol. III, no. 10 (June 1971).

15. Ibid.

16. J. S. Mbiti, *New Testament Eschatology in an African Background* (Oxford University Press 1961), p. 29.

independent judgement and this may obviate the conservatism of clergymen trained mainly under foreign missionary control'.[17]

In reaction to two of Agbeti's three points an English theological educator observed: 'I can see no reason why a black African will necessarily encourage the Africanisation of [the seminary]. Many black Africans, particularly black African priests are much more conservative than their white counterparts . . . In fact what is embarrassing to any European minister in Ghana is the rigid conservatism with which many Ghanaian clergy of all denominations defend liturgical and pastoral practices which were fashionable in Europe several generations ago.'[18] It seems to us that Agbeti's concerns are as valid as those behind the rejoinder. Evidently, the African theologian who has been so trained as to have become unaware of his African background is not likely to fulfil the dreams of those who would see a necessary equation between an African theological leadership and relevant theological education. And yet, a European is more likely to perpetuate the traditions in which he has been brought up in his own country; it may be doubted whether he will be able to feel himself sufficiently into the African religio-cultural situation to contribute meaningfully to theological education in Africa. An African theologian, *qua* African, is not necessarily best suited to provide suitable theological education; he should have rid himself of the false presupposition that the parameters of the theologising process have already been fixed for Christendom by the West. When Goba asks the question, 'How and what can white theologians who participate in the structure of Apartheid teach blacks about theology?' he also gives the answer: 'Only those white theologians who have become black by identifying themselves with the oppressed, black people's struggle for liberation, can be in a position to participate in black theological education.'[19]

It is quite clear that in the context of this study the question of

17. J. K. Agbeti, 'The Search for Theological Identity in West Africa', paper presented at the 1975 meeting at Ibadan of the West Africa Association of Theological Institutions.
18. J. C. Thomas, 'What is African Theology', in *Ghana Bulletin of Theology*, vol. IV, no. 4 (1973), p. 26.
19. Goba, op. cit., p. 20.

who are best suited to participate in theological education in Africa is one that is fairly easily answered: it is those who have a thorough understanding of African life and thought, and regard these as a formative factor of Christian theology in Africa. By this criterion it might very well be that some non-African theologians would qualify to participate in theological education in Africa, though I would think that theological educators in Africa would be predominantly African.

With regard to the suggestion that to realise its theological goals the Church in Africa should think in terms of Christian universities rather than seminaries, we are unable to see any real merit in the suggestion. While admitting that university Departments of Religion have a limited interest with respect to furthering the Church's specific goals, it is not clear to us why it should be suggested that teachers in secular universities may have a less adequate and authentic knowledge of African traditional religion, or that theological students cannot be exposed to 'critical and independent judgement' in a seminary. In fact, it would seem to us that there is more to be said for theological education in a secular university than in a so-called Christian university, for in the former theological students would at least have their theology tested in a heterogeneous set-up in terms of both the student and staff body, and academic disciplines.

If the training offered by seminaries in Africa has not been an unqualified success there are reasons for this, one of which concerns the calibre of staff and students. Some progress has already been made in this connection, even though a great deal more needs to be done. With the explosion of secular education in Africa it is only to be expected that at one level, at any rate, theological education should involve those with such basic education as would make them benefit from the kind of rigorous training that a well-staffed and suitably equipped seminary could offer. However, it is important that theological education should not be thought of exclusively in terms of residential theological schooling, especially since there is need to narrow the gap between the theologically trained and the rest of the Church, and here we have in mind both the educated and the illiterate laymen and laywomen. One of the little-commented-upon assets of the Church in Africa is the fast-growing body of laymen and laywomen, many of whom have a better general education than the average minister. So far the Church's educational efforts have not seriously engaged this group.[20] With respect to the illiterate and not so well educated members of the Church the issue of theological education has important ramifications relating to the question of language medium.

It is not often recognised that one of the drawbacks of Africa's educational drive is the use of the languages of her erstwhile colonial masters: mainly English, French and Portuguese. It is often assumed that after many decades of European rule and the adoption of European languages these are the natural media for the spread of education in Africa. There is something in this, of course; not only does the use of these European languages immediately establish a place for African countries in global interrelationships, but also it puts at the disposal of Africa a considerable store of literature and knowledge. Unfortunately, however, this is only one aspect of the matter, for generally speaking the use of foreign languages interposes a foreign medium between the material and its in-depth comprehension, with consequences which have been the subject of discussions in some West African universities for some time.[21] For many decades, some of the more widely-spoken indigenous languages have been taught in the schools; and now some of them are being taught at the university level. Most African countries have a number of unrelated languages, and the question of which could be adopted as the national language is one that often arises – and is as often shelved. In this respect, some East African countries have an advantage over West African countries, in that Swahili is spoken widely in that part of the continent; indeed, there are those who would want to see this language made the lingua franca for Black

20. See below p. 221.
21. In some quarters it has been suggested that the way forward would be to formalise the kind of imprecise English (or French, or Portuguese, presumably) which one often hears being spoken both in and outside the classrooms by Africans. The merits of this suggestion are not clear to us; in any case, the view that African languages should be made to play a greater role in education seems to us to have greater merit.

Africa. However that may be, for the moment African educationists are edging closer towards questioning about the extent to which African languages should play a participatory role in the educational process; some believe that the availability of some of these languages as university subjects is but a prelude to their featuring eventually as media of instruction.

Coming back specifically to the subject of this study, our own view is that the Church in Africa needs to work the local languages more into its theological education than it has done hitherto. There has been much tardiness in the development of suitable theological literature in languages which people speak in their daily living, whether in the universities or market places, in parliament (outside formal debates) or traditional gatherings, a failing which has further deepened the impression that theology is essentially a foreign commodity.[22]

As a result of the peculiar history of the Church in Africa, it is even more essential that theological education should be defined sufficiently broadly to cater for the whole Church. When people learn to think of their faith in the context of their total circumstances and in the medium of their own languages such immediacy would be added to the theologising process as would make theology a vital force in Church and society. It is evident that the views expressed here demand the development of new structures of theological education which would make seminary or residential training only one of the avenues which might be employed by the Church in Africa.

In the light of comments made in earlier chapters, there are other aspects of theological education which may be mentioned here. First, there is the need to study African life and thought, though not as presented by social anthropologists, however useful their studies may be. Theological educators in Africa have every opportunity to study traditional religion and life 'live', for – as we have noted – while the static humanity which the social anthropologist tends to picture is largely fiction, despite the modern forces and the changes that have been brought about, the traditional ways of life

22. It is interesting to observe that the attempts made in the early decades of the century to produce theological literature in one of Ghana's main languages, Twi, were discontinued, and have not since been revived.

and thought have not disappeared, and there is no indication that they ever will. There is a distinctive life-style which needs to be fully appreciated. A beginning has been made in some seminaries where theological students have the opportunity to prepare research papers dealing with life in African societies as part of their training. Indeed, much work is being done in French-speaking West Africa where several seminaries publish the results of their research.[23] Such serious study of African traditions should influence the presentation of theological subjects. Thus the study of the Old Testament would involve also an examination of the extent to which biblical life and thought are related to African life and thought.

Second, the delimitation of theological subjects should be such as to emphasise the wholeness of theology rather than its parts. Traditionally, theological education has proceeded on the basis of a supposed distinction existing between systematic theology and pastoral theology, the former being considered to be an 'academic' subject and the latter a 'practical' subject. This distinction is such an 'article of faith' that university Departments of Religion do not as a rule have a place in their system for 'pastoral' theology, while in seminaries the two subjects are usually presented in such a way as to imply that they are self-sufficient entities. This distinction is detrimental to the development of meaningful theology, for it implies a distinction between piety and Christian involvement in society. Later in this chapter further comments will be made on the falsity of such a distinction; for the moment it will suffice to observe that the perpetuation of this distinction has impoverished theology and accounts for theological treatises that have nothing to do with the actualities of life. Theological educators in Africa (and elsewhere) will have to draw lines of demarcation in such a way as not to continue to promulgate this falsification of the nature and purpose

---

23. See my review, 'Research in the History of Religions in West Africa' in *Religion*, special issue on the occasion of the XIIIth Congress of the International Association for the History of Religions, August 1975. The present situation with respect to the study of African life and thought is not entirely satisfactory. Often African religion is taught in the penultimate or final year, when it would be best to teach it in the first year as part of the fashioning of a foundation for a distinctive theological approach.

of theology. There is no reason why university Departments of Religion should not offer the so-called practical subjects. Some would feel that there could be no room in a secular university for such subjects, but our contention is that the implications of theology for societal interrelations should be considered as an indispensable aspect of 'systematic' theology. As an immediate corrective measure, theological educators at the university Departments of Religion and seminaries might consider arranging as a curricular activity inter-disciplinary seminars for the purpose of underlining the unity of theology.

The vicissitudes of the presentation of church history in Departments of Religion in African universities further illustrates the point being made. Much has happened since the early nineteen-fifties when the study of church history made room for the study of the life and thought of the national Church only as an after-thought. It has for some time now been recognised that the method of presenting church history whereby one starts from the story of the Church in the Mediterranean, then in Europe, then surveys the formation of missionary societies and the coming of missionaries to Africa, and then lastly ranges over some aspects of Church growth in Africa has very little to commend it; not only does it turn the subject into mission history but also it fosters the view that the fact of the Church in Africa itself is at best of secondary importance, not deserving to be seriously investigated. Greater emphasis, surely, needs to be placed on the Church in Africa, with a backward glance at the earlier *extra*-Africa developments.[24] Indeed, the advisability of sticking to the title church history, given its traditional connotations, might be examined.[25] It is essential that theological education

24. For other comments on the subject see Walter Cason's 'The Teaching of Church History in Liberia' in *Ghana Bulletin of Theology*, vol. II, no. 3 (December 1962), pp. 36f.
25. When the decision was taken by the Department for the Study of Religions, University of Ghana, to revise its Church History syllabus in such a way as to place greater emphasis on the Church in Africa, the greatest difficulty experienced was not over whether or not the change was desirable; the question over which there was protracted indecision was how much of the pre-1792 history of Christianity was to be retained. It was not easy to forgo any part of what had come to be accepted as an indispensable part of Church history!

should give prime attention to the Church in Africa, without cutting it off from Christendom. Moreover, to study the making and life of the Church in Africa is to study also the Independent Churches as well as the interaction of religions in Africa, with reference to the three main religions, Christianity, Islam and African traditional religion. Much has been written about the Independent Churches, but the historic Churches have not been sufficiently challenged by their success, partly because there is a tendency to view them as being at best on the fringes of 'orthodoxy', and partly because – unfortunately – sooner or later some of these newer Churches begin to model their life-style after that of the historic Churches. One would hope that in taking another look at church history theological education would give greater attention to the life and thought of the *total* Church in Africa. Incidentally, the reference just made to the life and thought of the Church has wider significance. It is thus more useful to study history and doctrine together than to study them separately; for either by itself would give an incomplete understanding of the significance of the facts of history, and the teaching of the Church. Similarly, it may be wondered whether there is any real advantage in teaching biblical exegesis apart from biblical history.

A third matter of interest concerns theological literature. In recent years voices have been raised in Africa regarding the need to ensure that theological education in Africa is backed by a suitable body of theological writings. The West African Association of Theological Institutions, at its 1975 annual meeting at Ibadan, discussed the possibility of preparing a Bible commentary which would, among other things, build upon the hermeneutical as well as theological continuity between the Hebrew traditions and African life and thought. Of course, in studying the Bible much of the traditional critical tools would have to be employed, but it is essential that such critical work should lead to the raising of questions that enable the African student to relate the text and its meaning to his existential situation.

Finally with reference to the need for hermeneutical realism, there is another area of theological training which calls for urgent attention. In the seminaries known to us students are expected, as part of their training in preaching, to compose sermons in English (or French). Regrettably, no work has been done, as far as we know, regarding what a sermon should consist in. The preacher has the task of relating the Bible message to the circumstances of his audience; thus the question arises of the form which a sermon to an African audience should take in order to accomplish this goal most effectively. Whatever steps are taken to achieve this – and our purpose is not to give detailed directions – serious consideration should be given to employing the indigenous languages in the preparation of sermons since most African clergy preach mostly in one or other of these media.

In concluding this part of the discussion, I wish to take a look at the concept of theological *training*. The very concept of training has within it the seeds of misunderstanding and misjudgement, for it implies a programmed study by which others are expected to be shaped to a pre-determined standard. In this there is the unspoken assumption that seminary entrants have no previous theological formation whatsoever simply because they are yet to have *formal* education in that field. It must be said at once that it would be a very poor Church, indeed, if it succeeded in selecting for training those who had not at any time given any thought to their faith in the context of their lives, for such would hardly be Christians. Procedures for the selection of candidates for the Church's ministry often unconsciously assume candidates' inability to theologise, for more often than not all that they are expected to do is to give oral and written evidence of their ability to recall what certain authors have said on some theological themes. As I stated earlier, knowing what others have said can be useful, for it could actualise for oneself one's vague and unarticulated thoughts. Yet care must be taken not to assume that others' expressions of faith represent the totality of what could be thought or expressed. For those admitted to seminaries, then, training can be dangerous in the sense that it might, if unimaginatively carried out, programme the trainee to look upon theology as 'fossilised' Christian thought which sets the possessor apart from life as he knows it in his circumstances. Such misconception stands a fair chance of growing in Africa as increasingly seminary students are being prepared for written examinations adminis-

tered either internally or by external examining bodies. Paper qualifications, essential as these are in the modern world may, if not
adequately monitored, make the student look upon theological education as a pedagogical regimentation whose sole purpose is to
encourage thought rather than thought-action.

Theological training, in some form or other, is a necessity, but it
must be carried out in such a way as not to stifle original thinking.
Above all, it should be such as to unite theological students in
thought and action with the ordinary members of the Church who
would be doing more informal, and perhaps more relevant, theologising in their daily living than the seminarians.

Theology and the Congregation

It has been suggested in the foregoing that theological education
should have as an end-product the bringing of the clergy and his
congregation more closely together. It is necessary in this connection
to make some comments on the place of the Church as a body of
believers in the theological education carried out by the Church's
specialised agencies.

As presently conceived and executed, theological education
accentuates the separation between the theologically trained and
the rest of the Church, and implies that the influence of the Church
is channelled only through the clergy and the specialists. It needs
to be remembered that the minister of religion does not have to go
into the world for the Church to be experienced by those outside
it, for the laity are already in the world; if it had not always been
so the Church would have fared much worse in its history. There
is a real sense in which theology grows in the worshipping
community as an expression of its life and work. The Church, of
course, needs the theological innovators, but where the Church does
not recognise itself in the innovator's theology, then there is cause
for concern. If, as has been argued here, theological education
should be made to embrace the laity as well, then it becomes
imperative that theology should not be thought of simply in terms
of its place in worship in the Church, but more widely in terms of
its relation to the world at large in which the laity are already

living, working and serving in various ways. Of course, as long as the Church continues to cherish its foreign character, in consequence of which the idea will persist that theology is what is done through the medium of a foreign language, the tendency to polarise the Church between the theologians and the laity will remain. Every attempt must be made to involve the total membership of the Church, literate and illiterate, in the Church's theological concerns.

With respect to the literate, the Churches, both historic and Independent, can count among their membership many with the highest training in a wide range of professions. The presence of such people in the Church is treasured, but often for the wrong reasons. Generally speaking, there is a tendency to look upon these professionals as sources of income, and as enhancing the Church's image. The cause of the Church would be better served if its leadership saw in these professionals a facilitating factor in the actualising of the fullness of the Gospel message. Not only should such people be enabled through Christian teaching to see their Christian calling and their 'worldly' professions as complementing each other, but also they should be called upon from time to time to share their professional experiences with the congregation in order to sharpen the worshipper's awareness of the ramifications of faith in Christ.

Writing of the Independent Churches one critic has observed that they 'attempt to satisfy the religious needs of the illiterate people. They have moved back therefore from a religion based on the written word, to a religion based on the spoken word and visual images.'[26] It is not quite certain what precisely is being criticised here. If by 'written word' is meant the Scriptures, then the critic has misrepresented the facts. If it were true that the Independent Churches ignore the Scripture's authority, this would be cause for worry, of course, but apart from the possibility of the misinterpretation of Scripture – and this is not a peculiar failing of the Independent Churches – it is unwarranted to suggest that the Scriptures have been set aside. It would seem that the life-style of the Independent Churches in certain of its aspects disturbs the critic, and this would appear to be because he is unable to think himself into the

26. See p. 212 above, note 18.

situation of members of these Churches, many of whom are 'illiterate'. While it would be wrong to hold up every aspect of the life
and work of the Independent Churches as being worthy of emulation, these Churches have by and large succeeded in integrating
into their life and worship all classes of their membership, including
the unlettered, to a degree to which the historic Churches have yet
to attain. The leaders of the Independent Churches take the fears
of their members seriously, making them see the faith in relation to
various aspects of life which have much meaning for them. That in
the process the faith could be subordinated to human fears and
desires is a real possibility, especially where these fears and desires
are exploited by an unscrupulous Church leader for his own benefit.
In contrast to the worship life of these Churches, that of the historic
Churches has been so structured that there is insufficient awareness
among their members of its dimensions with respect to *extra*-
'Church' life and thought.

Theology and the community

In the course of this inquiry comments have been made to the effect
that theology has ever-widening concentric circles of interaction.
The Church is in the world, and therefore theology must take
account of the world. Theological courses must bring students face
to face with life in their communities. The Church's awareness of
humanity necessitates that the theologian should draw upon several
disciplines in ministering to society; a society's way of life, after all,
has economic, social, political, religious and other dimensions. In
connection with this certain issues arise which deserve serious
consideration.

First, sometimes one gets the impression that the theological
world is polarised between those who are pious but consider the
process of protest as not necessarily demanded by their theological
calling, and those who 'at the drop of a hat' would be out in the
streets protesting, but are otherwise uninterested in piety. This is
a false polarisation in the context of Scriptural teaching, and is
particularly unfortunate in the context of Africa where traditional
life and thought are intertwined: the Gospel does not set apart

salvation from works, and African traditional religion is with the African in all circumstances of life. It is essential, to use the terminology often preferred by Latin American theologians, that there should not be a shift from orthodoxy to orthopraxis to the extent that the former ceases to be a living reality that informs the latter. Sometimes one senses that with some being a Christian does not necessarily imply going to Church; it is enough, apparently, to go into situations of poverty and exploitation in order to influence public opinion with respect to the inequities of life. This attitude raises the issue of what is specifically Christian about socio-economic and political involvement, since social criticism is in fact done also by socialists, marxists and others who are outside the Church. The truth of the matter is that Christianity is based upon faith in Jesus Christ; to accept Christ is to be aware that true Christian involvement in the issues of life should necessarily have its springs in the life and work of Christ who did not compartmentalise reality into religion and life, but rather lived and taught in exemplification of there being an inseparable tie binding the two, the breaking of which changes the character of our convictions where either activism or piety is opted for, and impoverishes our religion and sense of humanity. To preach the Gospel should involve facing the issues that confront society, such as education, poverty, and dictatorships. It has been observed:

> Sometimes the Churches really do appear to behave like some kind of ecclesiastical UNDP (United Nations Development Programme). We must use this criticism in order to ensure two things. Firstly, to ensure that we really listen and hear the demand the world is making to the Churches. Secondly, we must always re-examine our role to see when we are tending to behave like a technical agency and not being an *inspired spiritual* catalyst.[27]

Secondly, it is not enough to seek to improve the social circumstances of society; it is more important that people should be aroused out of their inner apathy and be encouraged to be self-

27. Burgess Carr, formerly General Secretary of the All Africa Conference of Churches, in *Quest* (an Ecumenical Journal), vol. 3, no. 1 (February 1972), pp. 7–8.

reliant. This is a point which cannot be over-emphasised; it is one of world-wide significance, though it is of particular relevance in the African situation because of Africa's recent history. For many generations Black Africa served under colonial rulers who dictated to the African the kind of social, economic and political systems under which he should live. That master–servant relationship which characterised this period of Africa's history has, regrettably, persisted right to the present in this post-colonial period with the independent African governments taking the place of the erstwhile colonial rulers; there is still the tendency for the ruling governments to decide what is good for the rest of society. Once again the recent history of Ghana is of interest here. The military dictatorship under Acheampong proclaimed the policy of self-reliance in accordance with which the country would rely on its own resources and hard work; it just happens that Acheampong and his ruling colleagues lacked that far-sightedness and disinterestedness which would enable such a policy to succeed. It is a commendable policy, all the same, for if fully implemented it could remove the vestiges of that colonial mentality which saw government as the sole initiator of social and other programmes and the provider of amenities, with the people merely playing a passive and submissive role. The theological activism which does not take into account the need for recognising the dignity of a people runs the risk of perpetuating the master–servant relationship, thus making the people a pawn in a power game. It would be a pity if the Church in Africa, given the peculiar history of the continent, adopted policies which did not take account of the fact that true aid is helping others to help themselves.

For a further illustration of this, there is the matter of foreign investments, after which African governments hanker, especially as their countries' economies falter and stagnate. The temptation is strong to see in foreign investments the answer to Africa's economic problems, especially in these days when there is much talk of the need to have a just and equitable distribution of the world's resources. Foreign investments will make available much-needed financial and other resources for the generation of economic activity; however, foreign investments are likely to be much less crucial and longer lasting as to their effects than 'home' investment: the mobilising and motivating of the people with a view to getting them to face their problems squarely – this is the best investment any country could make. Not only would the people have the absolute freedom to define their goals realistically, having in view their best corporate interest, but also national pride would lend them determination and the will to achieve.

Matters such as these should engage the attention of the Church whose leadership should engender awareness within the general membership of the issues involved. The Church must be sufficiently *au fait* with economic developments so as to be in a position to think and act in theologically relevant ways, and where necessary to offer advice to governmental authorities. And the Church has the resources for serving society in this way since it has access, within its membership, to men and women with the highest professional training, as already indicated.

Thirdly, Christian attention has, in our time, centred a great deal on the poor and the oppressed, a concentration of emphasis which is exemplified by the granting of aid. Grants were made, for humanitarian purposes, by the 'Programme to Combat Racism' of the World Council of Churches (without specific authorisation by the Central Committee) to the political liberation movements in Rhodesia (now Zimbabwe) of which the 'freedom fighters' were part, a course of action which has seemed to some to be an unwarranted politicising of this world religious organisation.[28] I bring up this matter in order to raise some general issues regarding Christian concern for the poor and underprivileged in Africa.

The Christian Church today runs the risk of oversimplifying the issue of the poor, to the extent of making its concern faddish;[29] for, while we admit the biblical concern for the underprivileged and the

---

28. In 1981 the Salvation Army withdrew from the World Council of Churches for this reason.
29. A few years ago it was learnt, while visiting New York City, that a group of theological students from the city visited Mexico City to observe the situation of the poor and to meditate upon it. If the students concerned did not consider that New York City exhibited all the poverty that could be meditated upon then, they could hardly have known what to look for in Mexico City!

poor, as well as the fact that one of the characteristics of Christianity in the early days was the readiness with which slaves and others who did not count for much in society identified with the Church, it is essential that the Church in Africa should keep this concern in proper perspective. Thus when we speak of poverty, one of the questions that arise is, in whose eyes is a situation one of poverty?

It is essential that poverty should not be defined using foreign parameters. Poverty is not synonymous with cooking on a coal fire, or feeding babies at the breast, or living in a non-western type of house, or wearing just enough clothes to feel cool in the tropics, or eating non-western-type foods. It is when the norm of life is defined *solely* in the way implied in the last sentence that the preconditions are created for real poverty. Thus in Ghana and other African countries the desire to measure life by standards set elsewhere has resulted in a hankering after unessential commodities (officially labelled 'essential commodities') and ways of life. Thus the norm came to mean for countless Ghanaian mothers, literate and illiterate, feeding babies on baby foods from the West, and when Ghana's increasingly precarious foreign-exchange situation led to cuts being made in the number of items imported, considerable hardship was felt by those who could not find imported baby foods to purchase; to these breast-feeding was not an option.[30] Similarly, tinned mackerel (mostly imported) has become a much prized – and now a much-priced – item in Ghana, when it would have served the people's interests better to develop adequately the supply of fresh fish. Thus poverty may be the result more of thoughtlessness on the part of

30. The American Academy of Pediatrics has made a strong recommendation for breast-feeding. 'While the endorsement is expected to have a significant impact on infant nutrition in the United States, it was also directed to poor countries, where reliance on artificial formulas has aggravated the problems of infant malnutrition' – *Reader's Digest*, feature 'News from the world of medicine', (American edn, February 1979), p. 19. 'The drop in birthrates and the gradual return to breast-feeding in the industrialised West has led the infant food industry to push heavily into the Third World where the hazards of bottle-feeding are awesome.' See *Development Forum* (The United Nations University and the Division for Economic and Social Information DPI), Vol. IX, No. 3, April 1981, p. 15.

the government and people rather than of a desire on the part of government to oppress and relegate some sectors of the population to a degrading position. Indeed, one could say with considerable justification that much of Africa's poverty is self-induced.

These comments are not intended to exhaust the causes of poverty, however. Our intention is to make the point that the Church in Africa cannot afford to react in these matters simply in order to be 'with it' in terms of theological activism. To help the poor help themselves it might be important, indeed crucial, to let them face the issue of the extent to which they may have contributed to their becoming impoverished.

All this, finally, requires sharpening the definition of evangelism. Evangelism may be defined simply as proclaiming Christ. Though such a definition will be found acceptable by many, it needs to be more closely specified in order to avoid possible misunderstanding. It is essential, for one thing, that *the evangelist should not get in the way of the message.* He is a bad evangelist who, consciously or unconsciously, draws attention to himself in his preaching, for the evangelist is not at the centre of his message. To be sure, the message should be worked into the evangelist's very system, but it remains a fact that he is not at the centre of the message; that crucial position is Christ's. This means, secondly, that the *message of the evangelist should be about Christ, but in such a way that Christ speaks for himself.* The evangelist, being human, may set much store by his own wisdom, but that would be preventing Christ from speaking through him. For Christ to speak for himself, the evangelist must know something of the mind of Christ. Of course, it would be presumptuous for any one to claim to know the mind of Christ fully; we can only know Christ's mind in part, and this we are enabled to do through his own teaching and inspiration. Once this is realised, then the evangelist's work is defined for him as to the content of his message. As Christ presented God as one who was actively involved in the exigencies of our human situation, so the evangelist of today can do no more than proclaim a message which takes account of our contemporary life-circumstances. Christ's message was a 'whole' in terms of its encompassing the wholeness of human life; the evangelist must proclaim this wholeness to his contemporaries, if Christ is to be encountered as the *living* Christ.

Evangelism, then, assumes greater complexity in an increasingly complex world. The evangelist must be familiar with the life-circumstances of his people; he does not have to be a specialist in economics or political science or cultural affairs, etc., but he must be sufficiently conversant with socio-economic, political and cultural matters so as to enable his hearers to hear Christ, just as in Christ's day kings, fishermen, tax-collectors, prostitutes, etc., were challenged by him.

The Church in Africa must respond to Christ in such a way as to give recognition to the dignity of Africans as God made them and as he comes to them in Christ. This is a crucial task for theological education.

Select Bibliography

The publications listed here have been selected from a growing body of literature which has relevance for the study of theology in Africa. It is evident from this selection that the interested reader will have to draw upon sources which are varied if a fuller appreciation of the subject is to be achieved. Needless to say, however, no attempt has been made, in drawing up this list, to give an extensive representation of each and every aspect of the subject. Much attention is given here to publications which specifically discuss matters relating to the formulation of Christian thought against the background of African life and thought; this, of course, has meant giving some attention to the literature on African religion and culture and – to a much lesser extent – on the African socio-economic and political realities.

(Unless otherwise stated the place of publication for books in both bibliography and footnotes is London.)

Books

Anderson, G. H. (ed.), *The Theology of the Christian Mission*. New York, McGraw-Hill, 1961.

Anti, K. K. A., *Relationship between the Supreme Being and the Lesser Gods of the Akan*. Unpublished M.A. thesis, University of Ghana, 1978.

Appiah-Kubi, K. and Torres, S. (eds.), *African Theology en Route*. Maryknoll, N.Y., Orbis Books, 1979.

Arinze, F. A., *Sacrifice in Ibo Religion*. Ibadan University Press, 1970.

Ayandele, E. A., *The Missionary Impact on Modern Nigeria, 1842–1914*. Longman, 1966.

Baeta, C. G., *Prophetism in Ghana*. S.C.M., 1962.

— (ed.), *Christianity in Tropical Africa*. Oxford University Press, 1968.

Bareš, Alison (ed.), *Christian Theology and Theological Education in the African*

Context, a report of an All Lutheran Consultation at Gaborone, Botswana, 5–14 October, 1978.

Barrett, D. B., *Schism and Renewal in Africa*. Nairobi, Oxford University Press, 1968.

— (ed.), *African Initiatives in Religion*. Nairobi, East African Publishing House, 1971.

Becken, H-J. (ed.), *Relevant Theology for Africa*. Durban, Lutheran Publishing House, 1973.

— (ed.), *Salvation Today in Africa*. Durban, Lutheran Publishing House, 1974.

Beetham, T. A., *Christianity in the New Africa*. Pall Mall Press, 1967.

Boesak, A., *A Farewell to Innocence*. Maryknoll, N.Y., Orbis Books, 1977.

Bosch, D. (ed.), *Church and Culture Change in Africa*. Pretoria, N. G. Kerk-Boekhandel, 1971.

Bossman, H. L. and Burden, J. J. (compilers), *Bible Translation and the Old Testament in the Context of Africa*. University of South Africa, 1982.

Buthelezi, M., *Towards an African Theology*. Lectures given at the University of Heidelberg, West Germany, 1972.

Daneel, M. L., *Old and New in Southern Shona Independent Churches*, vols. 1 & 2, New York, Mouton Publishers, 1971.

Danquah, J. B., *The Akan Doctrine of God*. Frank Cass, 1968.

Davidson, B., *Can Africa Survive?* Boston, Little Brown, 1974.

Dickson, K. A., *Aspects of Religion and Life in Africa*. Ghana Academy of Arts and Sciences 1977.

— (ed.), *Akan Religion and the Christian Faith*. Ghana Universities Press 1965.

— and Ellingworth, P. (eds.), *Biblical Revelation and African Beliefs*. Guildford, Lutterworth, 1969; also Maryknoll, N.Y., Orbis Books, 1969. (The French version contains additional material: *Pour une théologie africaine*, Editions CLE, Yaoundé, 1969.)

Evans-Pritchard, E. E., *Witchcraft, Oracles, and Magic Among the Azande*. Oxford University Press, 1937.

— *Nuer Religion*. Oxford, Clarendon Press, 1956.

Fasholé-Luke, E. W., Hastings, A. and Tasie, G. (eds.), *Christianity in Independent Africa*. Rex Collings 1978.

Fortes, M. and Dieterlen, G. (eds), *African Systems of Thought*. Oxford University Press 1965.

Gailey, H. A., *History of Africa from 1800 to Present*. New York, Holt Rinehart and Winston, 1972.

Groves, C. P., *The Planting of Christianity in Africa*, vols. 1–4, Guildford, Lutterworth, 1958.

Häselbarth, H., *Die Auferstehung der Toten in Afrika*. Gütersloher Verlagshaus Gerd Mohn, 1972.

— *Christian Ethics in the African Context*. Ibadan, Daystar Press, 1976.

Hastings, A., *African Christianity*. Geoffrey Chapman 1976.

Hunter, G., *The New Societies of Tropical Africa*. Oxford University Press (reprinted) 1963.

Idowu, E. B., *Olodumare: God in Yoruba Belief*. Longman 1962.

— *Towards an Indigenous Church*. Ibadan, Oxford University Press, 1965.

— *African Traditional Religion – A Definition*. S.C.M. 1973.

Ilogu, E., *Christianity and Ibo Culture*. Leiden, E. J. Brill, 1975.

Iroezi, C. J., *Igbo World View and the Communication of the Gospel*. Unpublished D. Miss. thesis, Fuller Theological Seminary, U.S.A., 1981.

Jacobs, D. R., *Christian Theology in Africa*. 1966 (in private circulation, funded by the Theological Education Fund).

Kalu, O. U. (ed.), *Readings in African Humanities: African Cultural Development*. Fourth Dimension Publishers 1978.

Kato, B. H., *Theological Pitfalls in Africa*. Kisumu, Kenya, Evangel Publishing House, 1975.

Kraft, C. H., *Christianity in Culture*. Maryknoll, N.Y., Orbis Books, 1979.

Kudadjie, J. N. K. (compiler), *Report of the All Africa Conference of Churches Consultation on African Music*, University of Ghana 1976.

Kuuire, A., *Dagaati Solidarity and Salvation in the Light of 'Gaudium et Spes'*. Doctoral dissertation, Rome, 1976.

Markovitz, I. L. (ed.), *African Politics and Society*. New York, The Free Press, 1970.

Mbiti, J. S., *African Religions and Philosophy*. Heinemann 1969; New York, Doubleday, 1970.

— *Concepts of God in Africa*. S.P.C.K. 1970.

— *New Testament Eschatology in an African Background*. Oxford University Press 1971.

McVeigh, M. J., *God in Africa*. Boston, Claud Stark, 1974.

Moore, B. (ed.), *Black Theology: The South African Voice*. C. Hurst 1973.

Mugambi, J. and Kirima, N., *The African Religious Heritage*. Nairobi, Oxford University Press, 1976.

Mulago, V., *Un visage africain du christianisme*. Paris 1965.

Mveng, E. and Werblowsky, R. J. Z. (eds.), *Black Africa and the Bible*. The Jerusalem Congress on Black Africa and the Bible, 1972.

Nichols, B. J., *Contextualization: A Theology of Gospel and Culture*. Leicester, Inter-varsity Press, 1979.

Niebuhr, H. R., *Christ and Culture*. New York, Harper, 1951.

Nyerere, J., *Ujamaa – Essays on Socialism*. Dar es Salaam, Oxford University Press, 1974.

Ofosu-Adutwum, *Hebrew Prophetism and Spirit Possession in Africa – A Comparative Study of Inspiration in Two Religions*. Unpublished M.A. thesis, University of Ghana, 1977.

Okullu, J. H., *Church and Politics in East Africa*. Nairobi, Uzima Press, 1974.

Oosthuizen, G. C., *Post-Christianity in Africa*. C. Hurst 1968; also Stellenbosch, Wever, 1968.

Opoku, K. A., *West African Traditional Religion*. Singapore, F.E.P. International Private, 1978.

Phillips, G. E., *The Old Testament in the World Church*. Guildford, Lutterworth, 1942.

Pobee, J. S., *Towards an African Theology*. Nashville, Abingdon Press, 1979.

— (ed), *Religion in a Pluralistic Society*. Leiden, E. J. Brill, 1976.

Parrinder, E. G., *African Traditional Religion*. S.P.C.K. 1962, New York, Harper, 1976.

Pauw, B. A., *Christianity and Xosa Tradition*. Cape Town, Oxford University Press, 1975.

Ranger, T. O. and Kimambo, I. (eds.), *The Historical Study of African Religion*. Heinemann 1972.

Rattray, R. S., *Religion and Art in Ashanti*. Oxford University Press, 1959.

Sawyerr, H., *Creative Evangelism: Toward a New Christian Encounter with Africa*. Guildford, Lutterworth, 1968.

Senghor, L. S., *On African Socialism*, trans. Mercer Cook. Pall Mall Press 1972.

Setiloane, G., *Image of God Among the Sotho-Tswana*. Rotterdam, A. A. Balkema, 1976.

Shorter, A., *African Culture and the Christian Church*. Geoffrey Chapman 1973.

— *African Christian Theology*. Geoffrey Chapman 1975.

— *African Christian Spirituality*. Geoffrey Chapman 1978.

Smith, E. W. (ed.), *African Ideas of God*. Edinburgh House 1950.

Sundkler, B., *The Christian Ministry in Africa*. Liverpool, Charles Birchall, 1962.

— *Bantu Prophets in South Africa*. Oxford University Press 1961.

— *Zulu Zion*. Oxford University Press 1976.

Taylor, J. B. (ed.), *Primal World Views*, Ibadan, Daystar Press, 1976.

Taylor, J. V., *The Primal Vision*. S.C.M. 1973.

Torres, S. and Fabella, V. (eds), *The Emergent Gospel*. Maryknoll, N.Y., Orbis Books, 1978.

Turner, H. W., *Profile Through Preaching*, Edinburgh House 1965.

Weman, H., *African Music and the Church in Africa*. Uppsala, Svenska Institutet För Missionsforskning, 1960.

Williamson, S. G., *Akan Religion and the Christian Faith*. Ghana Universities Press 1965.

Conference Papers

Christianity and African Culture. Papers given at a Conference organised by the Christian Council of the Gold Coast, Accra, 1955.

Changing Africa and the Christian Dynamic. Papers of a Seminar for Mission Board Executives, The Centre for the Study of the Christian World Mission, the Federated Theological Faculty, University of Chicago, 1960.

Civilization noire et Eglise catholique. Papers presented at a Conference at Abidjan, Ivory Coast. Editions Presence Africaine et Nouvelles Editions Africaines, 1978.

Chapters in Books and Articles in Journals

Agbeti, J. K., 'Theological Education in Ghana.' *Ghana Bulletin of Theology*, vol. 3, no. 10, June 1971.

Allmen, D. von, 'The Birth of Theology.' *International Review of Missions*, vol. 44.

Appiah-Kubi, K., 'The Church's Healing Ministry in Africa.' *Ecumenical Review*, vol. 27, no. 3, July 1975.

Awolalu, J. O., 'Sin and Its Removal in African Traditional Religion.' *Journal of the American Academy of Religion*, vol. 44, no. 2, June 1976.

Bennett, R. A., Jr., 'Africa and the Biblical Period.' *Harvard Theological Review*, no. 64, 1971.

Bimwenyi, K. O., 'Le problème du salut de nos ancêtres ou le rôle salvifique des religions négro-africaines: le Christ – pôle d'attraction de toutes.' *Revue du Clergé Africain* (Zaïre), vol. 25, 1970.

Bosch, D. J., 'God in Africa – Implications for the Kerygma.' *Missionalia*, vol. 1, no. 1, 1973.

Burden, J. J., 'Magic and Divination in the Old Testament and their Relevance for the Church in Africa.' *Journal of Religion in Africa*, vol. 4, no. 1, 1971.

Cason, W., 'The Teaching of Church History in Liberia.' *Ghana Bulletin of Theology*, vol. 2, no. 3, Dec. 1962.

Cone, J. H., 'Black and African Theologies: A Consultation.' *Christianity and Crisis*, vol. 35, 3 March 1975.

— and Wilmore, G. S., 'Black Theology and African Theology.' H. J. Cone and G. S. Wilmore (eds.), *Black Theology – A Documentary History.* Maryknoll, N.Y., Orbis Books, 1979.

Dickson, K. A., 'Worship.' *Report of the Council of the Methodist Church in West Africa,* 1963.

— ' "The Methodist Society" – A Sect.' *Ghana Bulletin of Theology,* vol. 2, no. 6, 1964.

— 'Consultation of African Theologians, 5–19 January 1966 – A Review.' *Bulletin of the All Africa Conference of Churches,* April 1966.

— 'Vers une expression théologique africaine.' *Flambeau,* no. 26, May 1970.

— 'Christian and African Traditional Ceremonies.' *Practical Anthropology,* vol. 18, no. 2, March–April 1971.

— 'The Old Testament and African Theology.' *Ghana Bulletin of Theology,* vol. 4, no. 4, June 1973.

— 'Hebrewisms of West Africa – The Old Testament and African Life and Thought.' *Legon Journal of Humanities,* vol. 1, 1974.

— 'Towards a Theologia Africana.' M. E. Glasswell and E. W. Fasholé-Luke (eds.), *New Testament Christianity for Africa and the World.* S.P.C.K. 1974.

— 'African Theology – Whence, Methodology and Content.' *Journal of Religious Thought,* vol. 33, Fall-Winter 1975.

— 'The Methodist Witness and the African Situation.' T. H. Runyon (ed.), *Sanctification and Liberation,* Nashville, Abingdon, 1981.

Fasholé-Luke, E. W., 'The Quest for African Christian Theologies.' *Scottish Journal of Theology,* no. 29, 1972; also G. H. Anderson and T. F. Stransky (eds.), *Mission Trends, no. 3: Third World Theologies.* New York, Paulist Press, 1976.

Goba, B., 'The Task of Black Theological Education in South Africa.' *Journal of Theology for Southern Africa,* no. 21, March 1978.

Harjula, R., 'Towards a Theologia Africana.' *Svenska Missionstidskrift,* 1970.

Horton, R., 'African Traditional Thought and Western Science – I.' *Africa,* vol. 37, January 1967.

— 'African Traditional Thought and Western Science – II.' *Africa,* vol. 37, April 1967.

— 'African Traditional Thought and Western Science.' M. F. D. Young (ed.), *Knowledge and Control.* New York, Macmillan, 1974.

— 'African Conversion.' *Africa,* vol. 41, no. 2, 1971.

Ilogu, E., 'The Problem of Indigenization in Nigeria.' *International Review of Missions,* vol. 49, April 1960.

Isaac, E., 'Relations between the Hebrew Bible and Africa.' *Jewish Social Studies*, vol. 26, no. 2, 1964.

Isichei, Elizabeth, 'Ibo and Christian Beliefs: Some Aspects of a Theological Encounter.' *African Affairs*, vol. 68, April 1969.

Kato, B. H., 'Black Theology and African Theology.' *Evangelical Review of Theology*, no. 1, Oct. 1977.

Kaufmann, L., 'Theological Education in the 1970s.' *African Ecclesiastical Review* (AFER), Kampala, Uganda, vol. 15, no. 3, July 1973.

Kibicho, S. G., 'The Interaction of the Traditional Kikuyu Concept of God with the Biblical Concept.' *Cahiers des Religions Africaines*, vol. 2, no. 4, 1968.

Kinsler, F. R., 'Mission and Context: The Current Debate about Contextualization.' *Evangelical Quarterly Review*, vol. 14, no. 1, 1978.

Kurewa, J. W. Z., 'The Meaning of African Theology.' *Journal of Theology for Southern Africa*, no. 11, June 1975.

Long, C., 'Structural Similarities and Dissimilarities in Black and African Theologies.' *Journal of Religious Thought*, vol. 33, Fall–Winter 1975.

Lymo, C., 'Quest for Relevant African Theology.' *African Ecclesiastical Review* (AFER), vol. 18, no. 3, 1976.

Mbiti, J. S., 'Some African Concepts of Christology.' C. F. Vicedom (ed.), *Christ and the Younger Churches*. S.P.C.K. 1972.

— 'An African Views American Black Theology.' *Worldview*, vol. 17, August 1974; also J. H. Cone and G. S. Wilmore (eds.), *Black Theology – A Documentary History*. Maryknoll, N.Y., Orbis Books, 1979.

— 'Some Current Concerns of African Theology.' *Expository Times*, LXXXVII, 1975–76.

— 'Some Reflections on African Experience of Salvation Today.' S. J. Samartha (ed.), *Living Faiths and Ultimate Goals: A Continuing Dialogue*, Geneva, WCC, 1976.

— 'The Future of Christianity in Africa.' *Cross Currents*, vol. 28, no. 4, Winter 1978–9.

Messenger, J. C., 'The Christian Concept of Forgiveness and Anang Morality.' W. A. Smalley (ed.), *Readings in Missionary Anthropology*, Practical Anthropology, Tarrytown, N.Y., 1967.

Mshana, E. E., 'Nationalism in Africa as a Challenge and Problem.' *Africa Theological Journal*, no. 5, Dec. 1972.

Mulago, V., 'Le problème d'une théologie africaine revue à la lumière de Vatican II.' *Revue du Clergé Africain* (Zaïre.), vol. 24, nos. 3–4, 1969.

Mushete, N. A., 'La quatrième semaine théologique de Kinshasa et la problèmatique d'une théologie africaine.' *Cahiers des Religions Africaines*, no. 4, July 1968.

— 'Christianisme et authenticité en Afrique noire. Le cas zu Zaïre.' *Le Monde Moderne*, no. 12, Paris, 1976.

Mveng, E., 'A la recherche d'un nouveau dialogue entre le christianisme, le génie culturel et les religions africaines actuelles.' *Presence Africaine*, no. 96, 1975.

Ngally, J., 'Bible Studies from an African Perspective.' *Ecumenical Review*, vol. 27, no. 3, July 1975.

Nxumalo, J. A., 'Christ and Ancestors in the African World.' *Journal of Theology for Southern Africa*, no. 32, Sept. 1980.

Nyamiti, C., 'African Theology: Its Nature, Problems and Methods.' *Gaba Pastoral Papers*, no. 19, 1971.

— 'The Scope of African Theology.' *Gaba Pastoral Papers*, no. 30, 1973.

Ray, B., 'Recent Studies on African Religions.' *History of Religions*, vol. 12, no. 1, 1972.

Reyburn, W. D., 'The Message of the Old Testament and the African Church – I.' *Practical Anthropology*, vol. 7, no. 4, July–Aug. 1960.

— 'Sickness, Sin and the Curse: The Old Testament and the African Church – II.' *Practical Anthropology*, vol. 7, no. 5, Sept.–Oct. 1960.

Sawyerr, H., 'Sin and Forgiveness in Africa.' *Frontier*, vol. 7, Spring 1964.

— 'What is African Theology.' *Africa Theological Journal*, no. 4, August 1971.

— 'Salvation Viewed from the African Situation.' *Presence*, vol. 5, no. 3 1972.

Setiloane, G., 'The God of my Fathers and my God.' *South African Outlook*, Oct. 1970.

— 'Confessing Christ Today.' *Journal of Theology for Southern Africa*, no. 12, Sept. 1975.

Sidhom, S., 'The Concept of Sin in the African Context.' *Communio Viatorum*, vol. 9, no. 4, Winter 1966.

Thomas, J. C., 'What is African Theology?' *Ghana Bulletin of Theology*, vol. 4, no. 4, June 1973.

Thompson, P. E. S., 'The Approach to the Old Testament in an African Setting.' *Ghana Bulletin of Theology*, vol. 2, no. 3, Dec. 1962.

— 'The Anatomy of Sacrifice.' M. E. Glasswell and E. W. Fasholé-Luke (eds.), *New Testament Christianity for Africa and the World*, S.P.C.K., 1974.

Tshibangu, Th. and Vanneste, A., 'Débat sur la Théologie Africaine.' *Revue du Clergé Africain* (Zaïre), vol. 15, no. 4, 1960.

Turner, P., 'The Wisdom of the Fathers and the Gospel of Christ: Some Notes of Christian Adaptation in Africa.' *Journal of Religion in Africa*, vol. 4, no. 1, 1971.

Tutu, D. M. B., 'Black Theology.' *Frontier*, vol. 17, Summer 1974.

— 'Black Theology/African Theology – Soul Mates or Antagonists?' *Journal of Religious Thought*, vol. 33, Fall–Winter 1975; also J. H. Cone and G. S. Wilmore (eds.), *Black Theology – A Documentary History*, Maryknoll, N.Y., Orbis Books, 1979.

— 'Church and Nation in the Perspective of Black Theology.' *Journal of Theology for Southern Africa*, no. 15, 1976.

Vanneste, A., 'Théologie universelle et théologie africaine.' *Revue du Clergé Africain* (Zaïre), vol. 24, nos. 3–4, 1969.

Williamson, S. G., 'The Lyric in the Fante Methodist Church.' *Africa*, vol. 28, April 1958.

Wilmore, G. S., 'To Speak with One Voice.' *Christian Century*, vol. 92, Feb. 1975.

Interested readers may look up the *Bulletin of African Theology*, first issued 1979 (vol. 1, no. 1, Jan–June). This is the organ of the Ecumenical Association of African Theologians.

Index